# John Donne
# and Twentieth-Century Criticism

# John Donne and Twentieth-Century Criticism

*Deborah Aldrich Larson*

Rutherford • Madison • Teaneck
Fairleigh Dickinson University Press
London and Toronto: Associated University Presses

Associated University Presses
440 Forsgate Drive
Cranbury, NJ 08512

Associated University Presses
25 Sicilian Avenue
London WC1A 2QH, England

Associated University Presses
P.O. Box 488, Port Credit
Mississauga, Ontario
Canada   L5G 4M2

The paper used in this publication meets the requirements
of the American National Standard for Permanence of Paper
for Printed Library Materials Z39.48-1984.

**Library of Congress Cataloging-in-Publication Data**

Larson, Deborah Aldrich, 1954–
    John Donne and twentieth-century criticism / Deborah Aldrich
Larson.
        p.   cm.
    Bibliography: p.
    Includes index.
    ISBN 0-8386-3338-2 (alk. paper)
    1. Donne, John, 1572–1631—Criticism and interpretation—History.
2. Criticism—History—20th century.  I. Title.
PR2248.L35   1989
821'.3—dc20                                                                87-46423
                                                                                  CIP

PRINTED IN THE UNITED STATES OF AMERICA

To Chuck


For I had rather owner bee
   Of thee one houre, then all else ever.

# Contents

# Acknowledgments

I want to thank Elizabeth Story Donno, Professor Emerita, Columbia University, for her inspiration and teaching and Professor James V. Mirollo for guiding and instructing me through this manuscript from its conception through its final stages. Professor Anne Lake Prescott, Barnard College, read the manuscript many times, always providing valuable comments and suggestions. I also appreciate University of Missouri-Columbia Professor John R. Roberts's remarks on the early stages of several chapters.

The continuing assistance of Professor Peter Wolfe (University of Missouri-St. Louis) was invaluable, and I owe particular thanks to Professor Richard Cook, also of the University of Missouri-St. Louis, for his advice, support, and encouragement throughout the past sixteen years.

Ellie Chapman patiently copyedited the manuscript, and Marla Schorr typed versions of it more times than I care to contemplate, without a word processor and without letting my demands interfere with our friendship.

Billi and Ron Miller and Peggy Mulvihill helped with the completion of this work in more ways than they, I'm sure, realize.

And finally I want to thank especially Wayne Stillings for his counsel, my stepson Andrew for his patience and love, and my husband Chuck for his skills in proofreading, editing, advising, listening, and consoling.

# John Donne
# and Twentieth-Century Criticism

# Introduction

As a major poet, John Donne has attracted his share of scholarly disputes and probably more than his share of idiosyncratic, eccentric interpretations. John R. Roberts, Donne's most recent bibliographer, observes that during the last fifty years, the critics "have kidnapped Donne and have turned Donne studies into a self-perpetuating industry that nearly rivals the Milton industry" (1982, 66). In fact, throughout the twentieth century, Donne studies have been characterized by readers' love-hate relationships with the poet. In the first two decades of the century, many critics grudgingly accepted him as a major poet, not easily dismissed, even though they questioned the morality of his love lyrics and elegies and deplored the roughness of his verse. In the twenties, thirties, and forties, the New Critics disposed of these objections as they proclaimed Donne the forerunner of modern poetry. Reacting against this adoption of Donne, some scholars in the forties began to study the poet in the context of his time—its poetic traditions and thought. Complicating this chronological development are questions about Donne's life and its relationship to his verse, about his kinship with T. S. Eliot, and about his use of some poetic and philosophical modes current during the sixteenth and seventeenth centuries. The variety and quantity of answers proposed to these questions have made Donne studies particularly problematic.

One difficulty arises because even now, more than 350 years after his death, Donne still arouses strong passions in his readers. It is not simply that his poetry and prose move readers to feel the emotions that Donne as an artist tried to express, although both still do that; nor is it simply that Donne is an uneven writer who causes literary scholars simultaneously to laud and disparage him, although he does that. It is rather that Donne as a writer is so intimately at one with Donne as a lover, husband, and preacher that a surprising number who write about Donne's works identify the poet with the speaker of the poems. His real face merges indistinguishably with his masks.

As Wayne A. Rebhorn points out in *Courtly Performances,* no one in Renaissance society was ever alone; thus, it was necessary always to put on a mask and to play a part (1978, chap. 1).[1] In *Astrophil and Stella,* Sidney recognizes and often mocks this incessant posing, and scholars are quick to enumerate the roles Astrophil plays, to note Sidney's mocking of those roles, and, most important, to distinguish Astrophil from his creator, despite the strong biographical connection between Stella and Penelope Devereux Rich. Given the prevalence of this kind of posing in Renaissance poetry and given the lack in the *Songs and Sonets* of an amatory narrative with a documented biographical link between the poet and one real woman who appears in each poem, Donne's poems should be recognized as a group of mainly unrelated monologues, spoken by several varying and contradictory *personae* playing a number of roles. But apparently they are not; otherwise, scholars would not have been arguing for the last hundred years over Donne's rakish youth and his "conversion" to "sincere" love, nor would any one of his poses become the predominant one, as has often happened. Obviously, then, one—and perhaps the greatest—problem for Donne scholarship is his life and the roles that life seems to contain.

In addition, the questions about Donne's life are themselves double. First, there is confusion about how to interpret his personality. His personal letters, his actions, and his written and reported responses to events in his life are more complete than those of any of his contemporary poets, but Donne's are also substantially more susceptible to contradictory interpretations. Second, responses to his life and personality often color interpretations of his works, and consequently controversies about Donne's poems do not have the same flavor as, for example, those between Stanley Fish and Douglas Bush over *L'Allegro* and *Il Penseroso* or those that might arise over the allegorical interpretations of the first book of the *Faerie Queene*. Fish and Bush might disagree about the interpretation of a line of Milton's poetry, but neither argues about Milton's personality or personal life on the basis of two poems. They may launch personal attacks at each other but not at the poet.

Interpretations of Donne's works too frequently depend on whether the writer approves or disapproves of Donne's religion, his marriage, his supposed promiscuity, or his relations with patrons. The man, John Donne, seems to be, in the eyes of many critics, inextricably connected with the poet and the poems—and their critical analyses are likewise connected with their feelings toward the man. Of course, this is not true of all Donne scholarship. Some quarrels about some of Donne's poems result naturally from the practice of literary criticism and focus objectively on imagery, meter, historical sources, and tone. Disputes about "The Extasie" and "Aire and Angels" are often of this kind. However, the range of critical squabbles often extends far beyond a few poems and into the unknowable but enticing realm of Donne's personality. Is the "Valediction: of weeping" a cynical foreknowledge of unfaithfulness as William Empson has claimed ([1930a] 1962, 54–55) or a moving illustration of mutual faithfulness as others maintain (Ferry 1975, 86–90)? Are the *Anniversaries* the result of sycophantic pragmatism or of a profound philosophical questioning? Is the "Nocturnall" Donne's mocking of idolatrous love (Andreasen 1967, 152–60), or is it a portrayal of his own loss of self after the death of Anne or the Countess of Bedford? These controversies only skim the surface of Donne criticism. Even in the 1970s and 1980s, Donne's poems are more subject to impressionistic, biographically based criticism than are those of any other poet. It is true that no critic of the last decade would say of the *Elegies,* as Andrew Lang did in 1912, that they "do not win admiration for Donne's taste and temper, not to mention his morals" (285). Literary criticism has changed too much in the last seventy years for this kind of statement to be made. Neither would a contemporary critic attempt to explain the early love lyrics and elegies by creating a story about Donne's involvement with a married woman that is as blatantly fictional as Edmund Gosse's ([1899] 1959, 1 : 66–75). However, even granted the expected and predictable changes in Donne criticism and scholarship in the last eighty years, none of these factors explains satisfactorily the continuing interpretations of Donne's poetry through his life and of his life through his poetry.

The advent of New Criticism in the 1920s reduced biographical readings of most other poets. For Donne, however, the New Criticism was less successful in diminishing these interpretations. In fact, from the forties on it produced more such readings as scholars and critics rebelled against New Critical methods. Even more important, the New Critics, in establishing Donne as the model poet, linked his critical fate with theirs. When they lost favor, so did Donne.

It is true that the critical estimation of several poets fluctuated as a result of the New Critical methods. Milton, for example, suffered something of a decline as a result of T. S. Eliot's original censure of him. With Eliot's retraction, however, Milton's popularity rose among adherents of New Criticism and has remained high ever since. Those who disapprove of Milton's politics or of his personality usually say so directly, somehow avoiding the confusion between discrediting the poet as a man and maligning obviously superior poetry because of that dislike. Even those who do confuse the two issues express their confusion in terms of taste rather than critical acumen. And these critics are in the minority. George Herbert's poetry illustrates the opposite trend. Before 1920, it was often faulted for its overly ingenious conceits. Readily adaptable to New Critical analysis, Herbert's poetry was, however, strangely neglected by this group. In fact, by the 1930s, Herbert had been dissociated from the metaphysical school, and this was one reason his popularity remained high even after the reaction against New Criticism had begun. Thus, in the forties and fifties, his poetry could be read according to New Critical dogmas without the stigma of being New Criticism's darling. This was not so of Donne.

T. S. Eliot, in writing about Donne and metaphysical poetry in 1921, initiated a phase in Donne's twentieth-century critical reputation that is difficult to underestimate. Because Eliot himself was a writer who revolutionized modern poetry, his championing of Donne dramatically increased interest in the earlier poet among Eliot's followers—the New Critics. Metaphysical poetry—always defined in terms of Donne's poetry—was admirably suited to the critical methods of such writers as Cleanth Brooks, Allen Tate, and Robert Penn Warren. They modeled some of their own poetry on Donne's and elevated him to the status of ideal poet. For a while, and for some, even Shakespeare was inferior. Eliot and, more significantly, his followers enhanced Donne criticism by concentrating on metaphor, meter, and diction divorced from Donne's biography. However, their adoption of Donne as their mentor also caused a serious and substantial backlash. In the forties and fifties, even those who admired Donne felt it necessary to deflate his importance. His originality, once so highly praised, now received no tribute; certain poems came under attack as being too witty or illogical or immoral. Furthermore, attacks on Eliot's critical comments often involved attacks on Donne, or attacks on Donne sometimes ended with a slam at Eliot. Thus, coupled with biographical problems and interpretations, the New Critics' extolling of Donne added to the perplexities and contradictions of Donne scholarship.

Donne's biography and T. S. Eliot and the New Critics have confounded Donne scholarship most intensely. However, other problems also beset the scholarship. First is the question of genre, or historical tradition. Whereas some would contend that Donne broke completely with the Petrarchan tradition, writing instead intellectual, masculine verse and overturning the poetic conventions followed throughout the sixteenth century, others insist that Donne has specific and readily identifiable affinities with the Petrarchan tradition. Similarly, Donne's exact relationship to Neoplatonism has been debated *ad nauseam,* raging most fiercely around "The Extasie" and "Aire and Angels." It is possible to see both as belonging to the Neoplatonic tradition or as overturning and mocking that tradition. The *Satyres* and the *Elegies* also are either firmly rooted in classical traditions or significantly divergent from these traditions. Thus, much of the confusion in Donne criticism depends on which side of Donne's work one wishes to emphasize.

In this regard, Donne has been treated differently from other Renaissance poets. When, for example, Milton scholars discuss Milton's modifications of the epic tradition in *Paradise Lost,* they do not disparage the final accomplishment. But in Donne's case, any deviance from the established tradition becomes a potential reason for disapproval of the work. *The Anniversaries,* for instance, can be placed in the Renaissance elegiac tradition or in the Ignatian meditative tradition (or in a combination of both). Unfortunately, they fit neither tradition as neatly as do Milton's

*Lycidas* and Southwell's "Burning Babe," respectively. Thus, the *First Anniversarie* is frequently criticized as a failed poem when, in fact, it may be that Donne was concerned with issues other than traditional elegy or meditation. Similarly, whether the "Epithalamion made at Lincolnes Inne" is a successful poem or not depends on whether it is a parody of the wedding poem tradition or a poor imitation of Spenser. The study of Donne's poetry according to genre or historical source is a tricky one because few of Donne's poems correspond exactly to the traditions. Trying to make them fit is like working a jigsaw puzzle not knowing whether there is one piece missing or one piece extra: if the former is true, the puzzle will be a failure; if the latter is true, the puzzle is a success with a little extra surprise.

The problems are the same in a consideration of Donne's relationship to his contemporaries' beliefs. What attitude does he express toward women in his poems? Was he a sexual or philosophical libertine? Did he, despite an outward conversion to Anglicanism, secretly remain a Catholic all his life? Did he reject or embrace the "New Science"? If he rejected it, what precisely were his ties with medieval philosophy and religion? The way a reader of Donne answers these questions determines her or his reaction not only to individual poems but to Donne's poetic powers, his life, and his worth.

Obviously, Donne is a complex poet and man. His life and poetry seem capable of invoking extremes of responses, from idolization to passionate hatred, from discovery of his sources to proof of his uniqueness, from joy in his many moods and forms to outrage at his cynicism and egotism. However, the purpose of this study is not to determine the accuracy of a certain school or decade of criticism—a difficult and unrewarding endeavor with any poet and especially so with Donne. Nor is it to propose a "new" reading of Donne's works—almost an impossible task, given the vast number of critical analyses already in existence. Nor is it to defend Donne as a poet, scholar, and preacher against his often-notable twentieth-century challengers. Rather, my purpose is to determine why Donne's poetry provokes such a range of critical and emotional responses, why it is apparently so difficult to read Donne's poetry objectively without reference to his life and personality, why his works, more than those of other poets, proved congenial to the New Critics, why his poetry is difficult to classify, and why his attitudes toward women, religion, and science have been so controversial.

# 1

# The Image of Donne from 1633 to 1897

The controversies about Donne's life and works began even before the first edition of his poetry was published in 1633. Some of the questions and problems confronting twentieth-century readers also challenged seventeenth-, eighteenth-, and nineteenth-century readers. Furthermore, commentary on Donne's poetry from these centuries has been partially responsible for some of the debates concerning his works today. Although the ultimate source of literary controversies about Donne is the poetry itself, three points that bear on pre-twentieth-century criticism also help explain the incongruities. First, Donne's extant comments on his own poetry are few and in general the result of a literary pose rather than a serious literary theory applicable to his works, while the statements on his poetry by his most famous contemporary commentator, Ben Jonson, are subject to varying interpretations. Second, from the seventeenth century on, Donne's meter was criticized as too irregular and harsh, leading some readers to label Donne a poetic rebel, the guiding spirit of a new "metaphysical" school of poetry, a school that quickly produced as many detractors as adherents. Third, ethical judgments of Donne's life, wit, and morality—seemingly separable issues to us—often become confused with critical considerations of the poetry, thereby causing the speaker of the poems and the poet to coalesce as a single personality. Each of these three features of seventeenth-century commentary has played some part in shaping twentieth-century literary criticism of Donne's works.

Scholars today might have an easier time resolving disagreements about the poetry if they could determine what Donne thought of his own verse. If Donne did explain his poetic theories, few extant works documenting such theories survive. It was not unusual for sixteenth-century poets to scorn or disown their love lyrics, to treat their verses as trifles not connected to the business of getting on in the Elizabethan world and, consequently, to pretend that they used little art or skill in writing them. Emphasizing the last practice, George Puttenham wrote that the poet dissembles "in the subtilties of his arte, that is, when he is most artificiall, so to disguise and cloake it as it may not appeare, nor seeme to proceede from him by any studie or trade of rules, but to be his naturall; nor so evidently to be discried as every ladde that reades him shall say he is a good scholler, but will rather have him to know his arte well, and little to use it" (G. Gregory Smith 1904, 1:186–87). Thus, the ideal poet should appear to use no art but rather to write with gracefulness and *sprezzatura,* disclaiming the importance of anything less than an epic or ode. Philip Sidney, for example, following this practice, calls his *Defense of Poesie,* undoubtedly the most important document in English Renaissance literary criticism, an "incke-wasting toy" (G. Smith, 1:206). Sidney's disclaimer is, of course, a pose, just like the pose any number of his contemporaries adopted to give the impression that poetry came to them effortlessly without the aid of art. That this was not the case is evident from the numerous poetry writing manuals and critical treatises defending the high nature of poetry.

Donne is unusual because he disdains even the pose. Nowhere in his poetry or prose does he claim that poetry is a trifling thing. In fact, it seems possible that his masculine lines and tough conceits are intended to show just the opposite—that poetry is difficult and more serious than his predecessors and contemporaries liked to pretend it was. If the reader must work to interpret the poem, then, if one presumes a skilled writer, it is probable that the complexity of thought forced the poet to work when he wrote it. By refusing the pose of a courtly maker, Donne may have been according love poetry a higher position than did his fellow poets.

Unfortunately, however, only a few of Donne's comments on his own poetry are extant—if, indeed, he wrote more than have survived. He does not remark in these that he modeled his satires on Juvenal or that he read Ovid before beginning his elegies. He never explains his motives for obscurity as does Chapman. By 1601, he had written a number of poems, but he seldom mentions them specifically, and the ones that he does name are poems now considered "minor"; he never refers specifically to any of the *Songs and Sonets.* It is as though they never existed for him or—and this probably is the case later in his life—as though he wished they did not exist. If he formulated a theory of poetry, it has not survived. Although Lynette McGrath has shown that by piecing together Donne's comments in his sermons one can discover a theory of poetry very similar to Sidney's (1980, 73–89), Donne's comments are more applicable to the poetry of the Scriptures than to the kind of poetry—secular or religious—he had written. And this is the main problem with McGrath's theory and with any attempt to apply Donne's scattered remarks to his own poetry. Sidney wrote his *Defense* about ten years before the publication of *Astrophil and Stella* but probably while he was writing these sonnets and the first draft of the *Arcadia.* Thus, Sidney was formulating a theory of poetry (or possibly simply expressing an already-formed theory) while he was engaged in his own creative art. On the other hand, Donne wrote sermons commenting on the nature of poetry at least thirteen years *after* he wrote the majority of the *Songs and Sonets* and at least four years after the *Anniversaries.*

That Donne in the later part of his life saw poetry as "Counterfait creation" (*Sermons* 1962, 4:87) which could direct and inspire men to good is
certainly evident in his *Sermons* (3:144). He also recognized the possible
dangers of poetry and may even have repented of his own poetry (2:88).
However, that the statements on poetry in his *Sermons* have any direct
bearing on any of Donne's poetic practices or on any of his poems from
the *Songs and Sonets* to the *Holy Sonnets* is far from certain. In fact, they
encourage just such a split as that initiated by Donne and emphasized by
Walton—the rakish Jack who repented of his lasciviousness and became
Dr. Donne. Finally, then, Donne's remarks about poetry in his sermons are
of very little use in interpreting his own verse.

Furthermore, from Donne's few secular references to his works, one
cannot tell how he wanted the reader to interpret his comments. "I did
best when I had least truth for my subjects," for example, has caused
modern scholars confusion in its possible applicability to the *Songs and
Sonets*. This, Donne's most overt and most often quoted comment on his
own poetry, is more confusing than helpful in what it tells us about
Donne's attitudes toward his verse.[1]

If Donne was, as many through the centuries have claimed, the leader of
a new school of poets that overturned Petrarchan conventions, there is no
evidence that he was conscious of his status. In extant works, he offers no
negative judgments on Spenser's sonnets, Shakespeare's plays and poetry,
or contemporary poetry at all; nor does he do so implicitly by singing the
praises of his own kind of poetry. The closest he comes to critical commentary is "The triple Foole":

> I am two fooles, I know,
> For loving, and for saying so
>     In whining Poëtry;
> But where's that wiseman, that would not be I,
>     If she would not deny?
> Then as th'earths inward narrow crooked lanes
> Do purge sea waters fretfull salt away,
>     I thought, if I could draw my paines,
> Through Rimes vexation, I should them allay,
> Griefe brought to numbers cannot be so fierce,
> For, he tames it, that fetters it in verse.
>
> But when I have done so,
> Some man, his art and voice to show,
>     Doth Set and sing my paine,
> And, by delighting many, frees againe
>     Griefe, which verse did restraine.
> To Love, and Griefe tribute of Verse belongs,
> But not of such as pleases when 'tis read,
>     Both are increased by such songs:

> For both their triumphs so are published,
> And I, which was two fooles, do so grow three;
> Who are a little wise, the best fooles bee.
>
> (Donne 1967a, 98–99)[2]

Not much attention has been paid to this poem, undoubtedly because Donne's pose is so obvious. But, especially given the few available remarks by Donne on his poetry, it is worth mentioning since it suggests the difficulty of determining Donne's reactions to his verse.

In "The triple Foole," the poet-speaker seems to identify his own poetry, either this particular poem or previous ones, actual or hypothetical, with "whining Poëtry"; that is, presumably, with the sonnets of the Elizabethan poets against whom Donne should, according to some critics, be rebelling. To counter "whining Poëtry," he will write lines that are like the "earths inward narrow crooked lanes," possibly a reference to the ruggedness of his meter. He knows, though, that even these lines will be set to music, which will please the ear and thus release the pain of love that should be fettered by the verse. Furthermore, verse that "pleases when 'tis read" is not a fit form for love and the pains love produces. Could this be a commentary on the kind of poetry Donne was writing or believed he was writing—verse not intended to please the ear but to imprison the passions?[3] If it is, the tone of the poem reveals self-mockery more than disdain of others' verses. The poet is two fools, who then grow to be three, the ultimate of fools, by even attempting to frame love and grief in verse. If this poem does mock the Petrarchan sonneteers, it mocks love poetry as a whole—or at least the abuses of such poetry—and those who write it even more.

Two verse letters to Thomas Woodward, himself a minor poet, provide little more illumination:

> Now if this song be too harsh for rime, yet, as
> The Painters bad god made a good devill,
> 'Twill be good prose, although the verse be evill,
> If thou forget the rime as thou dost pass.
>
> (Donne 1967a, no. 114, 25–28)

and

> Haste thee harsh verse as fast as thy lame measure
> Will give thee leave, to him; My pain, and pleasure.
> I have given thee, and yet thou art too weake,
> Feete, and a reasoning soule and tongue to speake.
>
> (Donne 1967a, no. 115, 1–4)

In these lines, Donne points to a characteristic of his verse that readers have observed and criticized for nearly three and a half centuries—his

sometimes-irregular meters. However, while Donne may be acknowledging that his verse was different from his contemporaries' poems, he is
more probably adopting a conventional stance: one poet who writes to
another must lessen his own merit to the other's praise.[4] Neither these
lines nor "The triple Foole" yield evidence to critics interested in proving
a poetic revolution.

If Donne does not, then, offer any overtly negative comments on his
fellow poets by extolling his own "revolution" in poetry, he does not offer
any positive ones either. Even Ben Jonson, who admired some of Donne's
poetry and with whose poetry Donne was no doubt familiar, is not praised,
except in a commendatory Latin poem, prefaced to the first edition of
*Volpone*. Like the poems to Thomas Woodward, this poem probably
reflects Donne's courteous sociability and his desire to pay tribute to his
friend more than his taste in poetry. Even so, there is an interesting
disparity between what Donne praises in Jonson's poetry and what
Donne's contemporaries praised in his. Donne writes: "no one is such a
follower of the ancients as you / because you, restorer of the old follow
those you approve" (6–7), and later "Genius and toil render you equal /
to the ancients" (13–14). However, to at least one of Donne's contemporary
admirers, Thomas Carew, Donne's poetry was praiseworthy because he
had "the lazie seeds / Of servile imitation throwne away; / And fresh
invention planted" (Donne [1633] 1970, 389).[5] In the quarrel between the
"moderns" and the "ancients," Carew favors the former, at least in his
praise of Donne's verse:

> . . . thy strict lawes will be
> Too hard for Libertines in Poetrie.
> They will repeale the goodly exil'd traine
> Of gods and goddesses, which in thy just raigne
> Were banish'd nobler Poems, now, with these
> The silenc'd tales o'th'Metamorphoses
> Shall stuffe their line, and swell the windy Page,
>                                    (Donne [1633] 1970, 387)

There are evident differences between Carew's view of Donne's verse and
Donne's expressed view of poetry, but neither poetic statement provides
the modern critic with a satisfactory explanation of how Donne or those
most acquainted with his poetry saw his relationship to the poetry of his
day.

Ben Jonson's comments on Donne, as reported by Drummond of
Hawthornden, contribute to the puzzle of what Donne meant his poetry to
be and of how his contemporaries regarded him as a poet. Both questions
have influenced Donne's critical reputation in the twentieth century. For
example, Jonson's contention that Donne "for not keeping of accent

deserved hanging" (Jonson [1619] 1966, 4) has, in the last three and a half centuries, encouraged those objecting to Donne's "harsh" meter and his "crabbed" style. Their criticism gains authority from Jonson even though his disapproval was probably leveled primarily at the *Satyres* and even though many of what Jonson alleged to be grossly misplaced accents are in fact deliberate, experimental metrical patterns. Similarly, Jonson's assertions that Donne is "the first poet in the world in some things" and that he had written "all his best pieces err he was 25 years old" (6–7) raise questions about what Donne had written by 1597, what Jonson had read, and what of the extant poetry he would have considered best. If in the first statement the emphasis is placed on "some," then there is an obviously implied criticism of other "things." What these are specifically cannot be known.

The early critical history of the *Anniversaries* most clearly indicates how Donne's and Jonson's comments can influence twentieth-century controversies. Immediately after the publication of the poems, Donne, traveling in Paris with the Drurys, received word, probably from George Garrard, about their unfavorable reception in England. Responding to this criticism, Donne wrote to Garrard:

> Of my *Anniversaries*, the fault that I acknowledge in myself is to have descended to print anything in verse. . . . but for the other part of the imputation of having said too much, my defence is that my purpose was to say as well as I could; for since I never saw the gentlewoman, I cannot be understood to have bound myself to have spoken just truths. . . . (Gosse [1899] 1959, 1:303–4)

Later he wrote to his friend Henry Goodyer:

> I hear from England of many censures of my book of Mistress Drury; if any of those censures do but pardon me my descent in printing anything in verse . . . I doubt not but they will soon give over that other part of that indictment, which is that I have said so much; . . .(1:305–6)

In 1619, six years after the *Anniversaries* were published, Jonson remarked, according to Drummond, that "Donne's Anniversarie was profane and full of Blasphemies [and] that he told Mr. Donne, if it had been written of ye Virgin Marie it had been something" (Jonson [1619] 1966, 4). These pieces of evidence seem to indicate a decidedly unfavorable contemporary reaction to the *Anniversaries*. Frank Manley, whose edition of these two poems was published in 1963, interpreted the information in this way: "The *Anniversaries* were never very popular. As early as April 1612, Donne received letters from England criticizing them in the same way they have been criticized ever since: that they say too much, that the praise is too fulsome, the imagery too extravagant" (6–7).[6]

Others, however, interpret the information differently. In 1973, Barbara Lewalski argued that Jonson's remark, although unsympathetic, indicates that the *Anniversaries* "made a deep impression on him" (1973a, 308). Agreeing with O. B. Hardison, she further argues that the uneasiness in Garard's letter and Donne's response "has to do rather with Donne's aristocratic sense that the role of the professional poet is beneath him than with any question about the subject or the execution of the *Anniversary* poems" (Lewalski 1973a, 307; Hardison 1962, 163–66).

Providing additional evidence for Hardison's and Lewalski's theories about contemporary reactions are the numerous seventeenth-century imitations of the *Anniversaries.* For example, A. J. Smith notes that as early as 1612–13, one year after the publication of the *Second Anniversarie,* John Webster echoed the *Anniversaries* in the *Duchess of Malfi* and other works (1975, 36–37). Elegies on the death of Prince Henry also show the influence of the *Anniversaries:* "Some writers simply take over lines and ideas from those poems" (A. J. Smith 1975, 37). One example from a half dozen cited by Smith begins: *"He, He* is dead, who while he lived, was a *perpetuall Paradise"* (Price 1613, 25). If Manley's theory is correct, the objections to the poems would seem to have arisen not from the poems themselves but from the subject. Manley's hypothesis that from the seventeenth century to the twentieth the *Anniversaries* raised objections because "the praise is too fulsome, the imagery too extravagant" might indicate that Elizabeth Drury was not an elevated enough subject for Donne's hyperbolic conceits but that the conceits, taken out of context, provided superb material for imitation. Hardison's and Lewalski's conclusions are easier to reconcile with the number of imitations, but that both conclusions can coexist indicates that Donne's and Jonson's comments on Donne's poetry often prove more confusing than illuminating to twentieth-century studies of Donne.

Donne's comments on poetry and Jonson's opinions of Donne's works are certainly important; a more important source of controversy about Donne's poetry, however, is the notion that Donne began a new school of poetry. This perception of Donne, evident as early as 1633 and persisting through the next three centuries, has often been tied to condemnation or approval of his "rough" meter.

After Donne's death, elegists were less enigmatic than Jonson in their comments on the "Monarch of Wit." Overt praise for his poetry increased, at least in extant works. Carew's "An Elegie upon the death of the Dean of Pauls" is certainly the most famous of the elegies praising Donne because of its perceptive analysis of Donne's poetry. According to Carew, Donne had begun a new kind of poetry of "rich and pregnant phantasie" and "masculine expression," which with its "strict lawes will be / Too hard for Libertines in Poetrie" (Donne [1633] 1970, 386–87). In 1924, Nethercot said of these lines: "To Carew's mind, then, Donne was a reformer in both subject matter and style, as well as a conscious innovator in versification" (1924, 175). Other elegy writers, even while offering evaluations of Donne's poetry, praised him in conventional ways. That is, Donne, "hovering highly in the aire of Wit, / Hold'st such a pitch, that few can follow it" (Arthur Wilson in Donne [1633] 1970, 397). He was "the Prince of wits, 'mongst whom he reign'd, / High as a Prince" (Mr. R. B. in Donne, 400). Izaak Walton asks,

> Is *Donne,* great *Donne* deceas'd? then England say
> Thou 'hast lost a man where language chose to stay
> And show it's gracefull power
>
> (Donne, 382)

Henry King laments that

> Widow'd invention justly doth forbeare
> To come abroad, knowing Thow art not here,
> Late her great Patron
>
> (Donne, 373)

There are numerous other elegies that pursue a similar line of conventional praise. Nethercot notes:

> Very curiously, Donne's metrical peculiarities seem to have troubled no one between the time of Jonson and Dryden. Perhaps Jacobean and Caroline ears were better attuned than those of the Restoration to the rhythms in which men like Mr. Grierson find such individual harmonies; or, on the other hand, as practically all the Neo-Classicists believed, the early seventeenth-century ear may itself have been quite deaf to the beauty of "numbers." (1922a, 464)

If the 1633 elegists were undisturbed by Donne's poetic meters, the same cannot be said for subsequent generations of writers. In fact, before Dryden's famous observations in the 1690s, Donne's meter, as far as we know, had caused comment only three times—in Jonson's comment to Drummond that Donne "for not keeping of accent deserved hanging," in Carew's elegy, and in King's elegy (Woods 1982). After Dryden, anyone interested in holding Donne up for ridicule or blame could cite—if nothing else—his uneven, rough meter. In his late essays especially, Dryden saw Donne as a maleficent influence on other poets, especially Cowley ([1693] 1958, 604). Donne is, he says, a great wit—the quality that Dryden imitated—but not a great poet (661). It is, primarily, his versification that

damns Donne; however, even "were he Translated into Numbers, and *English,* he wou'd be wanting in the Dignity of Expression" (603). Donne, in short, is not "natural"; he depends on abstruse learning and "perplexes the Minds of the Fair Sex with nice Speculations of Philosophy" (604). Dryden's criticism of Donne is not surprising: the eighteenth-century aesthetic was dawning, and the metaphysicals could not but suffer, so different were they from poets like Pope, Dryden, and Johnson. However, in singling Donne out for special censure, Dryden emphasized the earlier poet's presumed rebelliousness. Dryden's specific objections to Donne's meter and to his "perplexing" love poems have been responsible for some unsympathetic readings from Dryden's time to ours. But in pointing to Donne as a bad influence on Cowley, Dryden suggested what became a commonplace later in the eighteenth century: Donne founded a new school of poetry; he was thus to be held responsible not only for the excesses of his own poetry but also for the often-greater excesses of those who followed him.

Eighteenth-century imitations and criticism of Donne bear out Dryden's opinion of him: although his poems are witty, his meter is deplorable. Therefore, as one might expect, the imitations of Donne's verse "regularize" his meter. Pope's reworking of the second and fourth *Satyres* is the best known of these adaptations, and throughout the eighteenth and part of the nineteenth centuries, readers preferred Pope's version because he "every where elevates the expression" (Chalmers 1810, 5:124) and because he "has shown the world that Dr. Donne's *Satires,* when *translated into numbers and English . . .* are not inferior to any thing in that kind of poetry" (Kippis [1793] 1974, 336). Of the many other regularizations of Donne's meter in the eighteenth century, those in Samuel Johnson's *Dictionary* reveal the most about the changing poetic taste, especially since Johnson criticized the meter of Donne's poetry or of metaphysical poetry as a whole only occasionally. In his *Lives of the English Poets,* he calls poetry in the half century before Dryden "savage" because of its "forced thoughts and rugged meter" (1825, 7:307–8) and objects to Cowley's metrical looseness (7:40). More telling than these statements, however, are Johnson's regularizations of two Donne poems and stated preference for Cowley above all other metaphysical poets. In his *Dictionary* ([1755] 1967), under "shroud" and "snow," Johnson uses two Donne passages to illustrate the words' meanings. As Donne wrote them they read:

> Whoever comes to shroud me, do not harme
>   Nor question much
> That subtile wreath of haire, which crownes my arm;
> ("The Funeral," 1–3)

and

> If thou beest borne to strange sights,
>   Things invisible to see,
> Ride ten thousand days and nights,
>   Till age snow white haires on thee,
>         ("Goe, and catche a falling starre," 10–13)

Johnson, quoting perhaps from memory,[7] "improves" the lines by giving them the couplet form of his age; he regularizes meter and rhyme, producing lines that have the same sense and please the ear—at least Johnson's ear—more than the original.[8]

Given these regularizations, it is not surprising that for Johnson, Cowley "excelled his predecessors, having as much sentiment and more music" (*Lives,* 7:18), for in Cowley he finds the rhymed couplet to which his ear is attuned. Johnson often couples Donne and Cowley in his praise or blame: their thoughts are sometimes "worth the carriage," but more often both err in producing "combinations of confused magnificence" (7:17). Nevertheless, Cowley excels among the metaphysicals because his lines approach the eighteenth-century heroic couplet as Donne's frequently fail to do.

More injurious to Donne's future reputation, however, were Johnson's statements on Donne as a rebel. If Dryden began the criticism of what he saw as Donne's poetic rebelliousness, Samuel Johnson codified it. His dicta on the metaphysical poets have been quoted and questioned from his time until now, and they have done much to shape studies of the earlier poet. Although he could praise Donne's learning or individual poems, Johnson, like Dryden, saw his influence on later poets as wholly damaging:

> This kind of writing [metaphysical poetry], which was, I believe, borrowed from Marino and his followers, had been recommended by the example of Donne, a man of very extensive and various knowledge, and by Jonson, whose manner resembled that of Donne more in the ruggedness of his lines than in the cast of his sentiments.
> When their reputation was high they had undoubtedly more imitators than time has left behind. (7:17–18)

Johnson designated Ben Jonson as well as Donne as the leader of this movement. However, all his quotations in the *Life of Cowley* are from those poets whom modern scholars have designated "metaphysical"— Donne, Cowley, Denham. None is from Jonson. This is one of the reasons why on Donne and not on Jonson has been laid the blame for metaphysical obscurity and roughness. The second reason, which Johnson acknowledges, is that Donne combined his rough meter with a certain cast of sentiments that distinguished him from his contemporary.

For Johnson, Donne overturned all the conventions that make poetry worth reading:

> If the father of criticism has rightly denominated poetry . . . *an imitative art,* these writers will without great wrong lose their right to the name of poets, for they cannot be said to have imitated any thing: they neither copied nature nor life; neither painted the forms of matter nor represented the operations of intellect. (7:15).

The importance of Johnson's analysis of Donne and metaphysical poetry cannot be overestimated. For a century and a half after the *Life of Cowley,* Donne's rebelliousness was a cornerstone of scholarly work on the poet, although by the late nineteenth and early twentieth centuries, some were applauding Donne for the revolt Johnson had damned. Scholars like Arthur Symons (1916, 97), Frederick Ives Carpenter (1909, lvii), and Herbert Grierson (1909, 4:197) praised Donne for having scraped away the pretty sugar coating of the Petrarchan sonneteers.[9] Although one must feel grateful to those recognizing that "different" in Donne's case did not have to mean "worse," these writers also perpetuated the myth that Donne was always outside the mainstream of Renaissance literature. Thus they continued to focus attention on Donne's meter, conceits, and wit rather than on his place in tradition.

Even the attempts in the twentieth century to meliorate Johnson's criticism of the metaphysicals have reinforced the notion of Donne as a rebel. William Keast, for example, contends that Johnson was not nearly as critical of Donne and the metaphysicals as modern scholarship insists he was. In fact, Keast writes, Johnson did not single out these poets for blame; rather, when he defined wit, he defined it in poetry in general. His objection to the metaphysicals was simply that they had too much. The same can be said of his other complaints against the metaphysicals (1950, 65). In addition:

> What Johnson criticizes is the characteristic manner of a school—of "a race of writers"—which in individual poems may not predominate or may be assimilated to a compelling effect. And who will say that he has not hit off accurately the distinguishing aims and characteristics of this school? (68)

This is especially so if one looks at the works of Cleveland and Cowley, but even Donne is not exempt, for "If we leave aside all considerations of Donne's influence on the development of the language, of his contribution to the sophistication of the lyric, and of his fascinating personal history, how many great poems did he write?" (69). Thus, simply put, Keast wonders how many of Donne's poems are truly great if we forget about Donne the rebel and Donne the lover. His answer: "I venture to think they are but few" (69). Keast's comments are important for several reasons. First, they indicate the lengths to which scholars may go to bring Donne down from the exalted position accorded him in the 1920s and 1930s; Keast remarks near the beginning of his essay that "we may ask ourselves how far our disappointment with Johnson's treatment of the metaphysical poets reflects genuine deficiencies in Johnson and how far it reflects merely our present conviction that Donne is a greater poet than, say, Gray or even Milton" (60). Second, they show that, Keast's defense aside, Johnson probably did not approve very much of metaphysical poetry. But finally, even if Keast is correct in his revisionist version of Johnson's attitudes, the eighteenth century and the two succeeding centuries believed Johnson was severe with the metaphysical poets and used that severity as a guideline for assessing Donne's poetry. Perhaps *because* Johnson's definition of wit seems so appropriate to Donne's poems, it has continued, in spite of new developments in Donne studies, to be a forceful presence in the twentieth century from Gosse in 1899 to Carey in 1981.[10]

W. C. B. Watkins takes a different position. According to him, Johnson actually was partial to Donne's love poetry, admired the metaphysicals in many respects, and was mainly troubled by the versification, which did not meet the poetic standards set down by Dryden and Pope (1936, 81–82). Johnson wanted to admire Donne more than he did in writing but was prevented by the arbitrary criteria of his age. Donne's poetry was so different and Donne himself was so much the rebel that Johnson was forced to disguise his admiration.

However, whether these scholars are correct or not, Johnson's criticism had a negative influence on the reception of Donne's poetry at least in the eighteenth century. For instance, five out of seven writers, picked at random from the eighteenth-century section of Smith's *Critical Heritage,* criticize Donne's meter (1975, 243–49). What Carew had intimated of Donne was still accepted as truth—he was a leader of a new school of poets and one of the distinguishing marks of this school was rough, "masculine expression" (Smith 1975, 94); however, in the eighteenth century, this was considered a flaw rather than a virtue. His rebelliousness, which in the 1920s would be exploited as his main attraction, was in the eighteenth century turned against him. Nathan Drake, an essayist and doctor who, according to A. J. Smith, expressed "extreme views on literature" (258), nevertheless typifies lay treatment of Donne during the eighteenth century. For Drake, Donne is witty and erudite, but his versification is deplorably harsh and his conceits are cold even in his love poems (Drake [1838] 1969, 298). Even worse, he "may be considered as one of the principal establishers of a school of poetry founded on the worst Italian model, commencing towards the close of Elizabeth's reign, [which] continued to the decease of Charles the Second" (Drake, 298).[11] It was bad enough that Donne was a poor poet; it was unforgivable that he attracted followers.

Most scholars agree that the nineteenth century romantic poets began a Donne revival.[12] Coleridge, especially, tried to rescue Donne from the censure of the eighteenth century and to put him in the mainstream of English poetry. In response to Samuel Johnson and other eighteenth-century critics, Coleridge worked most assiduously at justifying Donne's meter although he admired Donne in all respects. In addition, Coleridge's comments on individual poems reflect an admiration for Donne that, while generally laudatory, also allow for what Coleridge saw as lapses in Donne's poems: he wanted to give Donne his due without overdoing his praise. Thus he calls "A Valediction: forbidding mourning" "an admirable poem which none but Donne could have written" (*Notes* 1853, 255). But although the last two lines of "A Fever" are "just and affecting," all the "preceding verses are detestable" (*Notes,* 254). In "Aire and Angels," "the first stanza is able . . . the second I do not understand" (*Seventeenth Century* 1955, 523n). Coleridge's negative criticism is not indisputably "correct," but it demonstrates Coleridge's avoidance of idol worship. He refuses to raise Donne to the status of ideal poet, choosing rather to regard him as a mortal with weaknesses and strengths. His comment on "Aire and Angels" is a clearer, if not more illuminating, statement of the poem's difficulties than are those offered by later critics about the poem's meaning.

Many of Coleridge's remarks, however, are aimed at absolving Donne from the charge of irregular meter. Most famous is his declaration that "To read Dryden, Pope, &c., you need only count syllables; but to read Donne you must measure *Time,* and discover the *Time* of each word by the sense of Passion" (*Notes,* 249). He attributes many of the irregularities of meter in Donne's poetry to misprintings by those who did not know how to read his poems: to these printers, the lines appeared "anti-metrical," and as a result they printed them so. All Donne's verse, he asserts, is metrical; the songs are smooth, whereas "in the poems when the writer *thinks,* and expects the reader to do so, the sense must be understood in order to ascertain the metre" (*Notes,* 250).

Nevertheless, like those before and after him, Coleridge was interested in rewriting certain of Donne's poems. In his Notebook, no. 43, he used Donne's poetry for what A. J. Smith calls "a peculiar exercise of his own devising" (1975, 276). Defining his practice as that of a "Filter-poet," Coleridge lays out his plan: "By successive Chipping the rude Block becomes an Apollo or a Venus. By leaving behind I transmute a turbid Drench into a crystalline Draught, the Nectar of the Muses" (Smith, 276).

Using this rather puzzling method, Coleridge rewrites two lines from a verse letter to Henry Goodyer: "So had your body'her morning, hath her noone, / And shall not better; her next change is night" becomes "Our bodies had their morning, have their noon, / And shall not better—the next change is night" (Coleridge, *Collected Works* 1969, 1 : 107).[13] Although it is not clear whether Coleridge regarded these lines as faulty and in need of a "Filter" because of printing errors or because of Donne's inadequacies or because of a change in taste and time, his revision adds smoothness at least to the first line by removing the elision. Thus, like others, Coleridge also apparently wanted, in however small a way, to regularize Donne's meter. His famous quatrain on Donne strengthens this assertion:

> With Donne, whose muse on dromedary trots,
> Wreathe iron pokers into true-love knots;
> Rhyme's sturdy cripple, fancy's maze and clue,
> Wit's forge and fire-blast, meaning's press and screw.
> *(Literary Remains* [1836] 1967, 1 : 145)

Although this verse may have been written in a flippant spirit, it, more than Coleridge's positive comments on Donne, was recognized by some nineteenth-century critics as an apt assessment of Donne's verse.

That there was a revival of interest in Donne in the nineteenth century is indisputable; that this revival came about without a struggle is less certain. At least as many nineteenth-century writers objected to Donne's style as approved of it, but the revival seems stronger than it was because Donne's champions were not only more vocal but also more memorable to later generations than were his challengers. Coleridge, Lamb, and the Brownings have earned their own places in literature, whereas Edwin Percy Whipple, James Montgomery, and Francis Cunningham are known only by literary historians. Donne's detractors—and not all of them were as little known as the latter three—while out of the mainstream of nineteenth-century literary taste, demonstrate the ways in which even positive commentary on Donne can be used against him. Those who were intent on criticizing Donne ignored Coleridge's positive statements, referred only to his quatrain on Donne's verse, or disputed the accuracy of all of Coleridge's comments on Donne.

Those aware of the revival but unwilling to praise Donne simply ignored Coleridge. Their comments indicate that they felt obligated to mention Donne but wanted to do so in their—generally negative—terms rather than in Coleridge's. Thus Robert Southey, brother-in-law to Coleridge, mentioned his friend's opinion of Donne neither in his early censure of Donne nor in his later grudging acceptance of him. For Southey, "Donne could never have become a Poet, unless Apollo, taking his ears under his divine care, would have wrought as miraculous a change in their internal structure, as of old he wrought in the external of those of Midas" (1807, 1:xxiv). Perhaps Southey felt that to praise Coleridge for an opinion he himself did not share would smack of flattery but that to attack that opinion would endanger a friendship. Whichever is the case, he was followed in his neglect of Coleridge by John Aikin (1810), Alexander Chalmers (1810), James Montgomery ([1827] 1828), Robert Chambers (1843), H. Taine ([1863–64] 1873), and Willliam Hazlitt ([1818–19] 1930). Hazlitt's comments are representative of nineteenth-century censures of Donne's meter:

> Donne, who was considerably before Cowley, is without his fancy, but was more recondite in his logic, and rigid in his descriptions. He is hence led, particularly in his satires, to tell disagreeable truths in as disagreeable a way as possible, or to convey a pleasing and affecting thought . . . by the harshest means, and with the most painful effort. His Muse suffers continual pangs and throes. His thoughts are delivered by the Cesarean operation. The sentiments, profound and tender as they often are, are stifled in the expression; and "heaved pantingly forth," are "buried quick again" under the ruins and rubbish of analytical distinctions. It is like poetry waking from a trance: with an eye bent idly on the outward world, and half-forgotten feelings crowding about the heart; with vivid impressions, dim notions, and disjointed words. ([1819] 1930, 6:50)

Like several nineteenth-century scholars, Hazlitt took note of the revived interest in Donne only by continuing to depreciate his meter while ignoring his greatest defender.

Others, however, who chose not to ignore Coleridge decided to emphasize his "With Donne, whose muse on dromedary trots" to defend their censure of the poet's meter. Francis Cunningham, annotating an edition of Jonson's conversations with Drummond, quotes Coleridge's quatrain to show the "difficulty of reading" Donne (1875, 373–74 n. 7). Edwin Whipple, while praising Donne's intellect and learning, protests that Donne's verse is marred by obscurity of thought and ruggedness of meter ([1869] 1899, 231). He begins his account with Coleridge's dromedary.

The only adverse critic of Donne during the nineteenth century who paid any attention to the body of Coleridge's remarks was Henry Hart Milman, professor of poetry and dean of St. Paul's. In 1868, in his *Annals of S. Paul's Cathedral,* he called Coleridge's taste for Donne "one of his caprices of orthodoxy." Although Donne does display some excellencies, his poetry on the whole is "hard, harsh, inharmonious" (325). Thus those in the nineteenth century who cared to could still safely avoid the revival by ignoring its chief proponent.

However, despite these negative comments, acceptance of Donne's meter had gained considerable ground since the eighteenth century.

Nethercot argued in 1922 that the eighteenth-century "Neo-Classicists" attacked Donne's meter as vigorously as they did because they "concentrated their attention on those poems of Donne which best agreed in subject-matter with the spirit and taste of their own later age"—that is, his satires (1922a, 464). In the nineteenth century, some notable poets and scholars began to recognize why Donne's meter had been attacked and to appreciate his artistic skill. But, Nethercot maintains, "the exoneration of Donne from the charge of simple slovenliness in workmanship . . . had its real roots in the seventeenth century," in Carew's elegy (470).

A similar pattern can be observed in scholars' and critics' reactions to three other interrelated subjects: Donne's life, wit, and morality. These, especially in the eighteenth and nineteenth centuries, provided admirers and detractors with enough material to support their respective views, thus complicating interpretations of the poet and his work by confusing ethical and technical matters. As with criticism of his meter, this complication began in seventeenth-century responses to Donne.

Elegists expanded upon Donne's own suggestion that his life could be divided into two phases. Sir Lucius Carey, for example, praised Donne because:

> He conquer'd rebell passions, rul'd them so,
> As under-spheares by the first Mover goe,
> Banish't so farre their working, that we can
> But know he had some, for we knew him man.
> Then let his last excuse his first extremes,
> His age saw visions, though his youth dream'd dreams.
> (Donne [1633] 1970, 392)

Throughout his elegy Carey refers to Donne's split life: he is "Both . . . a doubly-named Priest, and King" (Donne, 389) and such a divine priest that we may excuse his earlier passions. The elegy written by a Sir Thomas Browne divides Donne's life even more obviously. The title, "To the deceased Author. Upon the *Promiscuous* printing of his Poems, the *Looser sort,* with the *Religious,*" puts the distinction most succinctly. Browne's too is an elegy of undoubted praise, as he predicts that the "looser" poems will guide those who read them toward the kind of conversion Donne presumably experienced. However, in praising Donne's poetry in these terms, Browne recognizes that Donne's early life was not exemplary and that he must justify his subject's *"Crimes"* and *"wantonness"* (Donne, 376). Jasper Mayne, praising Donne's obscurity, also remarks on his divided life: Donne's

> . . . carelesse houres brought forth
> Fancies beyond our studies, and thy play

> Was happier, then our serious time of day
> So learned was thy chance, thy haste had wit,
> And matter from thy pen flow'd rashly fit,
> What was thy recreation turnes our braine,
> Our rack and palenesse, is thy weakest straine.
> And when we most come neere thee, 'tis our blisse
> To imitate thee, where thou dost amisse.
>
> (Donne, 394)

He concludes this section of praise by apologizing to Donne: "But I do wrong thee, *Donne,* and this low praise / Is written only for thy yonger dayes" (395). Mayne's stance regarding his own poetic skill is conventional. However, the second line of this couplet suggests that Mayne's praise in this part of the poem is purposely and decorously low because his subject is Donne's early life and poetry. This assumption is reinforced when Mayne goes on to praise profusely Donne's sermons and religious poetry. Although these comments by Donne's elegists indicate that the supposed division of his life has been a subject of interest since his death, they have not had much effect on twentieth-century studies of Donne's life, probably because, until recently, they were not paid much critical attention.[14] That is not the case with Izaak Walton's *Life of Donne* and Richard Baker's biographical remarks.

For Walton, Donne's greatest achievement, his greatest and most profound victory, was his ministry. Although Walton outlines other events of Donne's life in some (often erroneous) detail, he declaims most eloquently on his friend's holiness and ministry. Perhaps his most moving description is of the newly ordained minister preaching:

> A Preacher in earnest; weeping sometimes for his Auditory, sometimes with them: always preaching to himself, like an Angel from a cloud, but in none; carrying some, as St. *Paul* was, to Heaven in holy raptures, and inticing others by a sacred Art and Courtship to amend their lives; here picturing a vice so as to make it ugly to those that practised it; and a vertue so, as to make it be beloved even by those that lov'd it not; and all this with a most particular grace and an unexpressible addition of comeliness. ([1670] 1927, 49).

Thus Walton's *Life* established the picture of the saintly Donne, which has enabled others to look principally at one or the other side of his life. Even in the eighteenth century, when Donne's reputation had reached a nadir, his ministry could still be praised. James Granger, for example, condemning Donne's thoughts as "much debased by his versification," still proclaimed with obvious justification that as a divine he "had great merit" ([1769] 1775, 1:260). In the twentieth century, Walton's emphasis has continued to influence studies of Donne by sometimes causing biographers to focus primarily on Donne's religious life while neglecting other influences. For example, in 1964, Frederick Rowe, a Methodist minister, published a biography of Donne, which probably would not have been written were it not for the poet's ministry. Concluding with five original sermons based on Donne's, he says that "Donne will help us find our way back to Christ and to his Church" (223). Certainly Rowe, like Granger, is justified in his emphasis, but Walton's laudatory comments do not proscribe others dealing harshly with Donne because of his religion. Sidney Dark, writing in 1928 when Donne's popularity was rising, provides an extreme example. For nearly fifty pages he says nothing positive about Donne except that he loved Anne More. Then, after quoting Walton's description of Donne's final days, he remarks that Donne's character is no mystery to him:

> He was a man of great parts, of outstanding talents, born in a time of change and meanness, and without the nobility of soul necessary to save him from the traffic of the age. There is no possible reason to doubt the reality of his later religion, but he left Rome to save himself from unpleasant consequences, and he took Holy Orders in order to earn a competence. (102)

Thus, despite Walton's laudatory description of Donne the priest, his account does not prevent the biographer from negatively interpreting Donne's ministry.

Besides reinforcing the notion that the poet's life was easily divided into two segments—rake and divine—Walton encouraged biographical interpretations of certain poems, "A Valediction: forbidding mourning," for example, which have persisted for three hundred years and which have encouraged similar interpretations of other lyrics. Furthermore, because of Walton's frequent factual errors, what he does accurately report must be tested and retested before it is believed. This was the case with Donne's friendship with Henry Wotton. Walton reports that the two were close friends, but because he errs so frequently, his account of the friendship was dismissed. Not until 1924, when Evelyn Simpson discovered letters from Donne to Wotton, was Walton believed (Simpson [1924] 1948, 291-92). Thus, despite a "life" written by a contemporary who actually knew his subject, the study of Donne's biography was hampered rather than helped.

Sir Richard Baker, who also knew Donne, raises somewhat different problems. Baker's biographical facts are too general and too obviously correct to be doubted. He notes that Donne was urged to become a priest by King James, that he was made dean of St. Paul's Cathedral, and that he was a "rare" preacher. The difficulty arises with Baker's description of Donne's early life: Donne upon "leaving *Oxford*, lived at the *Innes of*

*Court,* not dissolute, but very neat; a great visiter of Ladies, a great frequenter of Playes, a great writer of conceited *Verses"* (1643, 156). What, it has been asked, do "not dissolute" and "a great visiter of Ladies" mean? Do these terms refer to Donne's sexual conduct? Was he, in fact, a rake during his Lincoln's Inn days? The position, developed in the forties and fifties, that Baker's words do not substantiate the picture of Donne as a sexual libertine is probably the correct answer to these questions.[15] Yet Baker's comment for many decades cast doubt on Donne's morality and helped to cloud perceptions of his life and work.

During the nineteenth century, when Donne's reputation underwent something of a revival, his life—romanticized and interpreted through the love poems—became the ledge to which unsympathetic critics, still deploring the ruggedness of his verse, could cling as they felt themselves drowning in a sea of new praise for this once rather obscure poet. In fact, some critics could find nothing to praise but his life. In 1819, Thomas Campbell wrote that "the life of Donne is more interesting than his poetry" ([1819] 1875, 182), and this sentiment, so succinctly phrased, found expression throughout the century, leading to numerous speculations about Donne's marriage and love affairs. The accounts were sometimes highly sentimental, intended to draw readers to the more mellifluous of the *Songs and Sonets* while avoiding the more rugged or tasteless ones. Mrs. Anna Murphy Jameson in *Memoirs of the Loves of the Poets* included comments on Donne in a section entitled "Conjugal Poetry." Anne and John's story is "as true and touching a piece of romance as ever was taken from the page of real life." Donne, she continued, "is more interesting for his matrimonial history, and for one little poem addressed to his wife, than for all his learned, metaphysical, and theological productions" ([1829] 1857, 327). Others, not quite so avowedly sentimental, stressed Walton's hint of a converted life. His earlier immoral attitude toward women and his later affection for Anne are both evident in his poems and show the progress of his temper (Cattermole 1844, 1:118-22; Trench 1870, 408; Bellew 1868, 189; and Chalmers 1810, 5:123). The story of Donne's vision of Anne in 1611 was, in an age that appreciated Gothic tales of horror, seized upon as a sign of true passionate feeling (Ferriar 1813, 63; Leigh Hunt 1862, 2:148).[16] Finally, some notable nineteenth-century scholars simply found themselves at a loss when it came to Donne. Their friends obviously esteemed him, and yet they found little that was worthy of note in his poetry. Thus they turned to his life. William Hazlitt was one of these. While agreeing with Samuel Johnson's censure of the metaphysicals, he notes that there are "some beautiful verses to his wife, dissuading her from accompanying him on his travels abroad" ([1818] 1930, 5:83). Such accounts served to make Donne's life and works parallel in importance. If it was impossible to praise his poetry, then his life could be made more poetical than his verse. This emphasis on Donne's life by those unsympathetic to his verse has had an impact on critical evaluations of the poet. In both the nineteenth and twentieth centuries, it has increased speculation about his life, justified biographical studies of his poetry, and promoted amateurish and sentimental accounts of his life by those who have little knowledge of or appreciation for his poetry or his biography. Donne's life seems so accessible that the impulse to write a biography is, for some, irresistible.

Of course, Donne has been noticed in all of the centuries since his for more than the nature of his life. In the eighteenth century, the emphasis was on Donne's wit. Samuel Johnson in his often-quoted definition of metaphysical wit had an enormous effect on the reception of Donne's poetry in the eighteenth century although he was not the first to notice—or deplore—this quality. Both Lewis Theobald and an unidentified essayist in *The Guardian* early in the century remarked on Donne's wit. The former, in 1733, while admitting that "the Writer, who aims at Wit, must of course range far and wide for Materials," lashes out at Donne and the other writers of his age (including Shakespeare) for ranging too far from Nature and into the realms of science so that their wit is far-fetched and obscure. "The poetry of DONNE," he continued, "(tho' the wittiest Man of that Age,) [is] nothing but a continued Heap of Riddles" ([1733] 1949, 1:xlvi). In *The Guardian* (1713), Donne and Cowley were singled out as the most "defective" in their poetry of any writer of the age for their "redundancy of Wit." Richard Hurd, writing in 1753, more than twenty-five years before Johnson's *Lives of the Poets,* criticized metaphysical verse in words remarkably similar to Johnson's:

> This quaint combination of remote, unallied imagery, constitutes a species of entertainment, which, for its *novelty,* may amuse and divert the mind in other compositions; but is wholly inconsistent with the reserve and solemnity of the graver forms. (198)

He goes on to note that Donne was "fonder, than ever poet was, of these secret and hidden ways in his lesser poetry."

However, after Johnson's pronouncement that in metaphysical poetry "the most heterogeneous ideas are yoked by violence together" and that the reader of these poems, "though he sometimes admires, is seldom pleased" *(Lives* 1825, 7:16), criticism of Donne's wit increased. Joseph Warton seems to have been most profoundly influenced by Johnson's dicta. As A. J. Smith notes (1975, 17, 232), Warton was severely criticized after the 1756 edition of *An Essay on the Genius and Writings of Pope* for placing Donne in the second class of poets—those "such as possessed the true poetical genius, in a more moderate degree [than Spenser, Shakespeare, and Milton], but had noble talents for moral and ethical poetry" (in

A. J. Smith, 233). By the second edition in 1762, Warton had dropped Donne to the third class in response to critical outrage over his former classification. Donne was now placed with "men of wit, of elegant taste, and lively fancy in describing familiar life, 'tho not the higher scenes of poetry" (Warton 1762, 1:xi). After Johnson's censure of the metaphysicals, in the second volume of Warton's work (1782), Donne was a poet who "had degraded and deformed a vast fund of sterling wit and strong sence, by the most harsh and uncouth diction" (1782, 2:353). In this case, Warton probably included Donne at first because he appreciated his poetry but subsequently lowered Donne's rank because he had to defend himself against the prejudices of his time.

Although less explicit than objections to wit, criticism of Donne's "taste" also colored eighteenth-century strictures of the poet. Although "taste" is an ambiguous term in any age, most eighteenth-century readers who specifically mentioned Donne's lack of taste were referring to his "unnatural" conceits and hence to his wit or sometimes to his irregular meters; that is, to what they saw as his indecorousness. David Hume links Donne and the Elizabethan writers to the decadent ancients, none of whom possessed taste:

> Learning, on its revival in this island, was attired in the same unnatural garb, which it wore at the time of its decay among the Greeks and Romans. And, what may be regarded as a misfortune, the English writers were possessed of great genius before they were endowed with any degree of taste, and by that means gave a kind of sanction to those forced turns and sentiments, which they so much affected. ([1778] 1983, 5:150)

Hume earlier condemned the ancient Greeks for also possessing "bad taste": "amidst the most elegant simplicity of thought and expression, one is sometimes surprised to meet with a poor conceit, which had presented itself unsought for, and which the author had not acquired critical observation enough to condemn. A bad taste seizes with avidity these frivolous beauties. . ." (5:149). Similarly, an anonymous reviewer of Warton appears to be criticizing Donne's metrical harshness and his wit when he asks, "Did any man with a poetical ear, ever yet read ten lines of Donne without disgust? or are there ten lines of poetry in all his works? No" (*Monthly Review* 1756, 535).

But when Andrew Kippis, defending Donne against this anonymous reviewer, also criticizes the poet's taste, the meaning of the word takes on a slightly different connotation. Kippis writes: "Dr. Donne might have noble talents for moral poesy, and yet they might be perverted from being properly displayed, by his want of taste and neglect of harmony" ([1793] 1974, 5:336). His citing of Joseph Warton as a "far superior arbiter in subjects of taste" than Thomas Birch, who found fault with Donne's inharmonious versification and affected style, indicates that Kippis does see taste primarily as a consequence of decorum in wit and meter. However, by separating "want of taste and neglect of harmony" into two different but related faults and by linking taste with "moral poesy," Kippis suggests that another issue in the eighteenth century was Donne's impropriety in dealing frankly with romantic love, God, and death.

Consequently, improving Donne's decorum, under the guise of regularizing his meter, became the basis for some rewritings of Donne's verse. Two examples will illustrate my point.

The eighteenth-century adaptation of "Breake of Day" begins (in dialogue):

> *Damon. Silvia* 'tis *Day (Sylvia)* what if it be?
> *Damon,* what's that to you or me?
> *(Universal Spectator* 1733, n.p.)

Donne's poem begins: "'Tis true, 'tis day, what though it be? / O wilt thou therefore rise from me?" Donne opens with two perfect iambic tetrameter lines; the imitator with a very irregular iambic meter, the stresses in the first line falling on the first syllable of *"Silvia," "Day," "what,"* and *"be."* Obviously, if regularity were the sole concern here, Donne's first two lines could have been left intact and the whole first four lines given to Sylvia. The versifier seems to have had other aims. Those aims apparently were not only to regularize but to "prettify" the opening lines, removing the direct reference to "Damon" and "Sylvia's" having spent the night together. The implication is there, in the third and fourth lines: "Went we to *Bed* because 'twas *Night? /* Then should we *rise* because 'tis *Light?"* But the woman's direct reference to her lover's rising from her is eliminated. Likewise, the last two lines of Donne's poem, which deviate from iambic pentameter only in that the first foot of line 17 is a trochee rather than an iamb, are "regularized" not so much into strict iambs as into a more tasteful comparison. "He which hath businesse, and makes love, doth doe / Such wrong, as when a maryed man doth wooe" becomes "Gallants when *Men* of *Business,* far remove, / Give *them,* whose *only Business* is to *Love."* The stated objective is regularizing the meter; the underlying motive is propriety.

Similarly, one of the eighteenth-century imitations of the "Canonization" does not regularize the meter so much as it removes the force and immediacy of the situation. Donne's "For Godsake hold your tongue, and let me love" becomes "I Prithee cease to chide my harmless Love" (in A. J. Smith 1975, 172). The eighteenth-century version with its strict iambs is certainly more metrically regular than Donne's; however, the rest of the eighteenth-century poem differs so drastically from the "Canonization" that the two poems can hardly be said to address the same themes. Donne's "five gray haires," gout, palsy and "ruin'd fortune" become "The Sordid Pleasures which thoud'st have me prove" (Smith, 172). Thus, although Donne's versification was, to eighteenth-century ears, harsh and inharmonious, also objectionable were his language and his blunt descriptions of lovers' actions.

In the nineteenth century, those who praised Donne and his poetry were many and varied. Besides Coleridge, other major writers from Emerson, the Brownings and de Quincey to Swinburne, Dante Gabriel Rossetti, and Sarah Orne Jewett admired Donne for everything from verse that is "next to [the] Soul," an "instinct to beauty," and an "impassioned majesty" to his "quaintnesses" and his ability to create "perfect delight" with his poems.[17] The latter part of the nineteenth century also, of course, signaled the awakening of modern Donne scholarship. Augustus Jessopp remembered, in his 1897 biography of Donne, the beginning of his interest in the poet and divine:

> It is fifty years since, as an undergraduate at Cambridge, I projected and began to make collections for a complete edition of the works of Dr. Donne.
> In those days there was a great revival of the study of our seventeenth-century divinity, the result of the great Oxford Movement. . . .
> Perhaps it was just as well that publishers shrank from embarking in so ambitious a venture as I had contemplated; and soon circumstances intervened which took from me "the dream of doing and the other dream of done." (vii)

However, in 1872-73, only twenty-five years after the period Jessopp describes, Alexander Grosart undertook a new edition of all Donne's poems, the first attempt to do so from early manuscripts since the seventeenth century (A. J. Smith 1975, 468). The poems were published, as were so many of Grosart's editions, for private circulation, but the study of Donne did not remain a limited enterprise.

Minor scholars, such as Henry Alford (whom Gosse deplored for butchering Donne's works in his six-volume 1839 edition of selected prose and verse) (Gosse [1899] 1959, 1:x), as well as anonymous reviewers and editors picked up on the century's enthusiasm and took issue with their predecessors' disparagement of Donne. Although not denying his obscurity or his rough meter, these commentators saw in Donne's poems "the warmth and sincerity of genuine feeling" (*Gems of Sacred Poetry* 1841, 86) and "an innate vigour and freshness which will always secure them a high rank in our English poetry" (*Book of the Poets* 1842, 49).

Yet, just as many in the nineteenth century censured Donne as praised him. Some felt that Donne was being unjustifiably elevated to an exalted position in English literature. With some eminent exceptions, Donne's detractors were usually less well known than were his defenders; however, that they chose to deal with Donne at all is a measure of the poet's (sometimes negative) appeal and of his force.

As with his eighteenth-century critics, Donne's "bad" taste and "false" wit were his most objectionable characteristics, and, as in the eighteenth century, the two faults often merged indistinguishably. However, in the nineteenth century, objections to his language and subjects were more overtly stated than they had been in the preceding century. Even those who admired Donne were shocked by his poetry, as Grosart, for example, admitted in his preface to *The Complete Poems:*

> I do not hide from myself that it needs courage . . . to edit and print the Poetry of Dr. JOHN DONNE in our day. Nor would I call it literary prudery that shrinks from giving publicity to such sensuous things (to say the least) as indubitably are found therein. . . . I deplore that Poetry, in every way almost so memorable and potential, should be stained even to uncleanliness in sorrowfully too many places. (Grosart 1872, 1:ix)

He took, Grosart continues, the "responsibility of including Donne" for several reasons, among them that:

> Those whom these Volumes may be assumed to reach are "strong" enough to use them for literary purposes unhurt; and respect is due to the "strong" equally with the "weak."
>
> . . . . . . . . . . . . . . . . . . . . . . . . . .
>
> The moral and spiritual study of an intellect so remarkable and intense, and of an after-life so white and beautiful, is of profoundest suggestiveness. It is only truthful too, to give all known materials for right estimate and right solution of problems started by the Life and Writings of Donne. (1:x)

Alford also was uncomfortable with many of Donne's love poems. In the preface to his six-volume work, he apologizes for omitting a large number of poems but excuses himself by arguing that many of the poems do not "well consist" with his selections from the *Sermons* and *Devotions*. He wanted, he says:

> to avoid as much as possible the strange jumble of subjects and chronological arrangement, which appears in the old edition: where Hymns and Love-elegies, purity and licentiousness, the works of repentant age and unbridled youth are recklessly placed in company. This misrepresentation (for such it is) of the genius of a great man I have endeavored to rectify; and as the last class of Poems did not accord with the nature of the present work. I have omitted them altogether. (1839, 1:vi)

Less generously, an anonymous essayist, writing two years before Alford, complained that Donne's poetry suffers from "too much erotic fervour: he allows his imagination to run loose into the most prurient expressions" (*Penny Cyclopaedia* 1837, 85).

One minor but interesting reason why some nineteenth-century readers were shocked by Donne's verse was that a poor text occasionally made his poetry more seemingly prurient than it is. For example, both Alexander Chalmers' *The Works of the English Poets* (1810, 5:137) and Emerson's *Parnassus* (1875, 70) contain a version of "The Extasie" that is much more scandalous—and amusing—than what Donne wrote. For "Sat we two, one anothers best," both editions read "Sate we on one another's breast."

However, even when the text was good, Donne's poetry was for some too indecent to be designated literature. For the essayist who criticized Donne's "erotic fervour," a "rich vein of poetry" excuses or at least diminishes Donne's excessive sensuality (*Penny Cyclopaedia* 1837, 85). Edwin Percy Whipple, on the other hand, has no use for Donne or for his poetry, and delineates a clear cause and effect relationship beween Donne's wit, the morality of his poetry, and his life. In Donne's poetry, the "power of intellect" is

> perverted to the production of what is *bizarre* or unnatural. . . . The intention is, not to idealize what is true, but to display the writer's skill and wit in giving a show of reason to what is false. The effect of this on the moral character of Donne was pernicious. A subtle intellectual scepticism, which weakened will, divorced thought from action and literature from life, and made existence a puzzle and a dream, resulted from this perversion of his intellect. He found that he could wittily justify what was vicious as well as what was unnatural; and his amatory poems, accordingly, are characterized by a cold, hard, labored, intellectualized sensuality, worse than the worst impurity of his contemporaries, because it has no excuse of passion for its violations of decency. ([1869] 1899, 232)

If Whipple was the most outspoken on this subject, others also linked unnatural conceits, false wit (or excessive wit), and immorality. Donne, wrote Robert Bell in 1839, has intellect, imagination, and learning, but all these, which could be "subjugated by a just taste," are marred by his wit ("the art of clustering an enormous variety of illustrations together"), which makes his poetry "useless for all moral and poetical purposes" (1:50-51).

Palgrave also objected both to Donne's style and to his taste. As Kathleen Tillotson (1959) notes, Palgrave refused to include many of Donne's *Songs and Sonets* in the first edition of his *Golden Treasury* (1861) because they seemed to him unfit for the " 'younger person' " who might read the anthology (31). Despite some wavering, he rejected for his final edition (1891) even those of the *Songs and Sonets* that he admired, holding fast to his principle that no poem characterized by " 'More *thought* than mastery of expression' " could be included (32). Although he included three of Donne's *Holy Sonnets* in *The Treasury of Sacred Song* (1890), his remarks on Donne express exactly why Donne could not be neglected even by those who disapproved of him, why even those who, like Palgrave, had formed an early dislike of his poetry still returned again and again. These poems, he writes, "cover an extraordinary range in subject and are throughout marked with a strange originality almost equally fascinating and repellant" (33).

As Palgrave's remarks show, in each century since the seventeenth, Donne's life, his wit, and his subject matter, which ranges from sexual word play to God and Christ to a provocative combination of the two, have prohibited neglect of the poet. This combination of elements has drawn attention to Donne when others of his status in his generation could be ignored. It has also enabled those who objected to any revival of interest in his poetry to deal with his life or his morality rather than with his poetic worth. That is, if a nineteenth-century reader had difficulty reconciling what his contemporaries believed was valuable poetry with what he saw as poetry deprived of its function by tasteless comparisons, he could turn his discussion of Donne to the immorality of the elegy "Going to Bed" or to the biographical relevance of "On his Mistris" or to the rough meter of the *Satyres* rather than dispute the poetic elements praised by his contemporaries.

This pattern along with discussions of his meter and along with the remarks contemporaries and Donne himself made about his poetry has influenced twentieth-century reactions to Donne. In fact, pre-twentieth-century responses to the poet and the nature of Donne's work itself have had a rather circular effect on twentieth-century criticism: Donne's poetry excites numerous and various responses; these responses in turn have prompted those interested in Donne in the twentieth century to respond not only to the work but also to the frequently idiosyncratic, sometimes-apologetic critical interpretations of the almost three centuries preceding them. Thus, these three hundred years provide a context for exploring the complexities of twentieth-century Donne studies.

# 2
# "I did best when I had least truth":
# Biographical Criticism

Since Augustus Jessopp's biography of Donne in 1897 and, more particularly, since Edmund Gosse's in 1899, the life of John Donne has proven irresistibly fascinating to biographers. Following Gosse's *Life*, thirteen full-length biographies (including two fictional adaptations of Donne's life) and numerous essays, articles, and letters elucidating one facet or other of his life have been written. Donne's life attracts writers, R. C. Bald argues, partly because Donne is the first English poet about whom enough is known to write a modern biography. Accounts of Shakespeare's life, Bald continues, dwell on his times or on autobiographical readings of the *Sonnets;* there are gaps in our knowledge of Dryden's and Spenser's lives, and few of Milton's intimate communications to friends have survived. For Donne, however, letters and verse letters to friends, relatives, and patrons, certain undeniably autobiographical poems, and Izaak Walton's seventeenth-century biography all exist to help, or sometimes to hinder, the modern biographer in piecing together Donne's life (Bald 1970, 2). Nonetheless, much of the twentieth century's fascination with John Donne's biography arises from the seemingly contradictory nature of his life. Jack Donne the Rake and Dr. John Donne, dean of St. Paul's Cathedral, is certainly the best-known antithesis. But such antinomies as Donne the Catholic great-nephew of Sir Thomas More and Donne the Anglican preacher, Donne the poet who extolled "full nakedness" and Donne the sermon writer who condemned lust, Donne the worldly courtier and Donne the other-worldly divine also exist and continue to generate attempts to reconcile the apparent contradictions. The interest in and puzzlement over these biographical inconsistencies are in turn spurred on by what is still uncertain about Donne's life. To show how these two elements—the solid factual knowledge and the tantalizing gaps—work together to frustrate certainty and fascinate or puzzle biographers, I will begin by offering as a sample of the unusual dependence of biographical criticism on interpretation a relatively recent dispute among well-respected chroniclers of Donne's life over a matter seeming on the surface to be quite clear-cut and indisputable—the date of his marriage.

In December, January, or February 1601/2, Donne secretly married his employer's niece, Anne More. We can be as certain that the marriage took place during this three-month period as we can be about virtually anything that occurred almost three hundred years ago. The date, even taking into account the three-month variable, is also more exactly verifiable than many other dates in Donne's life or in the lives of his contemporaries, and so in which of the three months the marriage actually took place would not seem to matter to any but the most exacting of biographers. However, the month one prefers as the date for the marriage depends not so much on the rather ambiguous facts as on one's assessment of Donne's youthful activities and character. On February 2, 1601/2, Donne wrote to his unwitting father-in-law George More to inform him that "about three weeks before Christmas" [1601], he and Sir George's daughter Anne had secretly married (Gosse [1899] 1959, 1 : 101). This letter quite naturally has been the basis for the December dating of the marriage. Gosse, Jessopp, and all biographers until 1972, including Bald, accepted Donne at his word—all, that is, except one. In 1966, Lady Mary Clive in *Jack and the Doctor,* a semi-fictional, semi-scholarly account of Donne's life, wrote that Donne's letter to Sir George was "deliberately untruthful" because the wedding had taken place not in December but in January (56). Picking up on a hint in Clive's note of acknowledgement, Edward LeComte in 1968 examined the *Seventh Report of the Royal Commission of Historical Documents* (Loseley MSS, published in 1897), containing not the Court of High Commission ruling, which is lost, but a lower court ruling on the Donne-More marriage. LeComte concludes from this document that Donne pre-dated the wedding, which actually took place in January, because Anne was pregnant (1968, 168–69).

Replying to LeComte, Wesley Milgate, the editor of Bald's biography of Donne, contends that Bald examined this document and concluded that the marriage, although upheld in January, did, as Donne says, take place at the beginning of December 1601. Milgate ends by saying: "The conjectures of Lady Mary [Clive] and Professor LeComte are, in short, not only unproven, but also highly improbable in the light of Donne's character and the circumstances of the case; and the reputations of Ann and of Donne himself need not be blemished" (1969, 67). Interestingly, neither the December nor the January contention can be absolutely proven: the document in question is vague—according to LeComte purposely so (1972, 20–21)—and can fulfill the expectations of either of the two contenders. Milgate's dismissal of LeComte's theory relies heavily on "Donne's character," more specifically, on Donne's character as he interprets it, just as LeComte relies on Donne's character as he interprets it. Milgate, I would venture to say, is reluctant to believe a future dean of St. Paul's would impregnate a woman before marriage; LeComte believes firmly in the rakish youth who underwent an Augustinian conversion:

> The apology for Jack and Ann, if perchance their daughter Constance was born a little early (say around September first in 1602), is love. I do not doubt it was mutual and true and lasting unto the grave and beyond. Ann, as well as God, was to be thanked for delivering Jack 'from the Egypt of lust.'" (1972, 22).

I have outlined this controversy because it is characteristic of the way in which the certainties of Donne's life, the uncertainties of it, and the oppositions or paradoxes in it work together to create a particularly fertile ground in which the biographer can sow the seeds of imagination and speculation.

For the editors of *Etudes Anglaises,* who printed the first two of these three articles, this controversy illustrates the difference between nineteenth-century and modern biographies:

> D'un côté Lady Mary Clive et M. LeComte, résolument modernes dans leur conception de la biographie, ne font bénéficier leur sujet d'aucun préjugé favorable et prendraient même un malin plaisir à révéler qu'il n'était pas exempt de faiblesses humaines. D'un autre côté le regretté R. C. Bald et W. Milgate maintiennent la tradition anglaise du siècle dernier, respectueuse des gloires du passé et portée à leur accorder le bénéfice du doute. (Milgate 1969, 67n)

Given the range and depth of scholarship and the mainly objective tone Bald evinces in his life of Donne, it is difficult to take this equation of Bald with nineteenth-century biographers with complete seriousness; however, the point as applied to Donne scholarship as a whole is a valid one: the paradoxes inherent in his life make it tempting for even the most sophisticated critic to emphasize one element or aspect of the life while underestimating or understating another. And, of course, this kind of biographical dispute is not confined to these four scholars or to Donne's marriage. Rather, it touches Donne's future relations with his wife and children, his courting of patrons, his entry into the ministry, his performance as dean of St. Paul's, and virtually every other major event of his life.

Before examining the ways in which twentieth-century biographers from Jessopp in 1897 to John Carey in 1981 have concentrated on certain aspects of Donne's life to create sometimes-contradictory pictures of the poet, it is necessary to recount briefly the known facts of Donne's life.

John Donne was born sometime between January 24 and June 19, 1572, to Elizabeth and John Donne, a prosperous ironmonger. Athough little is known of his father's ancestry (he may have been of Welsh descent; he was certainly Catholic), his mother's side of the family had a long and illustrious history. Elizabeth was the daughter of Joan Rastell and John Heywood; her maternal grandparents were John Rastell, the author and printer, and Elizabeth More, the sister of Sir Thomas More. Elizabeth Donne's brothers, Jasper and Ellis Heywood, were well-known Jesuits in England.

Donne's father died in 1576, when John was four years old. Of the six children surviving their father, John was the eldest son and the third child. Six months after her husband's death, Elizabeth was married to Dr. John Syminges, a physician.

In October 1584, when John was twelve and his brother Henry eleven, they matriculated at Hart College, Oxford. Having been educated prior to this at home, the boys entered Oxford when they did to avoid taking the Anglican Oath of Supremacy, not demanded of students under sixteen years of age. During this time, Jasper Heywood, John's uncle, was imprisoned in the Tower as a Jesuit; Donne's mother, Jasper's sister, visited him there. Donne may or may not have accompanied her on these visits.[1] John left Oxford without taking a degree—also to avoid the Oath—and in 1588 and 1589 may have been at Cambridge. Between 1589 and 1592, he may have been traveling on the Continent, possibly in Spain. Unfortunately, Donne's life between 1588 and 1591 is not well documented. However, we do know that in 1588 Dr. Syminges, Donne's stepfather, died and that in 1590 or 1591, his mother again married, this time Richard Rainsford.

Between 1592 and 1596, Donne was at Lincoln's Inn studying law; however, Lincoln's Inn at this time was a place for young men to be educated in the life of London as much as in the law, and Donne left Lincoln's Inn with a knowledge of the law that was to serve him throughout his life but without taking a degree. In 1593, Donne's brother Henry was jailed for harboring a Catholic priest and died of the plague soon after his imprisonment. There is no written record of Donne's reaction. The years at Lincoln's Inn were poetically productive ones for Donne. He probably composed all the *Elegies* as well as two of the five *Satyres*[2] and an undetermined number of the *Songs and Sonets*. Although these probably circulated in manuscript, none was published.

In the meantime, Donne had reached his maturity and had inherited, in 1593, about three months before Henry's death, his share of his father's estate. This amounted to a considerable sum, since (after Henry's death) only he and his sister Anne, now married to William Lyly, remained of the six children who had survived their father. It may also have been during his Lincoln's Inn days that Donne began to stray from Catholicism. Perhaps he questioned the truth of the teachings of the Roman church;

perhaps he began to understand the inefficacy of following a minority religion while trying to make his way in the world. Whatever the case, by 1596 he was sufficiently attuned to the English cause to join Essex and Sir Walter Raleigh on a three-month voyage to Cadiz against Spain. One year later he again joined Essex's fleet to fight Spain.

After Donne returned to England in November 1597, he became the secretary to Sir Thomas Egerton, Lord Keeper of the Great Seal, possibly through the influence of the Lord Keeper's son, whom Donne may have met at Lincoln's Inn and with whom he sailed in 1596 and 1597. The Lord Keeper was apparently quite fond of Donne and entrusted much business to his care.[3] Donne, in fact, had living quarters at York House, where the Lord Keeper resided. Here he became acquainted and intimate with Egerton's family as well as with influential court officials. For example, it is possible that Donne came to know Sir Francis Bacon at this time and likely that he played a role in the imprisonment and trial of Essex after his Irish escapade.[4] During the years with Egerton, Donne probably wrote *Satyre 5* (and perhaps others), possibly some of the *Songs and Sonets,* and definitely *Metempsychosis* (1601).

At York House he also met Anne More, Egerton's niece. In 1597, Thomas Egerton, a widower with three children, Thomas, John, and a daughter, married Elizabeth, the widow of Sir John Wolley and a daughter of Sir William More of Loseley. She had one child, a son, Francis. Her brother Sir George was a widower with nine children. Before her marriage to Egerton, Elizabeth Wolley attended the Queen at court as one of her Maids of Honor, and her son lived with Sir George. To repay this kindness, Elizabeth after her marriage took her niece Anne, Sir George's third daughter, to York House to live with her. Anne and John thus had ample opportunity to become acquainted and to fall in love. However, on January 20, 1600, Elizabeth, Lady Egerton, died, and in October, Thomas Egerton contracted a third marriage, this time to Alice, Countess of Derby. Anne returned with her father to Loseley.

Sir George More, a man of considerable learning, played an active part in public affairs, eventually becoming the Keeper of the Tower. But, as Bald points out, "Sir George, for all his energy and public spirit, was, in fact, rather a bore" (1970, 129). He also had a fiery temper, although one of his sons-in-law described him as "little and good" (quoted by Bald, 130). In 1601, he was a Member of Parliament, and Anne accompanied him to London. She and Donne met secretly, perhaps several times, and were secretly married. The secrecy was essential because Sir George certainly would not have approved of such a marriage for his sixteen-year-old daughter: Donne was definitely Anne's social inferior. The marriage was witnessed by Christopher Brooke, Donne's friend since their Lincoln's Inn days together, and performed by Samuel Brooke, a newly ordained minister, Christopher's brother, and also a friend. At the end of the parliamentary term, Anne returned to Loseley with her father while John awaited the right moment to tell him. On February 2, 1601/2, Donne, ill at the time, wrote to Sir George to inform him of the deed. The letter was delivered by Henry Percy, Ninth Earl of Northumberland, who was on friendly terms with Sir George but who, nonetheless, was unable to temper Sir George's wrath. Donne and the two Brookeses were imprisoned; despite another letter from Donne, Sir George persuaded Egerton to dismiss him. The marriage was finally validated in April 1602, and although Sir George tried unsuccessfully to convince Egerton to take Donne back into his service,[5] he himself refused the couple Anne's dowry.

Fortunately, the reunited couple was taken in by Anne's cousin, Francis Wolley, and his wife Mary on his estate at Pyrford. During the years at Pyrford, Donne studied and probably helped Francis with his accounts. In 1603, Queen Elizabeth died; when the new monarch, James, visited Pyrford, he probably met Donne. In 1605, Donne traveled on the Continent. By 1606 he could afford—doubtless because Sir George had finally relented and paid at least part of Anne's dowry—to move his family to Mitcham, closer to London than Pyrford and thus more accessible to possible employers. By the time the Donnes left Pyrford, they had three children, Constance, John, and George. During the five years they spent at Mitcham, they had four more children, Francis, Lucy, Bridget, and Mary. With such a large family and with the certain knowledge that it would continue to grow (when the Donnes left Mitcham in 1611, Anne was only twenty-seven), Donne was obviously in need of employment, nor did he remain unemployed for lack of trying. Sometime between 1601 and 1608, Donne met and courted as a patroness Lucy, Countess of Bedford. In 1608, she stood as godmother to the Donnes' fifth child, who bore her name. One year later he became reacquainted with Elizabeth Stanley, now the Countess of Huntingdon by her marriage to Henry Lord Hastings. Elizabeth was the daughter of Egerton's third wife, Alice, Countess of Derby, by her first husband Ferdinando Stanley. Donne had been a great favorite of all three of Alice's daughters when he was at York House, but especially of Elizabeth, who called Donne her "prophet." Now he began seeking her patronage, although discreetly so as not to anger the Countess of Bedford.

Donne was reintroduced to the Countess of Huntingdon by Sir Henry Goodyer. Intimate friends for years until Goodyer's death, the two men made a practice of writing each other once a week on Tuesdays. It is from this correspondence that we learn much about Donne's life. Goodyer was also liberal with his often-limited funds, frequently loaning money to Donne.

With the new monarch came the possibility of court employment. In

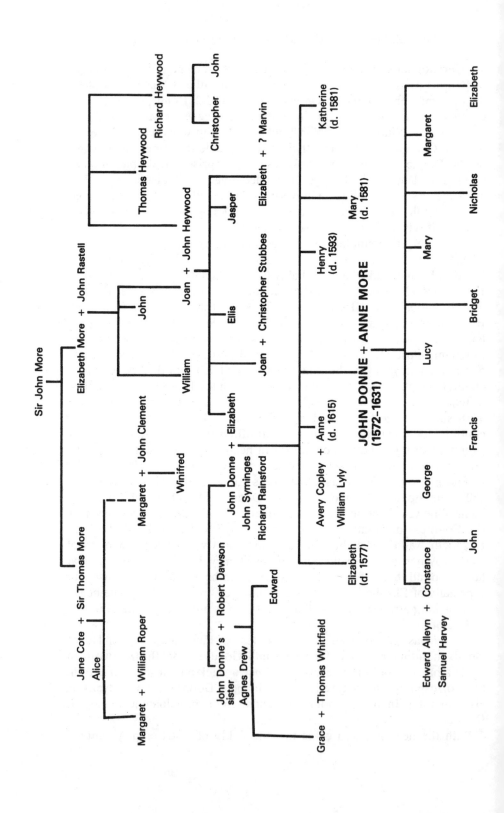

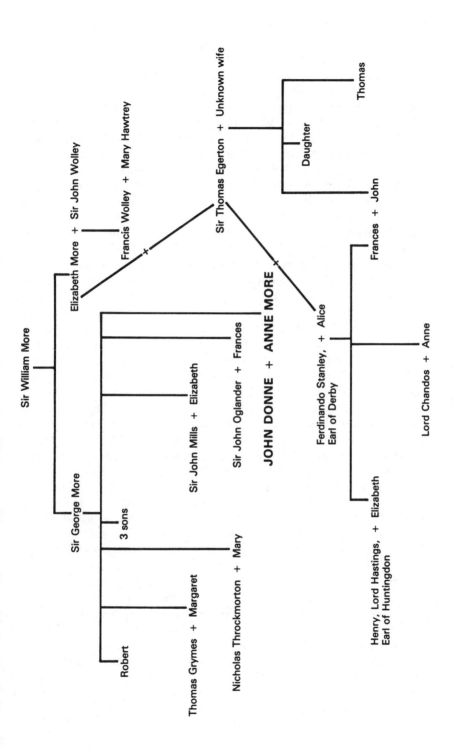

Sir William More

Sir George More

Elizabeth More + Sir John Wolley

Francis Wolley + Mary Hawtrey

Sir Thomas Egerton + Unknown wife

Daughter

Thomas

Frances + John

Robert

Thomas Grymes + Margaret

Nicholas Throckmorton + Mary

3 sons

Sir John Mills + Elizabeth

Sir John Oglander + Frances

**JOHN DONNE + ANNE MORE**

Ferdinando Stanley, + Alice
Earl of Derby

Henry, Lord Hastings, + Elizabeth
Earl of Huntingdon

Lord Chandos + Anne

1607 Donne attempted unsuccessfully to secure a post in the Queen's household. His petitionings for the secretaryships of Ireland (1608) and Virginia (1609) also failed.

Despite these disheartening failures and the frequent illnesses in his family, however, Donne continued to busy himself with study and writing, especially on religious matters. In 1607 or 1608, Donne wrote *Biathanatos,* a defense of suicide and a testimony to his despair during the early years at Mitcham; however, more orthodox work was soon to follow. By the time Egerton employed him, Donne must have been at least a nominal Anglican: it is inconceivable that the secretary to the Lord Keeper would be a professed, practicing Catholic. During the Mitcham years he assiduously studied the Anglican and Catholic controversialists as well as the church fathers. Sometime before 1607, he met Thomas Morton, the most impressive of the Anglican controversialists. By 1607, Morton was familiar enough with Donne and his studies to try to persuade him to take holy orders. Donne refused. Around 1609, however, he actively entered into the religious controversy of his time, which had intensified with the Gunpowder Plot in 1605 and the resulting new Oath of Allegiance required of English Catholics. The Pope and various Catholic writers condemned the Oath; finally, in 1607, James himself replied with *Triplici Nodo Triplex Cuneus or an Apologie for the Oath of Allegiance.* Thereafter, Catholics and Anglicans all over Europe wrote furiously defending their respective positions. In 1610, Donne, feeling perhaps that James's position had not been adequately defended, published *Pseudo-Martyr,* encouraging English Catholics to take the Oath and condemning for false martyrdom those who did not. In 1611, *Ignatius his Conclave,* a satirical attack on the Jesuits, was published in Latin and English.

Donne's literary efforts at this time were private as well as public. Along with numerous verse letters to the Countesses of Bedford and Huntingdon and to friends such as Henry Wotton, Donne also composed religious meditations such as the *Holy Sonnets,* "La Corona," and "A Litanie." Some of the *Songs and Sonets* may also belong to this period. Yet in spite of all his study and writing, Donne was still unemployed.

In 1611, however, his fortunes rose slightly. In December 1610, Elizabeth Drury, the only surviving child of Sir Robert and Lady Drury, died just before her fifteenth birthday. Donne had probably become acquainted with the Drurys through his brother-in-law William Lyly or through Joseph Hall. Following the fashion of the time, Donne composed a short funeral elegy for Elizabeth Drury, followed by the longer *First Anniversarie: An anatomie of the World.* Pleased with the poems, Sir Robert offered to have Donne accompany him and his wife to the Continent. Donne accepted, leaving the children and Anne, now pregnant with their eighth child, with her sister and brother-in-law, Frances and John

Oglander. While in Paris in 1612, Donne learned that Anne's baby was stillborn. He had by this time composed the *Second Anniversarie: Of the Progress of the Soule,* since both were published in 1612 and he was receiving news from England of their reception. After returning to England with the Drurys in September, Donne moved his family to a residence at Drury House.

The years 1613 and 1614 were particularly sad and frustrating for Donne despite better living conditions. In 1613, the Donnes' ninth child, Nicholas, was born but died before he was a year old. The family, including Donne, suffered repeated illnesses; in 1614 two more children, three-year-old Mary and seven-year-old Francis, died. During the same year, Donne sat in Parliament and made his final bid for state employment through James's current favorite Sir Robert Ker, Earl of Somerset. Once again he failed. In 1615, he entered the ministry and was appointed royal chaplain to King James, who also made him an honorary Doctor of Divinity. During the next two years, Donne was granted the rectories of Keyston and Sevenoaks and became Divinity Reader of Lincoln's Inn. The Donnes' tenth child, Margaret, was born in 1615; the eleventh, Elizabeth, in 1616; in August 1617, Anne Donne died after giving birth to the twelfth, her second stillborn child.

Donne preached frequently at Lincoln's Inn, where he was well known and respected, and at Sevenoaks and Keyston as well as at Court. Sometime bewtween 1615 and 1619, Donne probably composed the *Essays in Divinity,* a series of meditations and prayers (they may have been composed earlier). In 1619, James sent Donne, in part to improve his health, on a trip to Germany with Viscount Doncaster's embassy. A year after his return in 1620, Donne was made dean of St. Paul's Cathedral. For the next five years, he was busy with his preaching and administrative duties. Although he resigned his Keyston rectory (1621) and his Readership at Lincoln's Inn (1622), Donne continued to preach at Sevenoaks, at Court, at St. Paul's, and at a number of marriages, funerals, and state affairs.

In 1623, Donne arranged a marriage, which took place in December, between his daughter Constance, then at least twenty years old, and Edward Alleyn, who was fifty-seven. Alleyn, the famous actor, now retired, had met Donne and Constance through Margaret and Thomas Grimes, Anne's sister and brother-in-law, who were especially fond of their niece. Alleyn, six years older than his father-in-law, and Donne quarreled in 1625 over financial matters, but when Alleyn died in 1626, he left Constance a considerable sum of money. She married Samuel Harvey in June 1630.

Shortly before Constance and Alleyn's marriage Donne was seriously ill with a relapsing fever, possibly typhus (Lander 1971, 89), and composed the *Devotions upon Emergent Occasions,* published in 1624, the same year he became vicar of St. Dunstan's-in-the-West. On March 27, 1625,

James died; and since April was Donne's regular month of court preaching, he delivered the first sermon to the new King Charles. While the Court and all England were still in mourning, the plague struck London. Donne retired to the home of Magdalen Herbert, Lady Danvers, at Chelsea to wait out the epidemic. Donne had known her for years, but during the five or six months he spent there he was able to renew and deepen his friendship with her and her whole family, including her sons George and Edward. These months of retirement also gave Donne the opportunity to write out from his notes a number of sermons he had preached. After his return to St. Paul's in December, Donne continued to be active in the affairs of church and court.

The remaining years of Donne's life were busy but also filled with the deaths of friends. In January 1627, his daughter Lucy died unexpectedly at the age of nineteen. In March, Sir Henry Goodyer died, followed by the Countess of Bedford in May, Lady Danvers in June, and Christopher Brooke in February 1628. In 1630, while visiting Constance and her new husband at Aldoborough Hatch, Donne suffered from what was to be his final illness. Although he returned to London to preach his last sermon, *Deaths Duell,* at Court in February 1631, he was visibly ill, and his condition was perhaps worsened by the death two months before of his mother, who had lived with him at the Deanery for several years. At the urging of his doctor, he posed in his shroud for a portrait, which was to become a marble effigy.[6] He died on March 31, 1631.

I have presented Donne's life in this fashion to show, first, how much is known of his activities and, second, to contrast these bare facts of his life with the interpretations often given those facts.

In many ways Augustus Jessopp and Edmund Gosse laid the foundation for the contradictory interpretations of Donne's life in the twentieth century. Although the two worked closely together—Jessopp turned over all his notes on Donne to the younger Gosse when he realized he could not write a complete biography—each emphasized different elements in Donne's life. Jessopp admits, with a refreshing if somewhat naive frankness, in the preface to his biography, *John Donne: Sometime Dean of St. Paul's* (1897), that he could never feel

> much enthusiasm for Donne as a poet; and it is as a poet that Donne's fame has chiefly come down to us. Who was I that I should undertake to deal with the life of the man whose poetry I had not the power of appreciating at its worth? There must be some deficiency, some obliquity in my own mind. . . . I have dealt with Donne as one of the great *leaders of religion* in his time; it is from this point of view that this volume should be read. (viii–ix)

Thus, Jessopp was interested in one aspect of Donne's life—his ministry and the events leading Donne to preach God's word. There is nothing intrinsically unjust in this approach to an author; it can be likened, for example, to Christopher Hill's concentration on Milton's political rather than poetic life. However, this particular emphasis caused Jessopp a number of problems that are not unique to his work but that many biographers of Donne have faced.

First, if biographical interpretations of an author's work are in fashion, and the critic is presented with a collection of often explicitly sexual love poems by a man who becomes, twenty or so years later, one of England's most eloquent ministers, what can the biographer do to reconcile these two elements of his subject's life? One course he can take is to follow Walton in proposing an Augustinian conversion for Donne. Another course, the one Jessopp chose, is to dismiss the majority of verse as low quality work: "[I]t is difficult to believe that these earlier poems were not loved for the poet's sake rather than the poet for the sake of his verse" (19). Thus poems containing such provocative lines as "Licence my roaving hands, and let them go" or "Some that have deeper digg'd loves Myne then I, / Say, where his centrique happinesse doth lie," can be relegated to amateurish dabbling. There are, Jessopp must admit, "some few exquisite passages" in Donne's early poems (19), which, he implies, though more circumspectly than later biographers, were written as a result of Donne's love for Anne More (22). In this way, Jessopp, following Izaac Walton's lead, states that "A Valediction: forbidding mourning" was written for Anne before Donne left for the Continent with Drury (77) and assumes also that the elegy "The Perfume" was written for Anne during courtship when they feared her father's disapproval (22).

Concentrating as he did on Donne's religious life, though, Jessopp could safely afford to pass over the poems rather quickly. However, even in the early prose works, similar problems arise. In a religious biography, what is one to do with a future minister's disquisition on suicide? Jessopp makes quick work of *Biathanatos,* treating it primarily as an intellectual exercise. Although Donne was overwrought and depressed, his approach to the question of suicide was casuistical rather than personal:

> That the temptation to put an end to his own life ever presented itself to Donne in the form of a possible course of action—much less as a deliberate purpose to which his will inclined—must always appear incredible to any who have learned to know the man and to appreciate the true nobility of his character. (62)

To biographers of the turn of the century wanting to emphasize Donne's religious character, both the secular poems and *Biathanatos* proved embarrassments to be somehow explained away.

Two other large areas of Donne's life mystified these early biographers—his refusal to enter the ministry at an earlier age than he did and his sometimes excessive court flattery. Donne was encouraged by Thomas

Morton to take holy orders as early as 1607. Although the Donnes were at this time living at Mitcham, they had very little money coming into the house except for Anne's dowry. They had four small children, and, in June, when Morton probably made his offer, Anne was at least seven months pregnant. Donne's refusal can be, and has been, seen as sheer lunacy, overwhelming ambition for greater prospects, or extreme devotion. Jessopp, of course, chose the last:" [H]is conscience he would not tamper with; and to enter the ministry of Christ's Church only for the hope of gain,—that he could not and would not bring himself to do. It might be the call of man, it was not the call of God" (57–58).

To explain the flattering prose and verse letters Donne sent to hoped-for or actual patrons and patronesses in his search for state employment, Jessopp draws a picture of Donne used by the king's favorites for their own purposes. Donne, he argues, knew by 1610 that he would enter the ministry and decided that it would flatter James to be told of his decision through Jame's favorite, Rochester. Donne then wrote to Rochester of his intention to take holy orders, but Rochester, actively promoting the scandalous and very messy divorce of Lady Frances Howard and the Earl of Essex in order to marry Frances, suppressed the letter and used Donne for his own purposes, as a kind of legal secretary: "In spite of himself he [Donne] was compelled to play the part of courtier, and to do the work of a court poet at the bidding of his patrons" (83). Jessopp's account is factually inaccurate. The letter to which he refers was written in 1613, not 1610; Donne is somewhat vague about just what kind of employment he was asking for from Rochester; and he never served as Rochester's secretary (Bald 1970, 273ff). But even if Jessopp's facts were correct, his story still shows to what great lengths he was willing to go to make those facts match the religious character he proposes. To suggest that Donne would allow himself for five years to be controlled by Rochester when he had a calling from God to enter the ministry would seem to speak more of Donne's weakness than of his devotion; yet this is how Jessopp reconciled the flattering ambition with the religious vocation.

Thus Augustus Jessopp's biography of Donne presented at the dawning of the twentieth century the conflicting aspects of Donne's life that have continued to fascinate and plague later biographers choosing to emphasize one facet of his character to the exclusion of others.

Edmund Gosse, whose *Life and Letters of John Donne* was published in 1899, two years after Jessopp's biography, was, like his predecessor, interested in Donne's religious life; however, Gosse had a greater appreciation for Donne's secular works and gave equal emphasis to Donne's religious and secular interests. Although Gosse did not begin the practice of interpreting Donne's secular love poetry as autobiography, his account of Donne's licentious youth in a biography that remained for seventy years the most complete and authoritative record of the poet's life certainly encouraged such speculation. Gosse claims in the preface to his *Life* that "to me, even to his last seraphical hour in his bed-chamber at St. Paul's, Donne is quintessentially a poet" (1:xi); however, readers of Gosse's biography soon realize that he was more interested in Donne as a distinct personality than in Donne as a poet,[7] and this interest, quite naturally, influenced Gosse's perception of Donne's poetry and life.

Studies or analyses of a poet's life through his work were considered during Gosse's time and after a legitimate form of scholarship, even though objections were sometimes raised to excesses. Gosse, however, rejected biographical interpretations of other Elizabethan lyricists, specifically Drayton and Spenser, because they were following the literary tradition of embroidering upon imaginery love adventures. The biographical basis of their love stories, therefore, remains nebulous (1:61). Donne, according to Gosse, broke from tradition and wrote about actual events of his life: "We read Donne . . . to little purpose if we do not perceive that he was, above all things, sincere. . . . there is hardly a piece of his genuine verse which, cryptic though it may seem, cannot be prevailed upon to deliver up some secret of his life and character" (1:62). In this way, Gosse begins and justifies what has come to be the most famous error of his *Life:* the fabrication through the evidence in the *Songs and Sonets* and *Elegies* of an intrigue between Donne and a married woman. How else, Gosse wonders, can one explain the intensity, the realism, and the drama of the elegy beginning "Fond woman which would'st have thy husband die" or the startling malediction in "The Apparition"? It has become easy to ridicule Gosse's biographical theories, and rightly so: there is no conclusive evidence aside from the poems themselves—and they are more enigmatic than Gosse believed—that Donne was ever involved with any woman except Anne More (although he undoubtedly was involved in some sexual escapades). However, Gosse's interpretation of Donne's life through the poems has more theoretical relevance to the progress of Donne scholarship than has generally been recognized.[8]

Gosse himself was aware of the pitfalls of biographical interpretations of poetry: "The dangers of such a conjectural reconstruction of biography are obvious," but, he adds:

> in few cases in literary history is that method more legitimate than here.
> When Donne speaks of his personal experience, there is something so
> convincing in his accent, poignant and rude at once, that it is impossible
> not to believe it the accurate record of a genuine emotional event. (1:62)

With this statement, Gosse defines a problem (or a virtue) of Donne's poetry that has troubled any number of scholars and critics. There is a quality about it—whether the direct address, the intellectual wit, or the force of the personality behind the speaker—that makes the poems *seem* true, *seem* the record of actual events. If Gosse appears simplistic and old-fashioned in his analysis of the "events" of the *Songs and Sonets* and *Elegies,* he is followed in his method, if not in his conclusions, by other seemingly less naive scholars right up to our own day.[9]

Gosse then tries to justify his biographical approach by explaining one of the few comments Donne made about his poetry. In a letter to Sir Robert Ker[10] in 1625, Donne wrote: "You know my uttermost [in verse] when it was best, and even then I did best when I had least truth for my subjects" (1:62. Brackets are Gosse's). Gosse explains that the poetry Donne and his contemporaries thought "best" does not match modern readers' evaluations. Donne, he conjectures, would have considered his best poetry that which was filled with "metaphysical extravagance" and in which he "embroidered conceit after conceit upon a false or trivial first idea" (1:63). Therefore, what today are considered "best"—the love songs like "Sweetest love," "The Good-morrow," "The Sunnes Rising"—do reveal a true sequence of events because Donne would not have agreed with this appraisal. Despite Gosse's certainty, the question of Donne's evaluation of his own poetry is, of course, unanswerable.

Not only is it impossible to prove which poems Donne considered his best (unless additional evidence is discovered), but also it is difficult to determine what Donne meant by "truth" and how seriously he meant the statement. If he intended a personal poetic theory, what do his words indicate about the "truth" of the *Anniversaries* and the *Holy Sonnets,* most of which he wrote before 1625? Did he mean that these had little truth in them, that he did not consider them among this best, or simply that Ker had not read them?

More probably, Donne did not write these words as an all-inclusive poetic dogma. But because there are so few extant comments by Donne on his poetry, the words have been seized upon by scholars and critics throughout the twentieth century. David Novarr, for example, suggests they show Donne informing his friend Ker that "he no longer considered himself a poet, that his best days as a poet—when he was given to feigning—were in the past, and that as priest and as regarder of truth he was estranged from the Muse" (1980, 195). But, Novarr adds, the statement is "belied by the 'Hymne to God my God, in my sickness,' written not long before [1625] and written on the subject which was, above all others, full of truth for him" (204). Helen Gardner interprets the statement, at least in part, as a farther-reaching expression of poetic theory and uses it to discourage biographical interpretations of the poems usually assumed to be sincere expressions of Donne's love for Anne. Donne, she says, warns against any such easy "equations between the truth of the imagination and the truth of experience" in his letter to Ker (Gardner

1965, xx)—a conclusion with which William Empson, of course, disagrees (1966, 270).[11]

Gosse's conclusions, therefore, may be far-fetched, but he was trying to rationalize a troublesome area in Donne scholarship by answering in his own way a question that has continued to interest, and perplex, biographers and biographical interpreters. To solve the puzzle of this statement would tell us much about the biographical value of Donne's poetry.

Although Gosse's poetic evidence of an illicit love affair in Donne's early life has been widely rejected, his portrait of Donne as a licentious, rebellious youth converted to a holy, obedient servant of God in his later years occurs again and again in biographical studies of Donne over the next eighty years. In his desire to deal with Donne as a minister, Jessopp glossed over Donne's early life, concentrating on him as a rising wit in Elizabeth's court; Gosse, however, was intensely interested in Donne's whole character and thus expanded upon the Augustinian conversion suggested by Walton to explain the discrepancy between his versions of the young rake and the mature Anglican priest. Furthermore, Gosse's desire to understand and portray Donne's whole character allowed him to avoid some of Jessopp's errors caused by the latter's intense desire to keep the character of the dean of St. Paul's pure. Only recently has it been suggested that Gosse did not idolize Donne as much as Jessopp did,[12] and perhaps that is why Gosse was willing, unlike Jessopp, to treat Donne as a man rather than as a saint. For example, Gosse's account of Donne's relations with Rochester does not differ significantly in outward facts from Jessopp's. The difference arises, as it does so often with Donne, in the interpretation of these facts. Rather than treating Donne as a befuddled but sincere holy man, Gosse claims Donne dropped all ideas of entering the ministry after Rochester's "buying" of him (2:22). Donne, for Gosse, was a complex man with worldly desires and ambitions that could, and in Gosse's view did, corrupt him. He regards the whole episode as vile and degrading; he has few good words to say for Rochester and fewer still for Frances, but he does not try to camouflage what he believes was Donne's involvement with the two. His only apologies for Donne's actions are poverty and depression, and he mourns that this "whole period of Donne's life was ignominious, and his dependence upon Somerset [Rochester became the Earl of Somerset in 1613] degrading to his judgment and conscience. The reader cannot fail to observe a temporary deterioration of his character. Poverty and anxiety dragged his beautiful nature down into the dust" (2:54). There is idolatry here, of course, but with a difference: Donne is the active mover in this affair as in his earlier sexual intrigues, not the passive religious man trusting to the good will of others as he is in Jessopp's biography. The events remain the same; the man's character alone changes.

Having established Donne's character as licentious (in his early youth) and worldly ambitious (in his early years of marriage), Gosse somehow had to account for Donne's ministry and religious devotion in his later years. Jessopp had assumed that Donne throughout his married life aimed at holy orders but was sidetracked by unscrupulous patrons. Gosse, however, presents Donne's entry into the ministry as the natural outcome of Somerset's loss of favor with King James, of Donne's realizing his chances of court employment were slim, and of the King's specific pronouncement that he would prefer Donne only in the church. Gosse makes a sharp distinction, which today seems overly simplistic, between what he sees as Donne's worldliness and his holiness, dating his conversion three years after Donne took holy orders, when Anne died.[13] Before this, Donne had accepted God intellectually, which does not mean he was insincere or ungodly (2:99), just not passionately committed to his calling. With Anne's death, "which brought about the final process of sanctification and illumination" (2:101), Donne turned to God with his emotions as well as with his mind. Jessopp comments only that Donne was grieved and in his grief "rashly" promised his children never to remarry. This promise, in Jessopp's view, would have been better broken, both for Donne's sake and his children's (123). These two differing accounts of Donne's conversion perhaps best illustrate the difference in emphasis in Gosse's biography and Jessopp's. The latter's view is of a Donne wholly committed to the religious life but occasionally interrupted in his pursuit; the former's is of a Donne complex and changeable.

The errors in both accounts of Donne's life are many and are frequently compounded by what to modern readers seems an incredible naïveté, but I have not presented their inaccuracies and misinterpretations to ridicule either Jessopp or Gosse; both were important scholars, and Gosse especially opened the door on Donne scholarship if only because so many critics were anxious to reveal his mistakes. But even more important, their studies established the contradictory and argumentative tone marking the study of Donne since 1900.

Gosse's was the first of many biographies of Donne to differ substantially from Walton's account. According to Clement Wyke, one of Gosse's main reasons for undertaking such a biography was Donne's relative obscurity in the nineteenth century (1976, 809–10). Even though nineteenth-century scholars were noticing and praising Donne more than their predecessors had, they were relying on Walton's biography (or others not differing substantially from Walton's) and poor texts. Donne's letters had not been collected and edited since his son's self-serving efforts. Like every good scholar, Gosse wanted to do what had never been done before, but he had opened a treasure trove (or a Pandora's box): from 1899 on Donne had to be accounted for. Since Gosse's study relied heavily on

Donne's works for an interpretation of his life, it is not surprising that Donne scholarship in the first two decades of the twentieth century should exhibit a strong biographical bent. Of course, that kind of criticism was not unique to Donne: before the "New Critical" techniques of the 1920s and 1930s, the works of Milton, Shakespeare, Sidney, Gascoigne, and Spenser, to name only a few Renaissance writers, were subject to biographical interpretations or were the basis for reevaluations of these writers' lives. However, even when biographical criticism was the rule rather than the exception, some scholars endeavored to extricate certain authors from this limited approach. W. J. Courthope in 1903 objected strongly to reading too much of Milton's life in *Samson Agonistes* (3:411); Felix Schelling in 1913 protested against scholars who denied that Sidney's love for Penelope Devereux was the basis for *Astrophil and Stella* and who treated the sonnets as merely Sidney's dabbling in Petrarchism, although later he conceded that the characters in Shakespeare's *Sonnets* might be the result only of a fertile imagination with no biographical significance (59, 65). Thus various Renaissance poets were, by various critics, placed outside biographical interpretations. However, every critic in the first two decades of the twentieth century who took note of Donne was convinced of the autobiographical significance of at least the *Songs and Sonets* and the religious poems and often of the *Elegies* and *Satyres* as well. Had Donne been a less contradictory man, this would not have mattered. If he had been a more conventional minister like Herbert or if as little were known about his life as is known of Shakespeare's, biographical interpretations of his work would have either run their course and died or been substantiated. Instead, partially because of Gosse's claims and partially because of the nature of Donne's life and works, studies of him during these twenty years depended to a great extent on the critics' perceptions of Donne's character[14]—and the critics' perceptions ranged from romantic adoration to vehement hatred. Four factors disturbing to this generation of critics prompted these differing reactions to Donne's life as seen through his work. First, Donne seemed one of the most sincere and veracious of Renaissance poets. Second, he treated sexual themes with an explicitness shocking to even the most sophisticated turn-of-the-century scholars. Third, he did not follow the usual path for churchmen in either the seventeenth or nineteenth century. And fourth, Donne seemed to have rebelled against poetic conventions.

The concept of sincerity in Renaissance poetry as that term was used by early twentieth-century writers is anathema to present-day scholars. For the last fifty years, literary criticism has shied away from discussions of sincerity in sixteenth-century poetry, concentrating instead on literary conventions. To the early twentieth-century scholar, however, sincerity was not a forbidden concept. Just as the lesser Elizabethan sonneteers who closely followed the Petrarchan conventions were scorned for their obvious insincerity, the greater poets were praised both for the intensity of their passions and for their talent in conveying that intensity in poetry. When Donne was brought to eminence by Gosse and Jessopp, he presented scholars with a more complex set of problems than did Sidney, Spenser, or Daniel certainly, and perhaps even than did Shakespeare. Donne seems to offer in his *Songs and Sonets* and *Elegies* a clear account of an event or a series of events, if only the poems could be put in their "proper" order. He seems to offer the reader a complicated but tangible love story and yet he seems at great pains to keep this story the deepest of secrets. He offers no names in either the *Songs and Sonets* or the *Elegies*,[15] neither fictitious ones like Stella or Diana or Zepheria, nor punning ones like Will or Rich, nor even hints that the woman is not actual, such as those contained in the titles of Drayton's "Idea" or Daniel's "Delia." What motive for all this secrecy either in the late sixteenth century or today? An illicit love affair with a married woman was one possibility, as was a series of intrigues with several prominent women. Then, quite naturally, when Donne married, there was no need to use names—"sweetest love" or simply "thou" was sufficient.

Furthermore, although many shook their heads in dismay at Donne's hard conceits, the directness of his language and the songlike quality of some of his verse conveyed to these two decades of scholars a sincerity of emotion that was never questioned; and, in fact, by the first decade of the twentieth century, some scholars were beginning actually to associate obscurity and complexity with "fidelity to the truth of experience" (Joseph Duncan 1953a, 668). Seccombe and Alden in *The Age of Shakespeare* illustrate these points best in their discussions of Donne's and Sidney's poems: "Fantastic as he is, Donne writes of his own experience. Not that his lyrics are poems of pure passion. It is improbable that he ever loved simply. He had a passion for passionate experience, and, at bottom is always more intellectual than emotional" (1903, 1:66). If the sonnets in *Astrophil and Stella*, however, really do record Sidney's love for Penelope Devereux, they continue, it is odd Sidney needed so much help from Petrarch and Desportes to convey his experience. Furthermore, some of the sonnets are cold, although they add that, compared with other Elizabethan sonnets, Sidney's are "remarkably sincere" (1:13–14).[16] Sincerity was thus equated with the direct expression of passion that avoids conventions, and Donne was deemed more sincere than the Petrarchan Sidney.

Seccombe and Alden were not alone in insisting that Donne meant and, more to the point, had felt and experienced what he wrote about. Despite the suspect nature of biographical interpretations and assessments of sincerity in poetry, wrote Raymond Alden in 1920, one cannot avoid the belief that "Donne's love-lyrics were truly passionate in origin." And he qualifies his statement more than most when he adds that they at least give the *"effect* of directness or sincereity" (196). Horace Ainsworth Eaton in 1914 said that Donne's poems are pure lyric and that the "very essence of the lyrics" is "the quality of sincerity" (53–54). Virtually all writers on Donne during these twenty years not only did not doubt but in fact dwelt upon the sincerity and truthfulness of the poetry.

Were all of Donne's poems similar in theme to the song "Sweetest love" or "A Valediction: forbidding mourning," discussions of his lyrics would inevitably have ended in an encomium of praise for this sincere and passionate lover. However, this obviously is not the case. "Loves Diete," "The Apparition," and "Loves Alchemy," not to mention many others, had to be reckoned with. If Donne were as sincere in his poems extolling love as these writers believed, what can or should be said of his sincerity in the cynical love poems? One possibility is to discount the cynical love poems as youthful scribbles—games, pranks a young man about town might write to amuse himself and his friends, especially if they are just being initiated into sexual love. Herbert Grierson, for one, saw the relationship between Donne's poems and his life in this way. He writes that Donne's *Songs and Sonets* and *Elegies* "contain the most intimate and vivid record of his inner soul in these ardent years," 1592 to 1601 (1909, 4:208). However, when discussing the cynical love poetry, he qualifies his previous statement: "Realistic, Donne's love poetry may be; it is not safe to accept it as a history of his experiences" (4:210). Nevertheless, those simpler, purer lyrics, which are not cynical, were "in all probability . . . addressed to his wife" (4:211), for in these poems can be seen "the truth and intensity with which Donne sings . . . the joys of mutual and contented love" (4:212).[17] He continues by calling Donne's "moods" sincere and intense, though sometimes perverse and petulant" (4:213). Grierson here seems to be excusing Donne for his cynicism in some of the lyrics and elegies by denying their relevance to Donne's life while admitting that the "purer" ones (purer, that is, in emotion and sentiment) do record Donne's experiences with his wife Anne.

Grierson's comments delineats one of the major problems in biographical criticism at this time in general and biographical criticism of Donne in particular. Donne's lyrics, because of their often-abrupt openings, because of their colloquial tone, because of their frankness, seem assuredly realistic and even truthful, especially compared to a number of sonnet sequences from the 1590s, which often seemed, to early twentieth-century scholars, conventionalized emotion. No other poet, as Arthur Symons says (although some then and now would disagree with him), has "known as much of women's hearts and the senses of men and the passionate intercourse between man and woman" as Donne; "no one has ever rendered so exactly and with such elaborate subtlety, every mood of the actual passion" ([1899] 1916, 100). But if this is so and if Donne "sincerely" expresses his feelings for Anne More or possibly another woman—though this notion is seldom entertained—what can be said of the cynical love poems? They have the same abrupt openings, the same colloquial language, the same frankness as the more passionate love poems, and yet they express the sentiments of a man out of love and, more important, joying in the possibility of casual flirtations and love affairs. These poems, as well as the mutual love lyrics, seem "sincere." The question in the minds of Donne's early biographical critics was whether one can sincerely be a rake, whether one can sincerely lust after more than one woman. Given the popular, non-literary meaning (free from hypocrisy and dissimulation) today and in the early years of this century, one cannot; sincerity is connotatively associated with pure passions, not lustful ones. Thus, critics, like Grierson, had to distinguish between the pure and the unpure Donne, the sincere and the prankish Donne, and the serious and frivolous poems.

The problem of using "sincere" in describing Donne's poetry resulted then from a double use of the word. Some used it to indicate only a pure passion. For others, however, "sincere" meant simply true or genuine. Sincerity could therefore be associated not just with positive emotions like love (even illicit love is a positive passion for some) but with fidelity to any experience, whether positive or negative. For those less sympathetic to Donne than Grierson was or more strictly biographical in their interpretations, this latter alternative was almost universally accepted. For these, poems like "The Apparition" and "Womans constancy" were sincere because they show the true feelings of young Jack Donne devastated by a fickle woman, lashing out at her, or joying in sexual flirtations: "Controlled by fierce adolescent passions of body and soul, he wrote songs variously compounded—sensual, they are saved by a touch of higher feeling; mystic, they are kept human by the man in him" (Eaton 1914, 72).[18] Donne, these critics knew, had made a secret marriage with his employer's niece. The marriage cost him a court career and, for many years, any kind of career. Except for Grierson, who hinted that Donne may have hoped for preferment through his marriage (1909, 4:200–201), not one critic during these twenty years attributed Donne's marriage to anything but love of the most romantic kind, although some later critics do. If then, as most supposed, Donne was sexually prolific in his youth, his love for Anne More turned his life—and his poetry—to less cynical strains. That his love for Anne was enduring and that Donne was sexually faithful to his wife was never doubted even by Donne's most virulent detractors, although as little evidence existed then as now for this contention. But Donne's was an excellent story to romanticize, and this is exactly what happened. To reconcile his cynical with his mutual love lyrics, Donne was given a rakish, sometimes perverse, youth and a conversion to "pure" love through Anne.[19] Even Andrew Lang, one of Donne's severest critics during these two decades, declared that although the *Elegies* are addressed to women of imperfect purity and thus "do not win admiration for Donne's taste and temper, not to mention his morals," he did write some "charming songs" after meeting Anne (1912, 285). For a poet whose poetry is or appears to be more conventionalized than Donne's or whose poetry seems as realistic but more consistent in its emotional mood and tone or who makes a specific claim to truth or disavows it, the critical problem of reconciling poetry with the poet's life is not as acute as it is with Donne, whose poetry reflects in an unconventional form divergent and contradictory moods that his early biographers felt compelled to account for, either by dismissing the cynical poems or by reading from them the conversion of Jack to John.

It was not, however, only Donne's sincerity and truthfulness and the problem of reconciling passionate with cynical love poems that disturbed the early twentieth century; Donne's morals as expressed in some of his lyrics provoked other critics besides Lang to condemn or at least question the future dean of St. Paul's for his explicit language. Jessopp and Gosse, of course, had to deal with Donne's eroticism also, and Jessopp had done so by dismissing most of the love poems as the toys of youth while Gosse took them to be an explicit record of Donne's youthful amatory adventures. Probably because the intensity of Donne's love poetry seems to belie frivolous motives, most critics immediately following Jessopp and Gosse adopted the latter's proposal but with often differing results. When critics before 1920 read about pregnant pots, changed love as changed meat, travailing, sojourning, snatching, plotting, having, and then forgetting the whole love affair, they were often appalled, not just by the frankness of the language, but also by the kind of youthful experience in which these poems seems to indicate the future dean engaged during his youth. Not only was he sexually promiscuous, but he seemingly took great pride and pleasure in his adventures. Even sympathetic critics were taken aback by Donne's language. Seccombe and Alden are in general complimentary to Donne, praising him for his "fine ear" (1903, 1:74) and for "the originality [and] the essential sincerity of his love poems" (1:70). In fact, they go further than any others in excusing Donne's explicitly sexual language on artistic grounds, while also noting that these poems were the products of a licentious youth. A passionate poem, they say, is not pretty or tasteful, because passion itself is tender, brutal, and cruel. "So with Donne. His love poetry is sometimes positively ugly. It is abrupt, scandalous, ecstatic, fantastic, mocking, actual" (1:67). Yet, even with this defense, Seccombe and Alden were unwilling themselves to offend taste. Although they praise

"The Relique" as "one of the most extraordinary [poems] in English," and although they print the poem to demonstrate its beauties, they leave out lines three and four, "(For graves have learn'd that woman-head / To be to more then one a Bed)" (1:69). Perhaps they believed the scandalous nature of these two lines would offend sensibilities.[20]

Oddly, though, these two decades of critics continued to excuse Donne's verse for its sexual frankness, and whether reveling in its eroticism or reviling its crudity, they continued to discuss Donne with a fascination bordering sometimes on the voyeuristic and perverse. Arthur Symons seems positively gleeful in discussing this aspect of Donne's verse: "He exemplifies every motion and the whole pilgrim's progress of physical love, with a deliberate, triumphant, unluxurious explicitness which 'leaves no doubt,' as we say, 'of his intentions,' and can be no more than referred to passingly in modern pages" ([1899] 1916, 99). Quiller-Couch, also, is simultaneously drawn to and disgusted by the poems, which

> tell us autobiographically of wild living and licentious wooing: Th'expense of spirit in a waste of shame . . . and of shamelessness, we may add. They exhibit him as a genuine heir of the Renaissance, insatiable alike in carnal and intellectual curiosity: mad to possess, and having possessed, violent in reaction, crueller even than Horace to his castaways, then even more cruelly, cynically, cold in analysing the ashes of disgust. ([1918] 1930, 94. His ellipses.)

The " 'unpleasant' " poems "become actually significant when we recognize, though unwillingly,—since they must still shock our finer sensibilities—the fact that they are the genuine expression of a universal mood" (Eaton 1914, 64);[21] "there is nothing, not even the ugly and disgusting, which his verse will not say, no manner, not even the rudest, which it will not adopt to attain its almost impossible ends" and this is why he is so admired today (Bailey 1920, 320); Donne's "intensity of individuality . . . with all its disdain of amenity, makes his verse in these days of ours reveal more and more to those who ponder it most" (Wendell 1904, 125). These last two statements reveal not only how those in the early twentieth century felt about Donne's eroticism, but also why they were drawn to and repelled by it. Donne's verse was coming under critical discussion as the mores of the nineteenth century were being overthrown—although they were not yet conquered—and the new morality, first evident around the turn of the century, was slowly gaining ground. Donne, while often shocking, gave these decades the sexual explicitness in poetry that was coming to be a part of everyday life.

If Donne's sincerity in his love poems was often condemned but seldom questioned, the same cannot be said of his religious sincerity. The two most significant stumbling blocks in determining Donne's religious sincerity for biographers in any decade are his conversion to Anglicanism and his late acceptance of the ministry. The former is more an issue later in the century. For biographers before 1920, many of whom were Anglicans themselves, Donne's conversion to the state religion presented no real difficulties. Such was not the case for the latter problem. As we have seen, Jessopp and Gosse resolved this question in two very different ways, and the majority of later critics opted for Gosse's interpretation. Robert Lynd, for one, observes that Donne entered the ministry only after all worldly hopes were dashed by the fall of Somerset (1920, 42–43). Others take Gosse's assumptions further, contending that Donne was essentially insincere in his ministry. Gosse, of course, had theorized an intellectual acceptance of Anglicanism and the ministry in 1615 and an emotional conversion after Anne's death in 1617. An anonymous reviewer of the *Life and Letters*, however, missed this point and while praising Gosse as an "iconoclast" for finally revealing Donne as the unsaintly person he was ("John Donne and His Contemporaries" 1900, 231), went much further than Gosse in claiming Donne took holy orders because of "questionable patrons and more than questionable dealings" rather than out of any religious sincerity (229). Seccombe and Alden, who praised Donne's secular poetry, criticized his religious verse as "cold, tortured, and artificial," although Donne was not actually insincere in his religious belief, only never very profound (1903, 1:70).

Two factors combined to produce this kind of biographical criticism. The first, Donne's reluctance to enter the ministry and the motives behind his eventual taking of holy orders, I have already mentioned. The questions surrounding Donne's relationship with Somerset and hope for monetary gain still trouble Donne's biographers today; in the early twentieth century there were fewer facts, and Donne's motivation was subject to more speculation.

Second, even those who praised Donne for delaying his entry into the ministry[22] were troubled by a strain in Donne's religious poetry and prose analogous to the explicitly sexual language in his secular poems—Donne's interest in death and the grave. Quiller-Couch, who exhibits the highest praise for Donne's sermons, was disturbed and disgusted by the portrait of Donne in his shroud: "You may see the horrible silly picture in many editions of the *Life*. It is kept among the archives of St. Paul's. Reflex action, say I, of carnality *in exitu*. A very 'gloomy Dean' of St. Paul's at any rate!" ([1918] 1930, 109). That is, Quiller-Couch assumed the young Donne's fabled carnality disturbed the dying Donne as much as it did Quiller-Couch himself. As they did with the love poems, some early biographical critics praised a certain sentiment—in this case, Donne's sincere devotion to God and his open-mindedness—but then could not reconcile their interpretation of that purer sentiment with what they saw as contradictions in Donne's character—his seeming preoccupation with sickness, death, and the grave. Why, their comments on Donne's morbidity seem to ask, did a successful, sincere preacher have such profound doubts about his own salvation, and why did he seem to fear death as intensely as he did? Dismissing the prevailing fascination with death in the seventeenth century because Donne's seemed excessive and ignoring the possibility that Donne's sermons reflect simply a different religious style from, for example, Lancelot Andrewes's or Jeremy Taylor's style, they could only answer that Donne's nature was neurotic (Symons [1899] 1916, 89) or perversely rebellious.

This rebelliousness is the fourth element of Donne's life that simultaneously excited and disturbed his early biographers. Donne was a skeptic in religion and a revolutionary in love (Courthope 1903, 3:154); he had "strange personal characteristics which made him . . . unlike everyone else" (Garnett and Gosse [1903] 1904, 2:291); he was "a thoroughly original spirit and a great innovator" (Carpenter 1909, lviii); he was the "poet who challenged and broke the supremacy of the Petrarchan tradition" (Grierson 1909, 4:177). The list of comments during this period on Donne's rebellious life could go on, and their importance will be discussed more fully in chapter 4 on the attempts by critics to place Donne in or exclude him from Renaissance poetic traditions. However, these interpretations of Donne's life as one of conscious rebellion epitomize the difficulties of reconciling the Donne whom the early twentieth-century biographers thought they saw and wanted to see with the Donne who was objectionable to them. For example, biographers were supremely pleased with Donne as the poet who revolted against and undermined the Petrarchan conceits of the Elizabethan sonneteers.[23] But in the eyes of his early biographers, his genius in attempting this rebellion in his life through love, religion, and poetry outstripped his ability to write poetry. Thus the metaphysical conceits, seen after 1921 as separate from the poet's life, were before 1921 a measure of that life. Those most opposed to the wit and extravagance of his poetry were also most opposed to Donne as a person and delivered the severest biographical criticism—except, however, for Gosse, who, while retaining his fascination for Donne as a complex biographical subject, objected, four years after his biography of him, most strenuously to his poetic influence:

> Unfortunately, the genius of Donne was not equal to his ambition and his force. . . . What he gave to poetry in exchange for what he destroyed were almost wholly deplorable. For sixty years the evil taint of Donne rested on us, and our tradition is not free from it yet. . . . That Donne, in flashes, and especially in certain of his lyrics, is still able to afford us imaginative ecstacy of the highest order . . . must not blind us . . . to

the maleficence of his genius. No one has injured English writing more than Donne, not even Carlyle. (Garnett and Gosse [1903] 1904, 2:292)

Donne's rebellion was a good idea; however, Donne was not the man for it. A judgment of Donne's verse was thus tied inextricably to his life and, in the main, those who deplored his verse, deplored his life.

In 1921, however, criticism of Donne underwent a dramatic change.

"If Donne in youth was a rake, then I suspect that he was a conventional rake; if Donne in age was devout, then I suspect that he was conventionally devout. An observation which, even if true, is not necessarily destructive," wrote T. S. Eliot ten years after his seminal essay on Donne and the metaphysicals (1931, 10). Eliot, that is, did not care whether Donne had seduced fifty women or none in his youth or had taken holy orders for the sake of gain or devotion. However, in spite of the influence that Eliot exerted over the New Critics of the 1920s and 1930s and in spite of the way in which Donne's poetry became the paradigmatic focus for this group's critical methodology, it remains a curious fact of the history of criticism that Donne's life continued to be brought into numerous critical discussions of his poetry, no matter how strong the prevailing New Critical winds. There are three reasons why biographical interpretations hung on with such remarkable tenacity, and they involve paradoxes that Donne himself would have appreciated.

First, Eliot and the New Critics caused continuing biographical interpretations by provoking an iconoclastic reaction. They created a kind of literary hero of Donne that, in the eyes of some, needed to be knocked down, and this antagonism was often directed at Donne's life and character rather than at his poetry. Second, although Donne was the model poet for the New Critics' theories, many scholars reacted defensively to these theories as applied to Donne. Those who recognized the importance of Eliot's and his followers' work admitted that biographical criticism was passe, but then observed that nevertheless Donne's poetry demanded a biographical reading. Finally, and most important, Donne himself is the cause of these continuing biographical interpretations. The personality that emerges in his letters is often contradictory and slippery. Eliot's pronouncements on Donne and the New Critics' adoption of him certainly influenced biographical treatments of the poet, but it is Donne himself who most encourages biographical speculation.

The most excessive response to the New Criticism but probably the least important reason for continuing biographical interpretations is icon-smashing. Some critics and scholars, distresed by what seemed to them idealization of Donne by such critics as Cleanth Brooks and Allen Tate, were intent on proving, often through biographical treatments of his poetry, that Donne was neither a good poet nor a congenial man. This tendency is exemplified by a quarrel in the mid-1930s between C. S. Lewis and J. E. V. Crofts on one side, and Joan Bennett on the other. First, it must be noted that neither Crofts nor Lewis liked Donne as a poet or as a man. To Crofts, Donne was "alert, critical, ruthless," an "egregious and offensive coxcomb" ([1937] 1962, 78, 80). Even Donne's marriage to Anne More, always a rehabilitation of character for Donne in the eyes of his harshest pre-1921 critics, cannot redeem him in Crofts's view. Rather, the effect of the marriage on Donne's life has been "no more than sentimental conjecture, very difficult to square with the facts" (81). According to Lewis, Donne, because of his early Catholic training, never rid himself of "a medieval sense of the sinfulness of sexuality" ([1938] 1962, 101). If not a "nasty" person himself, Donne was at least unremittingly perverse about sexual matters (107).

Of course, it is the right of any critic or scholar to dislike a poet as a person, to object to his morality or his political views or his religion. Samuel Johnson could not tolerate Milton's politics and criticized his religion. However, strong-willed and opinionated as he was, Johnson was willing to grant greatness to at least *Il Penseroso, L'Allegro,* and *Paradise Lost* (1825, 7:121, 142). In more recent times, Ezra Pound's poetry has been praised, while his politics and his morality have been severely censured.[24] With Donne's love poetry, however, it is often difficult if not impossible for a number of critics to separate the *persona* of the poems from John Donne himself. Thus, in disliking the emotive situation in Donne's love poems, Lewis and Crofts must also dislike the man who was obsessed enough by sex or ruthless enough in his scorn of women to have written the poems. Lewis and Crofts insinuate that to have described the various emotions and experiences in the love poems, Donne must have felt them himself. Furthermore, since the experiences in the *Songs and Sonets* do not fit these critics' conceptions of what love poetry and love itself should be, Donne is relating not the universal experience of love, but the perverse, cruel, nasty thoughts and feelings of just one man. Therefore, he is a bad poet.

In answering these two, Joan Bennett eschews biographical interpretations of Donne's love poetry because it cannot be known when any of the *Songs and Sonets* was written or "how far the experience of which any one of them treats was real or imaginary" ([1938] 1962, 114). The second restriction seems clearly enough to have been prompted by the methods of New Criticism, yet I believe it would be fair to say that, unlike Crofts and Lewis, Bennett liked Donne as a man and liked his kind of poetry. She calls him "one of the greatest love poets in the English language" (122) and speaks warmly of the "nature and endurance of Donne's love for his wife" and of his reluctance on various occasions to part from her (115,

114). In addition, despite her own words of caution, she does use biographical facts (or her interpretation of those facts) as one weapon with which to
defend Donne against Lewis and, in the last two paragraphs of the essay,
against Crofts. To refute Lewis's bewildered wonder as to "what any
sensible women can make of such love-making" as is found in "The
Extasie" (Lewis, 103), Bennett cites the circumstances of Donne's marriage, the number of children he had by Anne, the length of their marriage,
and various letters in which he speaks warmly of her (115). Later, she
contends that "Donne came to know also the 'marriage of true minds,'
and many of his poems are about that experience" (119–20). Biographical
interpretation, it would seem, is difficult to escape from, even with a
conscious effort; and this literary quarrel is almost impossible to resolve
since it depends on an interpretation of the man behind the poems as
much as of the poems themselves.

In the first two decades of the twentieth century, scarcely a critic
questioned Donne's motives in marrying, his love for his wife, or the
sincerity of and passion in the poems that were assumed to have resulted
from that marriage. In the 1920s and 1930s, however, this attitude began to
change, largely because Eliot and those who followed him and modified
his critical comments into the school of New Criticism had made Donne's
poetry and Donne himself into a literary model. When Donne's bad taste,
lack of morality, and religious uncertainties were deplored in the early
decades of the twentieth century, his marriage could be put forward as the
redeeming biographical feature of a poet who was too important not to be
discussed but who, to many at least, was unpalatable. As Donne became
*the* poet to be read and studied, *the* hallmark of excellence in poetry, his
life became fuel for burning down the icon that Eliot created.[25] Idiosyncratic as they are, Crofts and Lewis, if they did not start the fire,
certainly fed the flames of the controversies surrounding interpretations of
Donne's life, which have continued throughout the twentieth century.

A second, defensive, reaction against the New Criticism's treatment of
Donne arose primarily from a critical term that was frequently used before
1921 to characterize Donne's poetry and that criticism even after Eliot
applied to it—sincerity. Cleanth Brooks in *Modern Poetry and the Tradition* wants, among other things, to enforce the separation of Donne's
personality from his poems: "Ultimately, it is not Donne's personality
which has fascinated the moderns," and only the "superficial critic" will
rationalize the "tremendous resurgence of interest in Donne" in this way
(1939, 11). However, Brooks is more than willing to grant sincerity to
Donne and the metaphysicals in general, especially in the religious poems.
Not to be confused with sentimentality, sincerity "reveals itself as an
unwillingness to ignore the complexity of experience" (37). Other writers,
however, continued to be willing to interpret the sincere quality of Donne's

poetry not just as a recognition of the complexity of experience but as a poetic portrayal of actual experience. The distinction between these two kinds of sincerity is an important one for all the metaphysical poets, but unfortunately it could be applied to any metaphysical poet other than Donne with less wrenching of previous critical foundations. With George Herbert's poetry, for example, one can accept at the same time both levels or kinds of sincerity. *The Temple* depicts the complex experience of the devout man in a wordly environment; it can also be the record of George Herbert's religious experience. The two levels of sincerity are not necessarily mutually exclusive. For John Donne, however, these two levels could not exist side by side as easily because of the experiences Donne depicts in his poetry. These are anything but homogeneous, nor were they in the 1920s and 1930s recognized immediately and without a struggle as experiences and emotions the "ordinary" man in love with a woman would have. Thus, whereas biographical interpreters and New Critics of Herbert's poetry could reach something of an undeclared truce in their readings of that poet, they could not with Donne.

Helen C. White, by no means a minor or particularly cranky or idiosyncratic scholar, put the argument for continued biographical interpretation of Donne's poetry most succinctly:

> Nothing is easier than to make the mistake of taking what a young poet says as literal fact. It is a standing temptation to read a man's biography into his verse, and *in Donne's case there is more excuse for doing so than in the work of most poets,* for his own verdict on his youthful license and what his contemporaries said of his life fully bear out the conclusions drawn from the poems themselves. (1936, 102. Emphasis is mine.)

It is particularly significant that White singled Donne out as a poet whose work is clearly autobiographical. With others, this kind of interpretation is a mistake; Donne's poetry, however, calls for it. The influence of the New Critics is clear; biographical criticism is out of fashion. But not when it comes to Donne.

White was not alone in her recognition (albeit tacit) of the forceful presence of New Criticism or in her willingness to make an exception for Donne. Pierre Legouis, for example, though more circumspect than White, was willing to grant an autobiographical reading to "The Extasie." The "supposition," he says, that Donne himself is the lover in the poem "contains no internal improbability" (1928, 70–71). J. B. Leishman more overtly threw his hat in with the biographical critics, yet even his comments show recognition that he was out of the mainstream of criticism. Although he sees the danger of looking for a record of specific events in Donne's love poems, he cannot regard them as "mere *jeux d'esprit,* or . . .

as 'academic exercises' " (1934, 12). He does, incidentally, go on to construct from the *Elegies* and *Songs and Sonets* an intrigue between Donne and a married woman, similar to that constructed by Gosse thirty-five years earlier, although he admits that the affair might not have happened exactly as he described it (20). Leishman's assumption that the alternative to autobiography is "academic exercises" points to one reason biographical interpretations of Donne's poetry continued even while the New Criticism was gaining ground. For some of these critics, rejecting autobiography in poetry as seemingly sincere as Donne's was equivalent to saying poetry had no purpose. If Donne did not write to or about a historical woman, then he must have been engaging in frivolous toys, *"jeux d'esprit."*

Obviously, Donne scholarship underwent a crucial change in the 1920s—a change affecting all subsequent work on Donne. However, biographical speculation both about the facts of Donne's life and about the degree to which the poems can be read as autobiographical accounts of that life has continued with remarkable persistency. René Wellek and Austin Warren in the *Theory of Literature* pronounce quite definitively on the value of biography deduced from literary works: "One cannot, from fictional statements . . . draw any valid inference as to the biography of a writer." "Even," they continue, "when a work of art contains elements which can be surely identified as biographical, these elements will be so arranged and transformed in a work that they lose all their specifically personal meaning and become simply concrete human material, integral elements of a work" (1956, 3d ed., 76, 78). This bastion of the New Criticism changed the course of reading and teaching literature. Despite classroom practices, however, biographical readings of Donne's poems never ceased. One reason for this, as Janel N. Mueller suggested in 1972, may have been the lack of a modern scholarly biography of Donne until Bald's was published in 1970. However, she predicted that this biography would eliminate the overabundance of biographical interpretations of the poems (236). Roger Sharrock, writing in the same year, took a radically different views of the role of biography in Donne scholarship. Unlike Mueller, Sharrock believed that after Gosse's *Life and Letters,* biographical interpretations of Donne went out of fashion but that the cycle was coming around again. To prove this latter point, he cites Bald's biography along with Helen Gardner's edition of the *Elegies* and *Songs and Sonets.* The return to autobiographical readings is a positive sign because "the well-bred indifference to autobiography or metaphysics leaves unanswered the yawning gap of question as to what this poetry is about" (1972, 37). It seems, then, that scholars disagree not only about the value of biographical readings of Donne's poems but also about the trend of such interpretations.

In a sense, both Mueller and Sharrock are correct in their assessments. The lack of a sufficiently scholarly and objective biography of Donne for the first seventy years of the twentieth century, when scholarship on the poet in all areas of research underwent a number of dramatic changes, certainly furthered speculation about his life as seen through the poems, especially since this was in large part Gosse's approach. In addition, Donne's life, easily romanticized and—as it has seemed to some—plainly chronicled in his verse, has attracted more than the usual number of non-experts and idiosyncratic critics, who claim a place in Donne studies and demand replies and rebuttals. However, Sharrock's contention is also valid in that well-respected scholars continue to indulge, albeit cautiously, in biographical interpretations of the poems. This point can best be illustrated by citing some of Donne's most prominent readers during the last fifty years.

John Sparrow on "Elegie: On his Mistris":

It is always difficult to know how far Donne's love-poetry can be used as evidence for his life, but of this poem, as of several others of his Elegies, it is impossible to believe that the occasion is entirely feigned. . . . The "mistris" was clearly one of the unnamed mistresses of Donne's earlier days. (1931, 142–43)[26]

Merritt Hughes on "The Extasie":

I believe simply that the poet felt himself to be expressing an established ideal which has been actualized dramatically in his imagination and perhaps in his life. (1932, 5)

George Reuben Potter:

If we may (as I rather think we may) read actual experiences into certain poems, Donne seems to have discovered that a married woman could make him feel jealous and ashamed. (1936, 16)

Douglas Bush:

Though we cannot assume that all the most serious and exalted tributes to love were addressed to his wife, a few of the best certainly or probably were. ([1945] 1962, 2d ed., 134)

Douglas Peterson:

The New Criticism has made us wary of using biographical material to recover poetic intention; but it is foolish to discount the circumstances and consequences of Donne's marriage as irrelevant to the view of love he expresses in the *Songs and Sonets*. (1967, 295)

R. C. Bald on "The Sunne Rising" and "The Canonization":

> It is possible, then, that these two poems express some of the moods of the early years of his marriage. (1970, 147)

Arthur Marotti on "The Extasie":

> My interpretation is unashamedly biographical; but for a poet like Donne who wrote primarily for his friends, such a perspective is, I believe, both inevitable and necessary. (1974, 143–44)[27]

The theme underlying each of these statements is that Donne is an exception to the New Critical strictures on biographical interpretation. Donne is different from other poets. His life and his poetry match at so many points that avoiding biographical readings is all but impossible, even though such readings in the case of Donne lead more often to confusion than to enlightenment, depending as they frequently do on a preconceived notion of the poet's attitudes and activities. "A Nocturnall upon S. Lucies day" is a case in point.

In 1912, Grierson suggested very tentatively that the "Nocturnall" was possibly written in 1612 when Lucy, Countess of Bedford, was seriously ill. Although disturbed by the sometimes sexual imagery in the poem and noting, alternatively, that the poem might have been written for Anne Donne, he agreed with Gosse that the poem mourns not an actual but an imagined death and therefore favored the Countess as the poem's subject (1912, 2:xxii–xxiii). Grierson was more cautious about biographical interpretations of the *Songs and Sonets* than most in his decade, yet he hardly entertained the notion that the "Nocturnall" may have been written with no actual woman in mind. Despite its tentativeness, Grierson's theory gained in prominence and magnitude as Donne's poetry was more and more studied. One obvious reason for accepting the Countess of Bedford as the woman of the poem is the title—even though it is not certainly Donne's. The second is the question of dating. Although R. C. Bald does not mention the poem in his biography of Donne except in a footnote disputing biographical interpretations (1970, 7n) and although Arthur Marotti maintains that the subject of the poem "cannot be identified either with Lady Bedford or with Donne's wife, for the poem's hyperboles grant her an extraordinary ideality" (1986, 234), these two are almost alone in their interpretations.[28] Most others, prominent scholars among them, insist on biographical interpretations of the poem. Since it seems as sincere in its emotional force as any poem Donne wrote,[29] it should logically be attributed to Donne's love for Anne, as the other "sincere" love lyrics are. To attribute the occasion of the poem to Anne's death, however, means that Donne must have written it in 1617—two years after taking holy orders. Those wanting Donne's poetic career to follow a consistent early-rake-and-later-divine pattern with no overlap between the two supposed stages have difficulty accepting Donne as a priest who still valued earthly love enough to write a poem about it. Thus, a pre-1615 date for the "Nocturnall" is the only possibility. More important, accepting 1612, the year the Countess of Bedford was seriously ill, as the date of composition enforces the conception of Donne the courtier. This picture of Donne is especially important to those wishing to emphasize his ambitious flattery, his misogyny, his continued interest in attractive women, or his public rather than his private voice.

Although Grierson's conclusions about the poem do not reflect negatively on Donne's character at all, he was quite interested in depicting Donne as a man with many friendships and connections at court—as a public man who wrote flattering poems to women in the "Troubadour convention." He describes Donne's relationship with the Countess of Bedford and with Magdalen Herbert as deep, though "Platonic, friendships (1912, 2: xxi–xxv)—harmless and natural for a man in Donne's position. Others followed this pattern. J. B. Leishman in *The Metaphysical Poets* associated "A Nocturnall" and "Twicknam Garden" with Lucy (1934, 55), although he later reversed his opinion of the former, becoming among the first to associate the poem with Anne (1951, 170–73). Richard Hughes attempted to solve the problem of imagery raised by Grierson by theorizing that the poem was written about Lucy when Donne was frightened at losing her friendship after she began leaning toward Puritanism in 1611. He suggests that Donne modeled the poem on the Roman breviary as a rebuff to Lucy's Puritan religious adviser and that this explains the imagery (1965, 60–68). Edward LeComte, though a bit more circumspect, also associated the poem with Lucy, despite his earlier warnings against finding exact women and experiences in the *Songs and Sonets* (1965, 50–57). She "drew Donne," he says, "to ecstatic freedom from misogyny" (114–15).

These readers are, in general, positively disposed toward Donne, wishing mainly to emphasize his public nature without disparaging his character. In their attempts, the "Nocturnall" becomes only one piece of evidence among others—letters in which Donne mentions Lucy, verse letters to her and to her friends and relatives—that prove Donne engaged in an active social life apart from his family.

Others, however, who see neuroses in his personality or dissatisfaction with his wife rely on the association of the "Nocturnall" and Lucy to bolster their pejorative views of the poet. Evelyn Hardy, very much concerned to show the events that traumatized Donne and formed his character, assumes the "Nocturnall" points to Donne's supreme devotion to Lucy and to "the measure of his gloom at her expected death" (1942,

127). To believe the poem might have been written for Anne, whom she described as too simple and normal ever to have comprehended her husband or to have allowed him to share with her "the deeper problems of his inner battle" (108), would destroy her created image of Donne as a misogynist. Doniphan Louthan, also believing Anne was too unaware of court life and fashion to remain attractive to her husband, objects to the "sinceritas heresy" in all of Donne's poems except the "Nocturnall" and "Twicknam Garden." In the former, he says, internal and external evidence points to a personal experience as the basis for the poem (1951, 141). He then constructs an elaborate theory (for which, he admits, he has "no biographical support") that shows Donne writing the poem as a kind of anti-epithalamion when Lucy married Edward Russell, third Earl of Bedford (in 1594). Donne, he believes, had wanted to be the groom (144)

The ease with which these two and other scholars and critics assume, often without bothering to prove, that the poem is addressed to or at least about Lucy epitomizes the mine field through which biographical interpreters of Donne's poems frequently wander. The association with the Countess of Bedford seems so obvious that proof would be superfluous. Even Richard Hughes, who supports his contention with evidence from the poem and from Donne's life, found it unnecessary to prove *that* it was written about Lucy, only *when* it was written about her. Judith Herz scoffs at what she considers the "highly unlikely proposition" that "A Nocturnall" could be addressed to either Anne Donne or the Countess of Bedford during her illness. Yet one does read the poem with the assumption (though not the certainty) "that they were written to, for, at the command of, or at the suggestion of the Countess of Bedford" (1986, 11). These arguments, though, are not totally convincing. Despite Gosse and Grierson, the tone of the poem is too dark to be mourning only the loss of friendship, no matter how deep; and it would seem a bit hasty, not to mention gauche, for Donne to eulogize Lucy before her death, no matter how severe the sickness. Furthermore, since Donne did write several verse letters to Lucy, why would he bother to mask her name at all in this poem? And why was it included in the first edition of the *Songs and Sonets* rather than with the other verse letters if it was indeed written for her? Louthan's theory could provide an answer to both these questions, but since it is, as he himself admits, unsupported by evidence, it must be discounted. Still, these readers do have Donne's friendship with Lucy and a form of her name in the title to support their contentions. This poem, like so many of Donne's, gives clues with one hand only to withdraw them with the other.

Those who reject Lucy and posit Anne as the poem's subject must take as their starting point the deep and long-lasting affection Donne had for his wife, which those favoring Lucy Bedford underplay. What distressed Grierson about the imagery of the poem leads them to the conclusion that the woman of the poem and Donne must certainly have been involved in a sexual relationship; and, therefore, since Donne's sexual fidelity to Anne is never questioned, she must be the subject. As Leishman was the first to point out, the third stanza of the poem is remarkably similar in its imagery to that throughout "A Valediction: of weeping," which, Leishman continues, can legitimately and naturally be assumed to have been addressed to Anne (1951, 171). Uncomfortable with the possibility that Donne the priest wrote secular verse, Leishman assigned the poem to Anne's miscarriage and Donne's vision of her when he was traveling with the Drurys in 1611 (172). Louis Martz, also trying to resolve the problem of the dating, shows that the "Nocturnall" is more religious in its presentation of a "midnight service, a 'Vigill,' commemorating the death of his beloved— his saint" (1954, 214) than most suppose and therefore could conceivably have been written after Donne's ordination. He offers as an alternative date 1606, the year of one of Anne's more difficult childbirths (215). David Novarr, theorizing that Donne wrote very little poetry—religious or secular—after his ordination, prefers Martz's 1606 dating because "it has more merit than those [suggestions], his own among them, which would date the poem after Ann Donne's death" (1980, 98n). One reason the suggestion has more merit is that it does not conflict with Novarr's thesis as any post-ordination date would. Helen Gardner, using textual and historical evidence, dates the poem as post-1614, and although no textual evidence proves the poem was written for Anne, Gardner sees a strong probability that it was (1982b, 195–96). John Shawcross, however, has been the most adamant in his insistence that the poem was written after Anne's death and about her death, dating it—with no concern over secular poetry during Donne's ministry—12 December 1617 (1965).[30]

But these readings are also somewhat problematic. Shawcross's evidence consists primarily of internal clues: the woman, he says, is "certainly dead" and therefore cannot be Lucy or Magdalen Herbert, since they died too late for Donne to be writing secular poetry. Thus Shawcross believes Donne could write secular poetry in 1617, despite what others say on that subject, but not as late as 1627. Martz's and Novarr's identification of Anne as the poem's subject depends on the poem's emotional force. Martz says it surely was written about Anne, because the concluding lines point toward the opening lines of "Since she whome I lovd" (1954:214–15). Thus, in a way similar to Leishman's method in *The Monarch of Wit* (1951), he proves that the poem is autobiographical by pairing it with another supposedly autobiographical poem.[31] Believing Anne Donne to be the subject of the poem is in many ways a more congenial interpretation of the poem than believing Lucy to be the subject but ultimately is no more provable.

The recurrent concern with dating "A Nocturnall" and the basing of whatever dating one chooses on Donne's supposed attitudes toward women in general, Lucy or Anne in particular, or his ministry continue in more sophisticated form the division of his character into libertine and dean, while pointing to the unique quality of Donne's poems. Bald notes: "Donne had a gift . . . for creating a situation and presenting it vividly by means of a few deftly economical touches" (1970, 6). But he cautions against assuming the poems are therefore autobiographical. He explains that Donne suffered from the same misinterpretations of his poems during his lifetime, citing George More's accusations that Donne had seduced a gentlewoman—accusations sometimes used to prove Donne's early licentiousness.[32] If Donne's poetry has been subjected since his own time to biographical interpretations and if, despite Bald's warnings, these continue today, the possibility of their stopping in the twentieth century is slim.

I have discussed the biographical controversies surrounding the "Nocturnall" at such length as an illustration of the flexibility of the poem when it is connected to specific events in Donne's life. The same biographical flexibility is present in certain other poems—for example, "The Blossome," "Loves Alchemie," "The Extasie," and the four valedictions—and contributes to the disputes about the poet's life. In addition, the known facts of Donne's life, apart from the poetry, also continue to provoke controversies. Naturally, the life of any author, especially if he lived before the eighteenth century, is subject to some biographical guesswork: some of the activities of Chaucer and Shakespeare, for example, may never even be known, much less accurately dated, and will continue to provide opportunities for research and dispute. The same is true of some of Donne's activities. For example, the years between 1589 and 1591 are a puzzle; although Bald shows that Donne was probably traveling then, he admits this is mainly speculation (1970, 52). Neither is it known precisely when Donne converted to Anglicanism nor, for that matter, in what month he was born. However, there are certain areas of Donne's life about which much is known, and yet even these produce various and opposing views of the poet and divine. To show how preconceived attitudes toward Donne have influenced presentations of his life, I will examine critics' and scholars' reactions to some specific, incontrovertible facts in four areas: his Catholicism, his relationship with his mother, the circumstances of and motives for his marriage, and his abilities as husband and father.

Donne was born into a Catholic family; he had as uncles two prominent Jesuits; his father died when he was four; his mother remarried twice; he wrote one extant letter to her when his sister Anne died in 1615; and his mother lived with him at the deanery for several years. These, in brief, are the facts, but much can be speculated about these facts. One issue that perplexes and interests biographers of Donne is not necessarily when he left Catholicism or even why (although both are themselves matters of considerably controversy and probably insoluable problems), but rather how he felt about himself after his "apostasy" and how his Catholic background influenced him. Donne himself is largely reticent on the issue. He notes in the preface to *Pseudo-Martyr:* "I have been ever kept awake in a meditation of Martyrdome, by being derived from such a stocke and race, as, I beleeve, no family (which is not of farre larger extent, and greater branches), hath endured and suffered more in their persons and fortunes, for obeying the Teachers of Romane Doctrine, than it hath done" (Donne, 1967b, 46). In his sermons he is often antipathetic toward the Jesuits but retains sympathy for some Catholic traditions (Simpson [1924] 1948, 107) and is more tolerant toward Catholics in general than toward the more radical Jesuits. However, the question remains of how Donne felt after renouncing the faith of his ancestors, and especially of his mother, particularly if, as some suggest, he left the Catholic faith for purely pragmatic reasons.[33] Those who are, in general, antagonistic toward Donne's poetry see in it his feelings of guilt, loneliness, and defensiveness; those who are, in general, sympathetic toward the poetry see in it sincerity and faith, even if at times that faith is struggling.

Clay Hunt is the most striking example of the former attitude. Although praising some—a very few—of Donne's lyrics, Hunt is overwhelmingly negative in his assessment of the religious poems, both for their "emotional poverty" and for their lack of the kind of "rich emotional and sensory texture" found in Milton's religious verse (1954, 134). Although he claims to except the three hymns, parts of "A Litanie," and the *Holy Sonnets* (of course, with these exceptions, not much religious poetry remains), he, in fact, finds most of the *Holy Sonnets* replete with "apoplectic literary seizures" and with "a blathering anxiety to Tell All" (135, 136). These tendencies, as well as the egotism and lordliness in the love poems, derive from Donne's Catholicism or, more accurately, from his break with that faith, which "evidently cost him something and left him with lingering feelings of guilt and apostasy" (171). Donne's negative remarks about Catholicism seem, to Hunt, forced. They are part of his desire to seem Anglican, but they have "deeper roots in Donne's defensiveness against himself, against a lurking sense that he had sold short his conscience at the counter of the World" (171–72). In his sermons, this tendency manifests itself in the preacher's lack of wit and humor, his "voluptuous abandonment to his necrophilous ardors [so that] one wants to minister to a mind diseased, possessed of the Green Shudders" (145). Donne, thus, suffered throughout his life from a neurotic sense of guilt that damaged him psychologically and, perhaps more important for the critic, weakened and marred the poetry.

Hunt is not alone in his assessment of Donne's religious trials as re-

flected in the poetry. His anonymous reviewer in *TLS*, while dis
with some of Hunt's censures of the secular poetry, asserted that
"must have felt that the death of his wife was a judgment on l
leaving the Roman Catholic Church" ("Poetic Tradition in Don     
March 1956, 164), thus enforcing Hunt's contention that Donne suffered
great anguish and distress as a result of his conversion. Although the
reviewer later admitted his statement was too strong, he still insisted
Donne must have retained doubts about leaving the Catholic Church
("Poetic Tradition in Donne" 11 May 1956, 283). E. M. W. Tillyard, like
Hunt, admits his distaste for Donne's poetry while recognizing the need to
understand and explore it (1956, 20–25). Donne, he says, is more interested in the process of thought than in things in and of themselves. This
lack of interest in action stems from Donne's early Catholicism. Since he
was always the outsider, he was more interested in thinking than in doing,
and this weakens his verse, especially in comparison with Milton's (37–
38).

Others, however, read Donne's religious verse and examine his life and
see just the opposite. Helen White, for example, looks at Donne's religious
writings and, while noting Donne's Catholic background and the problems
it caused (1951a, 355), focuses her discussion on Donne's spiritual
struggles with himself. Neither Hunt nor Tillyard, of course, overlooked Donne's spiritual struggles: Hunt, in fact, laid great emphasis
on them. However, White sees them in a considerably more positive
light: "[H]e saw human life as a struggle, and he plunged into that
struggle with characteristic vigor and energy" (357–58). Donne, she insists, could, because of his own weaknesses, minister successfully to
"others' sore need" and could, because of his positive thinking on sin and
redemption, lead his congregations to hope (365). Evelyn Simpson, in
examining the biographical information provided by the sermons of 1625
to 1628, also presents a very different view of Donne the preacher than
that posed by Hunt. For her, he was full of the hope and joy of redemption
until his world shattered and his hope turned to morbid melancholy when
his daughter Lucy and his dear friend Magdalen Herbert died (1951, 339–
57). Helen Gardner, in response to Hunt's *TLS* reviewer, vehemently
insisted that the *Sermons* and *Divine Poems* show Donne accepting the
Anglican position without dwelling in doubt and guilt on his early Catholicism ("Donne and the Church" 25 May 1956, 320); in another essay, she
and J. B. Leishman asked why the reviewer's statement that Donne saw
Anne's death as a punishment for leaving the Catholic church could not be
turned around: perhaps Donne felt years of married happiness were the
reward for turning to Anglicanism ("Poetic Tradition in Donne" 11 May
1956, 283).

Their question is, of course, a rhetorical one; however, to answer it provides some of the pieces in the puzzle of Donne's critical history. This problem, like so many others in Donne's life, depends not on the facts as they are known—the opposing sides are, after all, looking at the same poems and sermons—but on the antipathy or sympathy granted to Donne prior to interpretation of the poems or of his life. Perhaps, however, Janel Mueller is correct, and this kind of discrepancy in interpretation arises only because, when these critics and scholars were writing, there was no modern biography of Donne, and so facts were subject to more speculation then than after Bald's biography. Perhaps, but not in fact.

Bald, from the evidence of the *Holy Sonnets,* written during the Mitcham years, sees despair, but positive despair—despair that forecasts true conversion: "He passed through a spiritual crisis which was in large measure concealed from those closest to him. . . . But it is revealed clearly enough in the 'Holy Sonnets,' and in the sermons of later years he looked back with a particular sense of poignancy to the despair and suffering through which he had passed" (1970, 235). Bald is not always kind to his subject: he sees in Donne's actions immediately preceding ordination a certain worldliness, a desire to continue cultivating the courtier's arts, and, again, despair: "At no period in his life does he appear less unselfish, more self-seekinng" (301). But Bald also sees a positive change. By the time of Donne's death, doubts and uncertainties "were all banished by 'the testimonies of the Holy Spirit' which had been vouchsafed to him" (527). Even before this, however, Donne's emphasis in his sermons is "upon the comfort and joy of the Christian message, and upon the need for a positive and undespairing spiritual life" (484). Bald's seemingly fair and measured treatment of Donne's religious life—he dwells hardly at all upon the effect of Donne's early Catholicism, treating it merely as another aspect of the life of a multi-dimensional human being—would seem to leave no room for dissent. However, eleven years later, criticism returned to the question of Donne's Catholicism.

John Carey in *John Donne: Life, Mind and Art* (1981), in fact, devotes a considerable amount of space and energy to show just how much Donne's Catholicism and "apostasy" cost him in his early and later life. The *Holy Sonnets,* he says, are the "fruit of his apostasy. For all their vestiges of Catholic practice, they belong among the documents of Protestant religious pain, and their suffering is the greater because they are the work of a man nurtured in a more sustaining creed" (57)—that is, Catholicism. Both the religious and secular poems sprang from Donne's fear that he did not merit affection: just as women are inconstant, God will damn, and both fears resulted from his apostasy (57–58). Donne's early experiences with Catholicism affected him in other ways, too. Contending that Donne with his mother visited Jasper Heywood in the Tower—a visit that, according to Bald, never took place (1970, 64)—Carey insists this adventure is the basis for Donne's preoccupation with a colossal man in his youthful love poetry and that the ill effects of such visits colored Donne's later rancor against the Jesuits (20–21).

Is this contrast between Carey's interpretation of Donne's character and Bald's interpretation another, later, example of what the editors of *Etudes Anglaises* described as a modern's iconoclasm pitted against Bald's nineteenth-century hero worship? That seems unlikely since Bald is harsher in analyzing Donne's character immediately before ordination than many other scholars are. In reviewing Carey's work, Patrick Cullen admits to being at first "infuriated by its arrogance and its willingness to make conclusions out of mere speculations" (1982, 171), yet also sees it as a restatement of the "older view of Donne but in a new, romantic/psychogenetic context. The complex perspectivism valued in Donne's wit by another generation is Carey's inconsistency and dubiety—a complex response to his own circumstances and imagination" (173).

Adding a new layer to this controversy, Dennis Flynn in a 1986 essay applies Bettelheim's profile of a "survivor" to Donne's situation as a Catholic in Protestant England. Donne, as he watched other Catholics exiled or killed, would have been racked by the question "Why was I spared?" especially after his brother Henry's death. Trying to discover what in his life he had been spared to do, Donne, Flynn argues, turned to love, to friendship, and finally to the state religion (18–19; 23–24).

In a sense, Carey's portrait of the Catholic Donne and Flynn's are quite similar, but the brush strokes (as so often happens with Donne) differ: Carey's picture is dark with apostasy and guilt; Flynn's has subtler nuances and background. Typical of much Donne criticism, facts combine with possibilities and hints to fashion very different, even contradictory, Donnes. However, even though Eliot, the lack of a scholarly modern biography, and the perversity and obtuseness and crankiness of critics all play a part in biographical studies of Donne, ultimately it is the flexible, enigmatic character of the man himself that begs for multitudinous interpretations.

Donne's relationship with his mother has also provoked a wide and interesting range of speculation about his psyche, his attitudes toward women, and his views of religion. Most prominent scholars treat this relationship sympathetically. Bald sees Donne's relationship with his mother in his later years of life (the only period for which there is any real evidence of what his feelings for her were) as loving and sympathetic: "though his mother persisted in her recusancy, there is no trace of reproach or embarrassment on either side despite the fact that Donne was often moved to criticize the beliefs of her Church" during his ministry (1970, 316). He describes the letter Donne wrote to console his mother, now married to Richard Rainsford, after her daughter's death as "by far the most moving of all his letters" (316). Evelyn Simpson, forty-five years earlier, had seen the relationship in a similar light. The letter, she says, "shows that he regarded his mother . . . as one with whom he had a real spiritual sympathy" ([1924] 1948, 107). Helen Gardner concurs (1957, 564–65).

Others, however, are not as certain that the relationship was such a harmonious one. While these critics are, for the most part, interested in psychoanalytic studies of Donne or in debunking him,[34] their treatments are nonetheless important in the overall study of biographical interpretations of the poet, and they often point to provocative aspects of this relationship dismissed or ignored by more influential scholars. Both Evelyn Hardy in her avowedly Freudian study of Donne, *A Spirit in Conflict* (1942), and Lady Mary Clive in her more lighthearted biography (1966) found several problems in the letter to Elizabeth Rainsford that Bald and others find thoroughly sympathetic. Hardy suggests that in this letter Donne implies he is lost to his mother and that this alienation is the natural outcome of Donne's relationship with her in his childhood: "The alienation from his mother which would have begun at a very early age if, as I have suggested, he resented his stepfather's intrusion, or later, when she discovered his heretical and libertine trends of thought" would be magnified after his brother Henry's death (42), since Donne would have blamed her and her Catholicism for the tragedy. Clive is somewhat more generous in her analysis of Donne's mood when he wrote the letter:

> It was not easy. They had drifted apart and were divided by religious differences, and no very warm and comforting words sprang to his mind. Suppressing the memory of the occasions on which she had been tiresome and how she had given away her money to Roman Catholic causes, and recollecting her many bereavements, he began with a picturesque simile. (133)

What both Hardy and Clive are emphasizing are a few curious elements in a letter that on the whole seems sympathetic and generous. Donne writes:

> The happiness which God afforded to your first young time, which was the love and care of my most dear and provident father . . . God removed from you quickly, and hath since taken from you all the comfort that that marriage produced. All those children . . . He hath now taken from you. (Gosse [1899] 1959, 2:89)

This is an odd statement given that Donne himself was obviously still alive and perhaps does indicate, as Hardy suggests, some alienation between the two. Clive's rather mixed response to the letter depends on Donne's mentioning his dead sister only once and dwelling, she believes, for too long on his own poverty (134–35). Although Clive is often cavalier in her characterization of Donne, it is difficult to know how to respond to his promise that he will "be as strongly bound to look to you and provide for your relief, as for my own poor wife and children" and his emphasis on "the poorness of my fortune, and the greatness of my charge" (Gosse, 2:89). His relationship with his mother, though generally sympathetic, is perhaps more problematic than some scholars have deemed it to be.

Even without the evidence of the letter, Judah Stampfer can point to the psychological implications of a lost father and a remarried mother (1970, 41–42), and John Carey can speculate that Donne turned against the Jesuits with such vehemency because he may have resented the power his two uncles held over his mother and the love they commanded from her (1981, 21). This aspect of Donne's life, then, is no easier to pin down than his feelings about Catholicism. In both areas, Donne provides enough detail to encourage and confuse the biographer.

In the early twentieth century virtually all biographers of Donne were agreed on the sincerity of his commitment to Anne More. After Eliot, partially as a response to Eliot's treatment of Donne, such critics as C. S. Lewis and J. E. V. Crofts began to question the motives of Donne's love poetry. This trend has continued and becomes, in fact, even more interesting when opposite interpretations of Donne's motives for marriage and his abilities as a father and especially as a husband depend not on interpretations of the poems but on different readings of Donne's letters during the years 1601 to 1617.

The first letter to cause dispute about Donne's attitudes toward marriage and about his character is dated 2 February 1601/2, and is addressed to Anne's father, George More, to inform him of the secret marriage. He begins his letter with an apology:

> Sir,—If a very respective fear of your displeasure, and a doubt that my lord (whom I know, out of your worthiness, to love you much) would be so compassionate with you as to add his anger to yours, did not so much increase my sickness as that I cannot stir, I had taken the boldness to have done the office of this letter by waiting upon you myself to have given you truth and clearness of this matter between your daughter and me, and to show you plainly the limits of our fault, by which I know your wisdom will proportion the punishment. (Gosse, 1:100–101)

He then summarizes the circumstances of the marriage and outlines his reasons for not informing Sir George beforehand: "I knew my present estate less than fit for her. I knew (yet I knew not why) that I stood not right in your opinion. I knew that to give any intimation of it had been to impossibilitate the whole matter" (1:100). He ends with a plea that his father-in-law not allow anger to sway his reason and good sense.

Separated from his bride, sick, alone, frightened, Donne could almost be a character in one of Shakespeare's comedies, and it is tempting for biographers to romanticize the young lover and new husband who wrote this letter. K. W. Gransden calls it "disarming but unsuccessful" (1954, 15); Frederick Rowe notes that Donne in this letter and throughout the entire episode with Sir George "behaved . . . with a disarming dignity and candour" (1964, 7). Frank Kermode calls this and Donne's second letter to Sir George "dignified apologies" and implies that they succeeded in softening More's heart (1957a, 7); and Charles M. Coffin says:

> While naturally unable to conceal his anxiety for his own behavior, he is unselfish in his concern for his bride, and temperate in his address. . . . it is to his credit that he did not resort to obsequious apology nor allow the occasion to provoke him to unseemly anger. He simply insisted that his love was honest and sincere. (1937a, 23)

Others, however, take a dimmer view of the letter. To Lady Mary Clive it is "an extremely irritating letter, being off-hand, vague and evasive, triumphant, patronizing, and showing only too clearly that he was not in the least sorry for what he had done" (1966, 54). Robert Jackson more charitably calls it an "explanation," its "involuted syntax" resulting from a combination of anxiety and boldness (1970, 23), while to Edward LeComte the letter is tactless and blunt (1965, 82). For John Carey, it is an example of Donne's "self-absorption," his unawareness of how he was affecting those around him (1981, 71–72). Even Bald sees the letter as betraying "nervousness. Donne attempted to be at once respectful and firm, but succeeded only in achieving a certain jauntiness" (1970, 124).

One must wonder after examining these two sets of opposing responses if one group is right, the other wrong; if one group has caught the tone of the letter while the other has missed it. The discrepancy seems to arise from the lack of consistency between what Donne did and how he wrote about that deed. That is, his marriage, which the vast majority of critics and scholars believe was prompted by love rather than by ambition, was a romantic, daring, loving act, finding expression in the letter in such sentences as "But for her, whom I tender much more than my fortunes or life (else I would, I might neither joy in this life nor enjoy the next), I humbly beg of you that she may not, to her danger, feel the terror of your sudden anger" (Gosse, 1:101). However, the justification of his act also rather tactlessly informs Sir George that Donne has heard rumors of his vile temper and that no matter what Sir George may think, "it is irremediably done" (1:101). The inclination, and opportunity, to romanticize this period of Donne's life is so great that the two most popular options are to counter the tendency by emphasizing the tactlessness of certain phrases or to give in to the impulse by dwelling on the tenderness of others. If, as Evelyn Simpson insists, Donne should be seen as a split-personality only in so far as everyone is ([1924] 1948, 415), this letter emphasizes that split more than do the letters of many other authors.

Much the same thing happens in interpretations of the letters from Donne's married years (1601–17) and especially those from Mitcham (1601–11). If one is convinced Donne was too self-centered, egotistical, and aloof to be a good husband, then these letters can be used as supporting evidence. If, on the other hand, one is convinced Donne was deeply in love with Anne and content in his marriage, these letters can also be used to prove that. The contradictory responses these letters cause is due in part to their relative lack of newsiness. Donne sometimes drops a bit of information about a sick child or one of Anne's pregnancies almost like a subordinate clause and then goes on to other larger, more metaphysical issues, or, even more damning to some critics, he goes on to talk about himself.

In August 1608, Donne wrote to Sir Henry Goodyer, apologizing for not answering Goodyer's last letter and describing the numerous illnesses in his family. The following excerpt from the letter typifies a characteristic problem of Donne's letters during these years:

> And the reason why I did not send an answer to your last week's letter was because it then found me under too great a sadness, and at present it is thus with me. There is no one person but myself well of my family; I have already lost half a child, and with that mischance of hers, my wife is fallen into such a discomposure as would afflict her too extremely, but that the sickness of all her other children stupefies her; of one of which, in good faith, I have not much hope; and these meet with a fortune so ill provided for physic and such relief, that if God should ease us with burials, I know not how to perform even that: but I flatter myself with this hope that I am dying too; for I cannot waste faster than by such griefs. (Gosse, 1:189)

This letter is in many ways tender: Donne is obviously distressed by the sickness of his children and especially of his wife. He did not write because he was "under too great a sadness," and his concern for Anne is evident. However, there are other phrases and sentiments that seem, if one is predisposed to interpret Donne's character negatively, selfish and egocentric. Everyone is sick but him, and yet the focus of the last half of the paragraph is on his own distress: "I flatter myself with this hope that I am dying too." His assertion that "if God should ease us with burials, I know not how to perform even that" may not speak well of his fatherly concern; to some readers it seems almost a hope that some of the children will die.

These two strains in his letter or interpretations of it do not simply reflect my own confusion about Donne's tone and consequently his virtues or vices as a husband and father, but rather they reflect the dissension among critics and scholars who examine Donne's letters and read from them very different facts about his life as a married man. R. C. Bald treats Donne's feelings toward Anne sympathetically. The marriage, he says, was "a source of sustenance and comfort to him." Anne herself was an intelligent, compassionate woman who could give him not only love but also stability and companionship. Donne, Bald continues, "repaid her love not only with his own but with gratitude as well." To substantiate his view of the Donnes' marital happiness, Bald then quotes from a letter Donne wrote in 1614 to Sir Robert More, Anne's brother: "[We] had not one another at so cheap a rate as that we should ever be weary of one another" (1970, 326). John Carey, however, give a negative connotation to the very letter Bald sees as revealing Donne's love for and contentment with Anne. To Carey, it is simply Donne's putting the best face on the situation for Anne's family. In fact, Donne was, he asserts, bored with Anne: she was uneducated and unable to provide the social and intellectual stimulation Donne craved. He was never unfaithful, only sociable; and Anne could never fulfill this need, nor, Carey continues, did Donne expect her to do so (1981, 74–75). Although Carey posits a Donne shaped by "his desertion of the Catholic Church and his ambition" (14), his treatment of Donne is in many ways sympathetic; Cullen insists that Carey is not interested in debunking Donne but rather the generation of scholars who grew up under Eliot (1982, 171). However, to support his assessment of Donne's character, Carey must emphasize the egotistical, ambitious elements in the letters. Bald, on the other hand, although not always sympathetic to Donne, sees a more changeable man than does Carey and can read the letters as affectionate and generous.[35] The differences between these two biographies—although I would not wish to press the comparison—are similar to those between Jessopp's and Gosse's: Carey concentrates, as did Jessopp, on a certain element or theme in Donne's life; Bald, like Gosse, sees changes in his subject—he is sometimes worldly and ambitious but often loving and selfless.

These two are not the only scholars who read Donne's letters in contradictory ways, nor do unflattering interpretations of Donne's letters or, more generally, of his married life always depend on negative reactions to Donne's poetry or character, although they more often do than not. Evelyn Simpson, for example, depicts Donne as an "exacting husband, nervous, morbid, and subject to frequent attacks of illness" and notes that Donne gives no clear portrait of Anne in either his poems or letters ([1924] 1948, 72). Helen Gardner, on the other hand, sees him as "a good son, a devoted husband, a loving father, and a warm and constant friend" (1952, xxxvi), whereas J. B. Leishman, though much more tentative, suggests that Donne exhibits a "strange detachment" in his letters and that the tenderness for his wife revealed in them seems "more dutiful than spontaneous" (1951, 39). Sparrow (1923, x), Helen White (1936, 103–4), and Gransden

(1954, 17) find evidence of a loving husband; Louthan (1951, 149–53), Clay Hunt (1954, 175), Tillyard (1956, 4), and, of course, Clive (1966, 76, 110–13, 140) find evidence of boredom with and detachment from Anne as well as egocentricity in his relations with her. These last four, it should also be noted, do not think highly of the poetry or of the man who wrote it.

The problems posed by the letters are not unique in the study of Donne's life.[36] His relations with patrons and patronesses, especially with Sir Robert Drury, have provoked a wide range of differing responses, many of which dwell on Donne as a time-serving flatterer despite Bald's measured, objective examination of this issue in *Donne and the Drurys* (1959). His entry into the ministry prompts questions of motives; his retention of certain benefices after becoming dean of St. Paul's can be seen as self-serving (he should have relinquished all of them) or as progressive (many in higher positions kept more); his worries over money during his years as dean show either a grasping worldliness or the legitimate concern of a man with grown daughters needing dowries; his having Christopher Ruddy jailed for not kneeling in church is either an attempt to purify St. Paul's or an example of intolerance. The list could go on. So much depends in each of these examples on one's readiness to isolate phrases from his poems or letters or incidents from his life in order to create a unified personality that the totality of the man is too frequently overlooked and his life becomes, at times, what the biographer wishes to make of it.

This proposition—that Donne becomes, in some biographers' hands more than in others', a malleable bar of gold to be shaped according to the writer's purposes—leads us back to the beginning of this chapter; Donne is as fascinating a subject as he is because the facts of his life are more certain than the facts of the lives of any literary figure before him, and yet very little is known about his attitudes toward these events. Anne Donne died in 1617, but how did John Donne feel about the death? Is the "Nocturnall" a record of his feelings? The sonnet "Since she whome I lovd" almost certainly is, but to some it says more of the poet's feelings about himself than of his feelings for his wife. There are no extant letters on the subject. How did he feel about his mother? About Robert Drury? About his Jesuit uncles? About his Catholic upbringing? So much is known about the facts that a biography of Donne seems easy to write; so little is known about his attitudes that various assumptions are equally easy to make—and to support. The possibilities for motive and attitude searching are exploited more at the beginning of the twentieth century than at the end, but in spite of, and sometimes in reaction to, T. S. Eliot and the New Criticism, biographical studies of Donne have continued to flourish, both in interpretations of the poems and in readings of the life.

# 3
# Donne Refashioned: Eliot and the New Critics

In the 1920s an association of Donne and Eliot set in from which we have not yet quite recovered. The consequences of this association have not been wholly or even primarily harmful to Donne's reputation; however, Eliot's dicta on Donne and the metaphysical poets have determined the course of Donne criticism for the last sixty years. The catch-phrases from Eliot's early essays—dissociation of sensibility, direct sensuous apprehension of thought—in themselves would eventually have stimulated controversy: they are provocative terms. But these, coupled with the poetry of Eliot and his followers and with Eliot's later reversal on Donne and his sensibility, initiated in the twenties, thirties, and forties not only volumes of work on Donne but also work, even through the sixties and seventies, on Eliot's opinion of the metaphysicals, his poetry in relation to theirs, and his poetic theories as derived from Donne's poems. For a few decades, it seemed impossible to study one poet without at least mentioning the other.

Although interest in Donne had been growing through the late ninteenth and early twentieth centuries, Eliot's attention to and use of him caused an avalanche of response: Gosse and Grierson had shown Donne to be an important poet, but after Eliot's essays he quickly became the model poet. As I have shown, Eliot's interest in Donne prompted varying reactions from those who remained interested in Donne's biography. His influence elsewhere, however, was even more direct. Donne was quickly adopted, or "kidnapped," by a group of poets and literary commentators who based some of their poetic theories on Donne's poetry while at the same time forcing this poetry to fit their theories. These "New Critics"[1] fostered two complementary reactions to Donne. First, and most obviously, they caused the structure of Donne's poetry and of metaphysical poetry as a whole to be studied with unprecedented diligence and attention to detail; wit, paradox, conceit, and metaphor, instead of personality and biography, became the keys to understanding Donne. Furthermore, his conceits were no longer regarded as idiosyncratic extravagances but as elements essential to the structure of metaphysical and modern poetry. Although this kind of emphasis often led to the disparagement of the Victorians, the Petrarchan sonneteers, Milton, and even Shakespeare, the New Critics encouraged a more thorough and more intelligently positive study of Donne than had taken place before him. However, with this important work came also a good dose of idolization and idealization against which other critics and scholars reacted. Although their objections to the New Critics' perceptions of Donne often resulted in valuable studies on the poet as a follower of Renaissance traditions or on his philosophy as expressed in his poetry, some critics who were violently opposed to Eliot treated Donne as a proponent of the New Criticism, and even those who were sympathetic scholars of Donne tended to find fault with him in order to counter what they saw as "Donne-olatry."[2]

The study of these developments must begin with a few twentieth-century scholars, for twentieth-century interest in Donne did not begin with Eliot. Not only was Donne discussed and admired by such scholars as Gosse, Grierson, Felix Schelling, Caroline Spurgeon, and Rupert Brooke, but some scholars even before 1921 were reaching the same conclusions that Eliot was later to reach. Brooke, for example, in praising Donne in 1913, wrote that "when passion shook him . . . expression came through the intellect" ([1913] 1973, 101). Eight years later, Grierson, in the introduction to his *Metaphysical Lyrics,* noted that one characteristic of metaphysical poetry is "the peculiar blend of passion and thought, feeling and ratiocination which is their greatest achievement" (1921, xvi). However, these statements, similar as they are to Eliot's did not produce the popular and scholarly response that Eliot's did. Between 1915 and 1935, the number of studies on the metaphysical poets more than tripled (Raiziss 1952, 244). By 1939, popular—non-scholarly—interest in Donne was so lively that Richard Ince could publish a fictional account of the poet's life, and several works of fiction drew their titles from metaphysical works, *For Whom the Bell Tolls* being, perhaps, the best known of these.[3]

If Brooke and Grierson had noticed in metaphysical poetry the same fusion of thought and feeling that Eliot pointed to in 1921, why did this 1921 essay cause such a groundswell of popular and scholarly attention toward Donne? One answer is found in the rebelliousness accorded Donne by the early twentieth century. For critics like Arthur Symons, Frederic Carpenter, and Herbert Grierson, Donne overthrew the pretty conventions of the Petrarchan sonneteers to create a new kind of poetry. Before 1921, the value of this rebelliousness was frequently doubted; however, in *l'entre-deux guerres,* this aspect—or supposed aspect—of Donne's character and career became the justification for an overthrowing of pre-war poetic values. Because Eliot was a poet himself as well as a literary critic, he could and did use Donne's poetry as the basis and justification for the kind of poetry he was writing. The adoption of Donne by Eliot and the New

Critics had such an enormous effect upon Donne scholarship because he was brought to public attention not simply through the pronouncements of an academic in university circles but through the eyes and words of living poets who insisted on their affinities with Donne. Eliot, Tate, Ransom, and later Warren were effecting a revolution in poetry. They could not be overlooked by contemporary critics, and neither could Donne, upon whom they often modeled their poetry and poetic theories. Thus Donne, who twenty some years before had been charged with "dislocating" English literature, was now in the twenties a "modern" poet, a poet who, in Tate's words, was "still alive" three hundred years after his death ([1932] 1939, 325).[4]

Besides the specific adoption of Donne by the new generation of poets for their own aesthetic purposes, many who were interested in the literature of the 1600s projected their own *angst* onto the earlier period, especially after Eliot suggested the supposed parallels between the two centuries. Reviewers for popular magazines like *London Mercury, Dublin Magazine,* and *The New Statesman* as well as literary scholars could remark that "there is something in Donne that speaks to our present time" (Morley 1926, 206).[5] For an era coming to terms with Freud's theories of sexuality, Donne provided innuendoes and frank sensuality. What before had been tasteless vulgarities, often unprintable, became fashionable. A generation becoming disillusioned not only with traditional Christianity but even with traditional doubts about Christianity thought they had found a brother in Donne the skeptic, who had also expressed what seemed to them "modern," intellectual doubts about Christianity. The political and religious conflicts and the scientific advancements of the seventeenth century were, it seemed to many, mirrored in the world conflicts and the scientific progress of the twenties. From the perspective of the 1980s, these professed parallels between the 1920s and the early 1600s seem at best tenuous. Those who insisted on such parallels neglected both the religious skepticism and the burgeoning of industry in the nineteenth century, concentrating instead on the early seventeenth and twentieth centuries' doubts and scientific advancements. Sona Raiziss's 1952 compilation of opinions during the 1920s on seventeenth-century poetry points to the kinds of social, scientific, and religious similarities believed to exist between the two periods: "Society and the individual live in the furious common element of controversy. Like Donne, the indicative twentieth-century poet is at once highly self-conscious and objective; Yeats, D. H. Lawrence, Eliot, Auden, and Crane exhibit the adjacent contrasts of the material and the spiritual, the primitive and the subtle" (103).[6] Whether or not we today accept the validity of these parallels, to the poets of the twenties they seemed compelling. Yet, embarking upon their own literary revolution, they were not satisfied with mere surface comparisons.

Cleanth Brooks in *Modern Poetry and the Tradition* (1939) gives the articles of his literary revolution, which he notes is "of the order of the Romantic Revolt" (ix): "First, that things are not poetic per se, and conversely, that nothing can be said to be intrinsically unpoetic" (11): and, second, that, "the play of the intellect is not necessarily hostile to the depth of emotion" (13). Both of these clearly describe Donne's poetry as well as that of the "new poets." Brooks wrote this more than twenty years after the revolution had formally begun with Eliot and Ezra Pound's conscious decision to metamorphose English poetry. But in 1911, even before his first meeting with Pound, and nine years before he first published on Donne, Eliot had completed "The Love Song of J. Alfred Prufrock," and this poem also meets the criteria laid down by Brooks. Thus, that the revolution could have happened without the rediscovery of Donne is apparent; however, he provided a tradition, a justification, for the new poetry of the twenties and thirties. Without Donne's precedent the revolution would not have failed, but it would not have succeeded quite so decidedly.

Eliot's statements on Donne are well known. Throughout the twenties, he stressed Donne's intellectuality, his ability to think in verse, and his use of the rhythms of speech. These are also characteristic of Eliot's own poetry. To say that in Donne and the metaphysicals (as well as in the French symbolists) Eliot found precedent and justification for his work is not to imply that his admiration for Donne was only self-serving, only that in the Renaissance poet he had found an exploitable cohort. If Eliot had stopped with, or been able to stop with, admiration for and temporary adoption of Donne's poetic methods, he would probably have effected the same change of taste in favor of Donne that did, in fact, take place. However, for his purposes, praise of Donne necessarily involved disparagement of Milton, Dryden, and Tennyson. He could not have "defined" Donne's methods without comparison. To say that "a thought to Donne was an experience; it modified his sensibility" (1921, 669) is to say no more really than Brooke or Grierson had; however, Eliot's adding that "when a poet's mind is perfectly equipped for its work, it is constantly amalgamating experience" (669) makes clear his belief that an intellectual poet like Donne is the norm. Comparison with other poets is thus inevitable. Grierson noted that the language of Donne and the metaphysicals achieved a purity and naturalness lost in the later eighteenth-century poets, but he observed a similar purity in Wordsworth and Coleridge, and his criticism of other poets for failing to achieve this natural blend of thought and feeling is mild (1921, xxxi–xxxii). For Eliot, however, this merging was not only a characteristic of metaphysical poetry; it was an essential habit for a "perfectly equipped" poet. In that one sentence, Eliot set the stage for twenty years of "Donne-olatry." But to revolutionize poetic theory and to justify his own early poetry, it was essential to show also the dangers and causes of Browning's and Tennyson's "ruminating." Thus, "in the seventeenth century a dissociation of sensibility set in, from which we have never recovered; and this dissociation, as was natural, was aggravated by the influence of the two most powerful poets of the century, Milton and Dryden" (1921, 669). Language became more refined, but sentiment became cruder and finally lapsed into sentimentality. Hope for poetry flickered briefly with Keats and Shelley, who proved to be, nevertheless, "unbalanced." The only way to counter the insipidness of the Victorians was to bring modern poetry back to the unity of Donne's, just as Eliot believed he was doing in his own early poetry.

For a number of reasons, Eliot came, from the late twenties on, to write and speak more negatively of Donne than he had in his earlier criticism. He began to rely for a definition of "metaphysical" not on the fusion of thought and feeling—although this concept always remained important for him[7]—but rather on the relation between philosophy and metaphysics: "Donne, Poe et Mallarmé ont la passion de la spéculation métaphysique, mais il est évident qui'ils ne *croient* pas aux théories auxquelles ils s'intéressent ou qu'ils inventent à la façon dont Dante et Lucrèce affirmaient les leurs" (1926b, 525). Donne diminished in interest for Eliot and was replaced by Dante. Eliot even wrote, ten years after introducing the dissociation of sensibility, that "in Donne, there is a manifest fissure between thought and sensibility, a chasm which in his poetry he bridged in his own way" (1931, 8).

This turning away from Donne had several causes. First, in 1927, Eliot became a British subject and was confirmed in the Anglican Church: his need for order and stability was growing (Matthiessen 1947, 12). Perhaps it was for this reason that Eliot denounced Donne the sermon writer for his "impure motives," for being "a little of the religious spell-binder, the Reverend Billy Sunday of his time, the flesh-creeper, the sorcerer of emotional orgy" (1926a, 621). Lancelot Andrewes's sermons could provide Eliot with religious calm better than Donne's more turbulent ones could. Perhaps, too, Donne's poetry had served Eliot's purposes and he could now move on to other matters. Murray Roston believes that "Eliot's critical assessment [of Donne] was prompted to no small extent by a personal need, his search for a poetic model from the past on whose authority the range of contemporary poetic imagery and subject matter could be broadened beyond the self-imposed limits prevalent in the established poetry of his day" (1974, 3). If this assessment is correct, then Eliot could, once that need had been met, replace Donne with others who served more current needs. Perhaps Eliot simply became tired of Donne. By 1931, it was no longer unconventional to build one's system of poetry on the metaphysicals. In fact, just the opposite was true: Donne was so fashionable that Eliot could be more *avant garde* by noting that "Donne's poetry is a concern of the present and the recent past, rather than of the future" (1931, 5). In 1947, he could say with a disarming naïveté that the phrase "dissociation of sensibility" had had "a success in the world astonishing" to him (1957, 173). Whatever his motives, however, Eliot's loss of interest had little effect on the earlier poet's renown. Even he could not arrest the kidnappers of Donne.

René Wellek noted that Eliot actually had very little unqualified praise for Donne (1956, 438); however, the same could not be said of the majority of Eliot's followers. Donne became for them almost a cult figure. Idolization of a poet is almost always damaging to his reputation. Even if he is as great as Shakespeare, someone, like G. B. Shaw, will inevitably feel compelled, however unsuccessfully, to denigrate him. If he is only as great as Donne, there will eventually be repercussions. However, in the twenties and thirties, he was the most admired of poets. The idolization of Donne took two closely related forms: first, the depreciation of other poets in comparison with him, and, second, the elevation of his poetry to the supreme model for modern poets.

The first of these was a logical if excessive extension of Eliot's comparisons in his 1921 essay on the metaphysicals and was reinforced by his 1936 essay attacking Milton. On Milton was laid the primary responsibility for dissociating sensibilities, corrupting language, and thus diverting "the direct current of English poetry"—that written by Donne and his followers (1957, 156; 1921, 670). The charges were less direct, less developed in 1921 but became, nevertheless, ammunition for similar shots against Milton. The attackers could be gentle like Herbert Read: "[t]o compare his [Milton's] diction with Crashaw's (or Donne's) is to realize that what he took he polished, and that the lustre which he gave to English verse, though brilliant, is not vital" (1928, 80). Or more abrupt, like George Williamson: "Great as Milton was in learning, Donne was probably greater. In knowledge of the world they cannot be compared. Of all the explorers of the soul who come within the seventeenth century, Donne, and not Milton, deserves to stand nearest to Shakespeare" (1928, 432). F. R. Leavis devoted twenty-five pages to denigrating Milton. Although he insisted that in comparing him with Donne he was not "as seems . . . commonly to be thought lamenting that he chose not to become a Metaphysical" (1936, 55), it is quite clear that Donne along with Shakespeare is the norm against which Milton is measured. Donne and Shakespeare spoke; Milton only latinized. The Truth on a Hill passage from Donne's Third Satyre demonstrates "the Shakespearian use of English; one might say that it is the English use—the use, in the essential spirit of the language, of its characteristic resources" (55). That it would be heresy for any of Eliot's followers to contradict these attitudes toward Milton based on Donne is evident from Leavis's admonition to Allen Tate. The latter has in the past, Leavis says, told his readers that "Milton should be 'made' to 'influence poetry once more.' " but now, fortunately, Tate has renounced this opinion and returned to the fold (42). This dislike of Milton by Eliot's disciples is not surprising. After all, Eliot said that "Milton's poetry could *only* be an influence for the worse, upon any poet whatever" (1957, 157. Emphasis is Eliot's). However, among adherents of New Criticism, disapprobation of any poet who was not Donne swelled, and soon not only Milton and the nineteenth-century poets[8] but the Petrarchan sonneteers, other metaphysicals, and even Shakespeare were regarded as inferior. According to Alice Bradenburg, the Elizabethan sonneteer "deserves censure" for his "heavy stress on elaborate 'word pictures,' " whereas Donne demonstrates "an understanding of the powers and limitations of poetry" (1942, 1044). To George Williamson, the other metaphysical poets, much as he admires them, are derivative: all imitate Donne (1930).[9] John Crowe Ransom, perhaps a bit too iconoclastic even for the thirties, announced that "the thing which surprises us is to find no evidence anywhere that Shakespeare's imagination is equal to the peculiar and systematic exercises which Donne imposed habitually upon his" ([1938] 1938, 286). Shakespeare compared unfavorably to Donne? Leavis, Williamson, and Ransom are all eccentric in their own ways, and fifty years later their comments should perhaps be seen as no more than the preferences of an age rather than of all time,[10] but, in fact, these judgments had to be—and were—countered by those who appreciated Milton, Shakespeare, and Spenser more than they did the upstart Donne. The New Critics were attacked, but Donne's reputation suffered more.

What happened, in effect, was that those who opposed the elevation of Donne at the expense of other, often greater, poets felt it necessary to elevate or re-elevate Spenser, Shakespeare, and especially Milton and, in the process, to take Donne down a notch or two. Throughout the thirties, forties, and fifties, critics and scholars protested—often mildly or by implication—the depreciation of other poets in comparison with Donne;[11] however, the real harm to the poet came with attacks by prominent scholars who were not content merely to put Donne back in his place but wanted to push him far below his contemporaries in worth. The two most eminent of these were E. M. W. Tillyard and Douglas Bush.

It is not my intention to depreciate these two scholars for the sake of Donne, but rather to show how their defense of other poets slanted their perceptions of Donne. Tillyard is the more obvious in intention of the two. In *The Metaphysicals and Milton* (1956), he emphasizes the differences between Donne and Milton much to the former's discredit. That the comparison was prompted, at least in part, by the adulation of Eliot and his followers is evident from Tillyard's assertion that:

Donne, on the other hand, was a great innovator but with a narrower, more personal talent than Milton. He made people heed him, he stirred them up, he contributed to the age's vitality. But he remains the exception, and his admirers will do him no good in the long run if they pretend he was anything else. (74)

In fact, Tillyard's comparison depends on attacking Donne for not being Milton (as, of course, many of the New Critics had attacked Milton for not being Donne). But in doing so, Tillyard returned in a more sophisticated fashion to the same charges brought against Donne before 1921. Donne in the Holy Sonnet "Since she whome I lovd" is "self-centered." The sonnet is "about his own feelings and the state of his own soul and his hopes of what God is going to do for it. His dead wife, the nominal concern of the sonnet,[12] is not in the least characterized, she really has no existence (in spite of the elopement and the twelve children in sixteen years), and she is the mere passive vehicle of her husband's self-preoccupations" (4). Milton, however, in his sonnet "Methought I saw my late espoused Saint," treats his wife as "a real woman, doing her high honor" (8–9). Donne contradicts himself; he is too intellectual; he lacks Milton's social sense; he does not appeal to universal emotions. In short, although Tillyard never states this explicitly, Donne is inferior to Milton not only as a poet but as a man. His popularity has been only a fad, which, in Tillyard's Miltonic phrase, "cannot in the nature of things suffer no decline" (13). Tillyard's comparisons are cogent and valuable for what they reveal about the two poets. But what he neglects or purposely overlooks is that the two sonnets describe two different experiences. If Donne's sonnet is self-centered, it is so because he was not mourning a death as much as he was acknowledging the effects of the death on him. Milton's sonnet renders a more immediate and more emotionally charged situation than does Donne's, but this does not necessarily make it a better poem. Nor is Milton's sonnet noticeably less "intellectual" than Donne's; it is only that the intellectual activity required to remember the myth of Admetus and Alcestis is more congenial to Tillyard than that required to follow the intricate thought of Donne's sonnet. Tillyard comes close to acknowledging this when he admits that he prefers Milton and the Romantics to the "perplexities and the torture of Donne's mind" (20–25). Preferences in literature are commonplace, but because the New Critics established Donne as the gold standard of literature beside which all other poets were lead, Tillyard was obliged to treat at length a poet for whom he had little taste or sympathy. In other contexts, Tillyard could and did praise Donne's poetry[13] however, when forced by New Critical adoration of Donne at the expense of Milton to compare these two, he had to devalue Donne.

Douglas Bush's comments on Donne are more scattered and subtle than Tillyard's and thus more insidiously dangerous to the poet, especially since Bush was, in general, the more judicious scholar. His comments on Donne in *Mythology and the Renaissance Tradition* ([1932] 1963) are necessarily sketchy given Bush's subject. He is unhappy with the "uncritical cult" of Donne (206) and says that compared with Spenser's epithalamia Donne's are "sorry affairs" (233)—a comparison as unfair to Donne as a dismissal of the *Amoretti* compared to the *Songs and Sonets* is to Spenser, given the differences in style, form, and content. However, in later works, he focuses more intently on rescuing other poets from the cult of Donne. George Herbert, naturally linked with Donne by the New Critics, nevertheless was most often seen by them as derivative and imitative; he is mentioned only one time (and that in connection with hieroglyphic poems) in Wellek and Warren's *Theory of Literature* (1956, 3d ed., 143), and none of his poems appears in the 1938 edition of Brooks and Warren's *Understanding Poetry*.[14] For Bush, however, reacting against the Donne cult, Donne's religious poems pale beside Herbert's: "Whereas Herbert's can enter into and act upon our own being, most of Donne's religious poetry remains an external object of intellectual study. . . . can many of us really get inside them, or can they get inside us?" ([1957] 1958, 40). In his chapter on the Renaissance in *English Poetry: The Main Currents* (1952), the only section Bush begins pejoratively is that on Donne. True, he is somewhat critical of Spenser's sonnets, and he notes that some of the Elizabethan sonneteers are repetitious. Even Shakespeare's sonnets, he says, are tedious if read in one sitting (28–29, 40), but Donne is the only major Renaissance poet that he criticizes more than he praises. The rediscovery of the metaphysical poets gave criticism, he complains, a new direction that needs qualification and modification (56–57). "If he [Donne] fused thought and feeling, he did not always maintain the fusion through even a short poem . .;. Donne is a much smaller and in some ways less complex poet than Spenser. His technique is exciting but, once grasped, is fairly obvious, and other rewards are not inexhaustible, whereas Spenser continually reveals new depths and overtones" (57). The New Critics gave a standing ovation to Donne's difficulty and his many levels of meaning. Bush, in protest, demanded not just that they sit down but that they stop applauding as well. The same kinds of comments are evident in *English Literature in the Earlier Seventeenth Century* ([1945] 1962, 2d ed.),[15] where they are particularly unfortunate since Donne receives even less sympathetic treatment from C. S. Lewis in the sixteenth-century volume of the same series. Thus Donne remained an outcast in some substantial literary works because he was identified with his idolaters. Donne. who in his extant writing is virtually silent about contemporary poetry, suddenly became, through the work of the New Critics, the outspoken opponent of many poets, and in this way was left open to the attack of conservative but influential scholars.

That this trend was recognized even as it was developing is evident from Merritt Hughes's statement that his preference for Milton should not influence his critical perception of either that poet or Donne (1958, 69) and by Cleanth Brooks's assertion that

> in the present muddled state of scholarship–criticism, the charge that the critic is engaged in turning one poet into another—Milton into Donne—is to be expected. I suspect that Professor Douglas Bush, for example, might see it in that way.
>
> The new poetry and the new criticism, for Professor Bush, involve a disparagement of Milton; they tend to exalt Donne over Milton. And Milton's own fervent angel Abdiel could not resent this inversion of just hierarchy more indignantly than Professor Bush resents it. . . . Naturally, Professor Bush fixes upon T. S. Eliot as the Satan who has drawn off a third part of the host of Heaven (or at least a third part of the graduate students) from their proper allegiance. (1951, 4)

But, this defense aside, perhaps the hypothetical assessment Brooks posits for Bush is correct, since Brooks does proceed to turn Milton into Donne. His justification for doing so is that in recovering Donne's poetry, the critic has also recovered poetry itself. Thus it is natural to look for the same elements in other good poetry that we find in Donne's (3). This sentiment typifies the second reason for "Donne-olatry" and the second reason for opponents of the New Criticism to attack the poet. Donne became the model for all poetry.

The primary characteristic of Donne's poetry pointed to by the New Critics of the 1920s, 1930s, and 1940s was its "direct sensuous apprehension of thought." In his poetry was none of the emotionalism or sentimentality of a Shelley or a Tennyson. Here was a fusion of thought and feeling, irony, paradox, wit, passion refined by the brain; in short, Donne was admired for an intellectuality that corresponded exactly to the intellectual tastes of this three-decade period. Leavis observes that "Donne in his poetry could be intellectual and lyrical, cynical and serious, witty and intense at the same time. A modern's ways of feeling will be different, but are likely to be similarly complex" (1931, 347). Fausset sees the revival of Donne as suggesting "a taste for mental subtleties" (1931, 341). Bald praises Eliot for bringing back into poetry the "direct sensuous apprehension of thought" that had been missing for 250 years ([1932] 1965, 59); that is, since the time of Donne's imitators. These are only three of many such comments during this time. In fact, the comments on his intellect as revealed in his poetry are so numerous that hardly a pre-1950 writer sympathetic to Donne can fail to mention his ability to link emotion and thought through intellect. However, also important to Donne's later critical reputation was a less obvious, often unacknowledged praise of his obscurity and elitism—qualities cultivated by the "new poets" in their own work.

John Dryden complained that Donne "perplexes the Minds of the Fair Sex with nice Speculations of Philosophy" ([1693] 1958, 604). Many in the first two decades of the twentieth century objected likewise to Donne's hard conceits and obscure meanings. The following censure from 1903 is typical: "Eagerness for novelty and paradox leads the poets to obscurity of expression; and the reader is justly incensed when he finds that the labour required to arrive at the meaning, hidden behind involved syntax and unmeasured verse, has been expended in vain" (Courthope, 3:167). For Eliot, however, this difficulty or obscurity was an essential ingredient of poetry. He praised it in the metaphysicals and employed it in his own work:

> Poets in our civilization . . . must be *difficult*. Our civilization compre-
> hends great variety and complexity, and this variety and complexity,
> playing upon a refined sensibility, must produce various and complex
> results. The poet must become more and more comprehensive, more
> allusive, more indirect, in order to force, to dislocate if necessary,
> language into his meaning. (1921, 670)

For Eliot's followers, obscurity became one of the most important similarities between that poet and Donne. According to George Williamson, it
was one of the main reasons both poets received negative criticism (1927,
286). Essays justifying Donne's obscurity appeared. Eliot, everyone knew,
cultivated obscurity, and so Donne's obscurity must also have been conscious. John Sparrow tried in *Sense and Poetry* to distinguish between the
obscurity of the symbolists and of the metaphysicals (1934, 71–89), but he
was roundly attacked by Eliot's followers, who insisted that the obscurity
of both served the same artistic function.[16]

Furthermore, obscurity often leads to elitism. Both Donne and Eliot
were *poèts de coterie* (Cruttwell 1970, 33–34), and Eliot was often accused
of intentional obscurity in order to exclude from his poetry those not as
learned as he. Donne, in the minds of many, took on this elitist character.[17]
In fact, this conception of Donne was encouraged by the New Critics, who
saw definite advantages to linking their poetry with his. When Tate defined
"tension" in poetry, he did so by distinguishing between kinds of
obscurity: even Cowley's worse poetry is better than that of Edna Millay
or James Thomson ([1938] 1959, 78–81). By implication, the revolution in
poetry waged by Tate, Eliot, Ransom, and Warren even at its worst was
better than what poetry had been. If the public failed to understand that
poetry, then it was not the poet but the public "which inhabits the Ivory
Tower, separating its emotional life . . . from the actual world" (Brooks
1939, 68).

All of this could not help but affect Donne's critical reputation, and in the forties political events did little to stop Donne's fall from grace. During World II, the desire of the New Critics to judge a poem without reference to the poet's life and beliefs, their disavowal of the notion that a good artist must necessarily be a good man, led to numerous attacks on their aesthetic theories and their political views, especially after the War when in 1948 Ezra Pound was awarded the Bollingen Prize for poetry. Eliot's anti-Semitism was discussed; the selection committee, composed of Eliot, Tate, Warren, Aiken, Auden, and others, was accused of Fascist leanings; and the Library of Congress was even implicated (Hillyer 1949, 9–11, 28).[18] This kind of accusation naturally provoked heated responses, but the controversy went far beyond Pound; rather, "the emphasis shifted to T. S. Eliot, the new poetry, and the Higher Criticism" (Corrigan 1969, 294). This quarrel's effect on Donne was not dramatic; in fact, neither he nor metaphysical poetry was mentioned by name. However, because the feud was provoked by writers and editors of *The Saturday Review,* "the fact that a revolution in taste had occurred—finally penetrated even the densest popular minds" (Webster 1979, 124–25). Modern poetry was criticized in terms reminiscent of those used to fault Donne's poetry in the early years of the century. A letter writer in *The Saturday Review* asserted that "the really great poetry of the world is understandable, moving, quotable" and suggested that it is "about time we came down to earth" and forget this "modern craze" of reading "deep meanings into drivel" (Taylor 1949, 31). His comments apply equally well to Eliot or Donne, the latter of whom Sparrow notes is perplexing to the ordinary modern reader (1934, 76). William Barrett asks, "How far is it possible, in a lyric poem, for technical embellishments to transform vicious and ugly matter into beautiful poetry?" (Davis 1949, 347). Rossell Hope Robbins, whose aim is clearly to dethrone Eliot, refers obliquely to his elevation of Donne and the metaphysicals:

> Perhaps because of his attitude toward modern society, Eliot was attracted to the seventeenth century, the greatest period of literary production of the rising mercantile classes. Yet Eliot was attracted not by the virile and progressive writers, but those already showing decadent elements. His heroes are Webster . . . and Crashaw. (1951, 113)

His failure to mention Donne could be an indication of the high place accorded Donne in English literature, or it could simply indicate scholarly ineptitude. Yet, when *The T. S. Eliot Myth* appeared in 1951, the association of Eliot and Donne had been enough publicized that, for him and for his readers, the description of Eliot's "heroes" implied the inclusion of Donne, even though Eliot had long since lost interest in the earlier poet. Since this kind of comment was most pronounced in columns and books appealing to the nonexpert in literature, it harmed Donne only by continuing to stress his inaccessibility and justifying future criticism of him.

More significant for Donne's reputation than the furor over the Bollingen Prize were specific objections to Donne's poetry by men of letters. Poets who in their own work eschewed Eliot's poetic theories and practices disapproved also of Donne's poetry because in it they saw the germ of their rival's poetry. They dismissed both without examining the early poet in any terms other than Eliot's. A. E. Housman, for example, whose poetry could not be more at variance with Eliot's and Donne's, objected strenuously to metaphysical poems, which, he says, are "no more poetical than anagrams; such pleasure as they give is purely intellectual and is intellectually frivolous" (1933, 10). Furthermore, the metaphysical poets were too much taken with simile and metaphor, "things inessential to poetry" (10–11). Although his wording is careful, Housman blames Eliot, his followers, and their poetry for raising these unpoetical anagrams to their present stature (11–13). By asserting that poetry is not intellectual but physical (45), he distanced himself even more from Eliot's aesthetics and demonstrated his unwillingness to separate the "new poetry," which was so unlike his, from metaphysical poetry. He could see in the latter only what the New Critics had pointed to, and he disapproved of that without investigating further. In 1938, Louis Untermeyer, described by Conrad Aiken as "essentially a conservative poet" who objected to and refused to understand Eliot and his school (1919, 259, 265–68), labeled Donne's poetry humorless, "twisted, angry, and, finally, tortured" (15). He notes that it is no wonder "our perplexed and tortured age turns toward them [Donne's poems] as expressions of our own ingenious disorder. Sensual and cynical, the tormented spirit evades reality by retreating into wit, an escape that is as pathetic as it is preposterous" (15). Obviously, Untermeyer, like Housman, had no taste for the "mental subtleties" admired by the New Critics.[19] In 1946, James Stephens, who believed that love poetry should be simple, as a flower is simple, disliked Donne's verse because it is too passionate, too witty, and too dramatic ([1946] 1964, 202–5). In 1934, he had admitted that he was not "in sympathy" with Eliot's poetry (1974, 386). An attack on Donne more admittedly inspired by dislike of Eliot's poetry and criticism is evident in Karl Shapiro's *In Defense of Ignorance* (1952). In the middle of an iconoclastic assault on Eliot, Shapiro observes that "his intellectualization of feeling and taste led him to such twisted judgments as . . . the approval of Donne and the disparagement of Milton" (43). Metaphysical poetry itself is "inferior poetry . . . bordering on the freakish," and Donne is valued only because Eliot taught a generation that intellectual poetry is the best poetry. Donne's poems are about equal to Marianne More's (12–13)—a most unlikely comparison. Had Eliot not written as glowingly as he did of

Donne, it is questionable whether these poets would have bothered to mention him—so antithetical is he to their own poetry—but by writing on him, they added to criticism of Donne that depends on taste and literary feuds rather than on judicious analysis or scholarship.

As early as 1934 Merritt Hughes understood the danger that could befall Donne because modern poets were "kidnapping" him ([1934] 1975, 39). He cautioned that "the more absolute we make our estimate of Donne's wit, and of metaphysical wit in general, the less historically revealing becomes our appreciation of Donne" (41). It has been a long process—one not yet completed—to separate Donne and Eliot as Hughes advised and then to return Donne to his historical period. The most obvious manifestation of the first step involves explaining Eliot's phrase "dissociation of sensibility."

In 1941, John Crowe Ransom, rather heretically, declared of the assimilation of thought and feeling that, "having worked to the best of my ability to find the thing Eliot refers to in the 17th-Century poets, and failed, I incline to think there was nothing of the kind there" (183). Such a pronouncement by one of the New Critics should have ended the kidnapping and returned Donne to his proper place. However, in denying the association of thought and feeling in the metaphysicals and Donne in particular, Ransom established another pattern, almost as damning for Donne. After citing a passage from Chapman, Ransom notes that, although the poetry is not particularly metaphysical, it is still better poetry than Browning's, not because Browning reveals a "dissociation of sensibility" but simply because Chapman has greater imagination and perception (183–86). Donne's compass image, however, may be "dignified," but it is also very "awkward." Donne's metaphysical poems "offer us an art which has a very formal mode of composition, but in it the texture dominates the structure and all but threatens its life. . . . This poetry runs a great risk" (190). Eliot labeled Donne's poetry; Ransom showed the label to be wrong, but in order to enforce his criticism of Eliot, he had to show that one of Donne's finest poems, one that has easily passed Samuel Johnson's test for great literature, is itself bad poetry. The tone of Ransom's essay implies that Eliot deceived his disciples by making them chase after a quality that was never there and that Donne participated in the deception.

Not everyone wanting to disprove or discuss Eliot's phrase, of course, has been as harsh to Donne. Disputes about what Eliot meant by "dissociation" and "sensibility" are frequent, and Donne is often used merely as an illustrative example.[20] However, even these writers sometimes divert in one of two ways the course of Donne's critical reputation. First, they continue the association of Donne and Eliot, thus abetting the kidnapping by interpreting Donne in terms of the critic. For example, Robert Adams, writing in 1954, attempted to reconcile Eliot's two contradictory views on

Donne's "sensibility," contending that "the confusion is significant, not merely careless; the rather complex fact seems to be that Donne did suffer from 'dissociation of sensibility,' exploited the fact energetically, and felt rather strongly that he shouldn't—being in all respects like Eliot" (280). His statement, which makes "dissociation of sensibility" sound rather like a disease, implies that Donne understood the tensions in his life and poetry in much the same way that Eliot understood his own tensions—a perspective that continues to make Donne "modern." Malloch in 1953 sought to apply Eliot's phrase to all poetry while using "metaphysical" to characterize Donne's poetry. Thus he continued to define Donne's poetry in terms of Eliot (97, 100). This practice was so common during the fifties and early sixties that F. M. Kuna protested: the critic, he says, should decide if he wants to talk about Donne or Eliot. To do both leads to talking about neither poet but rather about poetic theory (1963, 243). Even when Eliot's phrase is not the chief subject, its ghost haunts Donne criticism. Bullough (1962, 41) and Woodhouse (1965, 55) in separate essays felt obliged to deal with the phrase and explain its relation to Donne. And they are only two of many who must take Eliot into account in their assessments of Donne.

The second effect is that Donne is paired with other poets for no reason other than an attempt to counter or support Eliot. Thus he is compared with symbolist poets (Block 1967), Browning, Dante (Eric Thompson 1952), Milton (H. W. Smith 1951), and others. Studies of influence and similarities and differences between poets are, of course, critical commonplaces. However, Donne's poetry does not become more understandable through these comparisons; he becomes merely a tool for understanding Eliot.

The most damaging repudiations of Eliot and his "dissociation of sensibility" have followed in Ransom's path. Mario Praz, for example, although astute in his criticism and generally sympathetic to Donne, traces Donne's rise to fame via Eliot and praises Clay Hunt's, *Donne's Poetry* for its revelations of both poets' limitations. Hunt in this book is himself iconoclastic, reveling in Donne's alleged morbidity, emotional poverty, and lack of wit. He disputes the applicability of "unification of sensibility" to Donne's poetry because "to suggest in any way that Donne's poetry comprehends a great range of human experience seems to me gravely misleading" (1954, 118–19). Praz seems to agree:

> Far from "possessing a mechanism which could devour any kind of experience," as T. S. Eliot would have it, Donne's sensibility was then extremely limited, and the fact that its limitations are in large measure those of the modern intellectual world, accounts for Donne's popularity in our time. (1961, 362)

The necessity for de-popularizing Donne for not, in fact, possessing what Eliot led a generation to believe he possessed is evident in both these writers. Eliot, they imply, was right in approving a unified sensibility, but Donne does not have it.

Frank Kermode takes a different tack. The focus of his argument is Eliot's poetic need for the term, the need other poets have also felt for "a critical moment after which everything went wrong," and the historical inaccuracy of this belief (1957b, 185). However, his essay also includes an attack on Donne. He may be able to wed thought and feeling, but the result is that a poem like "Batter my heart" is "indecorous, a mere grotesquerie, with no point unless it be that Three Persons can batter better than One" (188). [21] Kermode's theory about the poem, in the context of attacking Eliot, loses whatever literary objectivity it might otherwise have had. That Stephen Orgel, writing in 1971, had to insist vehemently that, in criticizing Eliot and showing a "disproportion between the facts and feelings" in Donne's poetry, he was *not* faulting Donne (241) is a measure of how persistently criticism of Eliot has caused criticism of Donne.

This habit has presented itself at least once even in the last twenty-five years. H. M. Richmond presents an extreme example in his "Donne's Master: The Young Shakespeare" (1973). The inspiration for Richmond's essay was a lecture given by F. R. Leavis in 1969 (569–72), defending Eliot against Leishman's criticism of him in *The Monarch of Wit*. Richmond in turn defends Leishman by showing that, as he had suggested, Donne learned from and was influenced by Shakespeare. What might have been a thorough, scholarly essay on sources and influence, however, turns into a characterization of Donne as a naive "devotee" of Shakespeare:

> It is scarcely an exaggeration to say that as distinctive a personality as Donne appears to have been psychologically conditioned by his master [i.e., Shakespeare], and that he is less capable of grasping and extending the sweep of the dramatist's genius, than of excerpting, elaborating and delicately perfecting a few flashes of character from among the many sparkling showers of personae thrown off by Shakespeare's virtuosity. (143–44)

Given Richmond's absolute gleefulness in finding for each of Donne's poems a source in one of Shakespeare's plays, this may be an extreme example; however, its late date, its direct renouncing of New Criticism, and its exaggerated emphasis on Donne as a "charming but derivative appendix to the Elizabethan drama" (144) indicate the harm Eliot and the New Critics' theories could have on Donne's reputation.

In 1951, Helen White noted that "the new criticism has accomplished a good deal, but it has a good deal to do before it will have Donne" (1951b,

2). Eleven years later, E. L. Marilla elaborated on this sentiment when he wrote that "if mere vagaries of critical pronouncement can bring him [Donne] into his current high esteem, what is there to prevent a continuance of such vagaries from thrusting him at any time into neglect or even oblivion as long as his real strength as a poet remains undefined?" (1962, 173). Since the 1940s, Donne scholars have labored to prevent what Marilla forecasted: they have tried to remove Donne from the influence of the New Critics. To do this, they have used, with varying degrees of success, three main methods: a return to biographical studies, a reinterpretation of Donne's skepticism, and a study of his place in Renaissance poetic traditions.

The first I have already discussed; however, let me note again that, from the thirties on, biographical treatments of Donne's verse often arise directly from antipathy to Eliot and the New Critics.[22] Often, readers who protest the New Critics' admiration of Donne are interested in showing that Donne was egocentric, overly ambitious, and sexually perverse. The three who come most readily to mind are John Carey, Clay Hunt, and Judah Stampfer, and their interpretations of the poet's life lose some objectivity because of their icon-blasting aims.

Similar to these are the critics who, again objecting to Eliot, attempt to define Donne's system of beliefs. This can take two forms: either a denial that Donne fits into the categories the New Critics attempted to place him in followed by a reinterpretation of his thought, or a repudiation of the New Critics coupled with an assertion that Donne was a much less attractive person than they believed him to be. Irving Lowe and William Rooney illustrate the first approach. According to Lowe in 1961, "[I]n the twenties and the two decades following, criticism was apt to approach Donne and other literary figures of the past with what was then the new interest in the psychological and experiential" (389) and therefore to read Donne and others as forerunners of modern skepticism (397). Thus Donne was turned into a skeptical fideist (390). In a reasoned, objective manner, Lower shows that Donne never doubted reason and faith, only knowledge (397). Similarly, Rooney in 1956, using New Critical methods, argued against Brooks's interpretation of "The Canonization." He criticizes Brooks for reading into the poem only those meanings he wants to see there (43), and he concludes that from this poem one cannot decide whether " 'Donne takes both love and religion seriously' " (47). Both writers, and examples of others could be added, protested New Critical interpretations of Donne without—as, for example, Ransom did—attacking the poetry itself. Neither of these is necessarily "right" in his interpretation of Donne. The point is rather that both, provoked by the picture of the poet established by the New Critics, used the techniques of the opposition to broaden the scope of Donne studies.

Unfortunately, however, the second alternative is also prevalent. Marius Bewley, for example, objected to the concentration in the twentieth century on Donne's *Songs and Sonets* and on his treatment of women. This emphasis, he believes, has ignored his attitudes toward religion. Nominally interested in examining Donne's cynicism in a different context than had the New Critics in extolling his skepticism, his essay shows that the *Anniversaries* are a "private joke," because Donne seems to be eulogizing Elizabeth Drury when, in fact, he is celebrating his own "apostasy" (1952, 622): "What, in effect, Donne does here is to transpose the profoundly serious theological problems to the level of a time-serving courtier's outrageous flattery" (633). It is in a statement such as this that the real purpose of Bewley's essay can be discerned. Once again, this is not a question of the rightness or wrongness of his interpretation. The symbolism of Elizabeth Drury has provoked wide and varied speculation, and Bewley is not the first or the last to identify her with either the Anglican or the Catholic Church. Even his reading of the *Songs and Sonets* as Donne's record of his struggles to escape from Catholicism (637)—while not widely accepted—is as possible as some other interpretations of the poems. John Carey, in fact, reads them in approximately the same way (1981, 37–45). Bewley's scholarship is, however, undermined by his tone. This essay is not simply an investigative study; it is an attack intended to remove Donne from "sentimentality" (619–20). His aim is not simply to show that the *Songs and Sonets* are about Catholicism; it is to show that Donne as he is revealed in his poetry was deceptive, egocentric, and venal and that scholars like Leishman and Bennett have been fooled into thinking him a lover when in fact his poetry demonstrates a "manichean [sic] hatred of the flesh" (641). His sympathy for C. S. Lewis and J. E. V. Crofts, "cooling cards"[23] for Eliot's enthusiasm for Donne, strongly suggests his lack of sympathy for the New Critics and their portrait of Donne.[24]

Doniphan Louthan in 1951 also wanted to discredit the New Critics' perception of Donne as "an iconoclast in revolt against Petrarchanism" (183), and he too sided with Lewis in believing Donne was self-conscious "to the point of neurosis and beyond" (128). Relying on an autobiographical interpretation of "A Nocturnall" and detailed readings of several of Donne's poems, he shows that the poet was "preoccuppied with sex" and cheerfully amoral (164). Thus, if objections to New Critical treatments of Donne opened the door to valuable reassessments of his thought and life, they also let in evaluations reminiscent of the moral objections of the first two decades of the twentieth century.

Ultimately these attacks on Donne because of his association with Eliot and the New Critics led to a revaluation of Donne by knowledgeable, sympathetic scholars who attempted to place Donne in the Renaissance poetic tradition and thus divorce him from the modern revolutionary of the twenties and thirties. Although the results were generally valuable, these scholars often found it necessary to distance themselves from New Critical idolatry of Donne by treating his poetry as less original than the New Critics had touted it as being. Their assumption often seemed to be that Donne had attempted the innovations the New Critics believed he had accomplished but had failed. To compensate, he had fallen back on sixteenth-century themes and poetic modes.

Rosemond Tuve, the first of these scholars, placed Donne in the tradition of the Elizabethans who preceded him, although Donne was not, of course, the main subject of her study. As an attempt to locate Donne historically, *Elizabethan and Metaphysical Imagery* is invaluable. Donne's poetry, she says, would be easier to understand if "we did not try to postulate for him a more 'modern' relation between informing concept and possible connotations" (1947, 228n.). As a rebuff to the New Critics, it serves its purpose with scholarship, judicious interpretations, and attention to detail. However, it leaves unanswered the question of why Donne *seems* so different from his contemporaries. For Tuve, apparently, he does not: "to leaf through Donne or Sidney or Carew is to make a list of the old conceits—fire and ice, sighs and winds. . . . But what poet (or lover) ever did otherwise than claim that the old ways of pleading his cause or praising his lady are insufficient?" (420). It is a mistake, she says, to interpret Ben Jonson's statement about Donne's perishing because he was hard to understand to mean he "headed an opposing school of poets who had given up the idea that poetry is to be understood" (229). Donne's conceits in relation to Renaissance theories of rhetoric and decorum are undoubtedly worthy of study. Yet Donne's poetry, as generations of readers have recognized, is different from Spenser's and Sidney's and even Wyatt's. His fire and ice are not their fire and ice, and his sighs are certainly not their sighs. It is frustrating to the scholar that Donne did not to our knowledge write about his poetic theories (if he had any) because this lack has permitted the contradictory views of Donne as a revolutionary and as a traditionalist.

Because of this lack, Tuve can assert that Donne was not creating a new poetic style but was conforming to the Renaissance doctrine of decorum. In her view, what is "sometimes mistaken by moderns for a new (and more modern) attitude toward grave and high matter for poetry" is no more than Donne's choice of a "middle or base style" for his poetry (236–37). If this is true, why, one might ask, did Donne choose to treat his poetic subjects in this lower style? For the half-century preceding him and during the time he was writing some of the *Songs and Sonets,* fire, ice, sighs, and winds had been versified in the high style. Did not Donne's low style, then, indicate something of an innovation in poetry? Furthermore, if Donne was introducing only "minor variations of decorum," which were not new because of the "great revolutionary achievement of the earlier Renaissance poets with respect to the decorum of styles" (234), why did Donne's contemporary Thomas Carew insist on his "fresh invention" and "masculine expression"? If the New Critics unfairly slanted our perceptions of Donne by emphasizing his rebelliousness, Tuve and her followers slanted them by emphasizing his traditionalism. Both views limit our understanding of Donne.

The effects of the latter perception can best be assessed by examining the work of two of Tuve's scholarly followers.

No one could doubt Helen Gardner's interest in and knowledge of Donne; therefore, when she deems one of his poems a poor work of art, the reader can be fairly certain that she does not do so out of a desire to demean the poet. In *The Business of Criticism,* this is her judgment of "Aire and Angels." She criticizes it, apologetically and tentatively, for ending with what she sees as a "slap in the face" to women (1959b, 68). Even after she takes into account several Renaissance works demonstrating the inferiority of women's love, the poem does not have, as a great poem should, a self-evident "unity of moral tone or feeling" because it begins by praising women and ends by degrading them (73–74). She is frankly confused by the poem (75) but sees it primarily as a poor work of art. Her judgment, however, depends in large part on her rejection of Leonard Unger's interpretation of the poem. For him the ending is a "calculated surprise"—witty and ironic (1950, 45). According to Gardner, if we read the poem in this New Critical way, then it is "artistically trivial" and Unger's defense of it is "desperate" (69). Although the disagreement itself is an interesting one, Gardner's motives for selecting the poem for analysis are, for my purposes, more important. She delights in other of Donne's poems ("Negative Love," "Loves Deitie"), but she seems to have selected "Aire and Angels" for analysis simply to prove its unsatisfactory nature in response to New Critical methods and enthusiasms. Her purpose in the chapter in which she discusses it is to show that asking relevant historical questions about a work and trying to grasp the writer's use of language are the keys to understanding a work (62). By failing to do this, Cleanth Brooks misinterpreted the naked, new-born babe metaphor in *Macbeth.*[25] Her examination of "Aire and Angels" reinforces this point and raises some thoughtful objections to New Critical techniques. However, it is unfortunate that to do so she chose one of Donne's most puzzling poems. Surely her purpose could have been served as well by reading one of Donne's more straightforward poems in a historical context. Her selection of this poem hints at a desire to show not only that the methods of Brooks and Unger are fallible but also that Donne's poetic value has been overestimated.

A. J. Smith's early essays on Donne followed a similar pattern. Seeking to explode the myth of Donne's "direct sensuous apprehension of thought," Smith portrays Donne as one of a group of poets who, unlike those who write for all time, are "so thoroughly of their time" that scholars must labor to make us grasp them. This second group is "perhaps not less worthy than the first," but misplacing Donne in the first group has led in the twentieth century to an "obsession" with his poetry (1957a, 260).[26] Smith's attitude is interesting. He admires Donne and enjoys his poetry. He calls "The Extasie" the work of a "strongly original and variously gifted personality" (1958, 374). However, Smith's often contentious tone sometimes undermines his discussions. In an essay on "Aire and Angels," for example, he dwells on Donne's reliance on stock situations and themes in order to counter the "Thirties school" and to show what Donne was "driving at consciously" ([1960] 1962, 174). In doing so, he brings Donne himself into the fray. In fact, "what was new about Donne's poetry—and it is new only in a limited sense—was that the poet found his means of witty presentation in a thorough-going application of argumentative techniques" (173). Not only is Donne's poetry new only in this limited sense, but, in fact, there is no serious, intellectual thought behind it. Donne was merely putting into poetic form "for quite orthodox ends the manners of a game with which every such frequenter of the Inns of Court would have been familiar" (173). Thus, Donne lacks the "modern" intellectualism praised by the New Critics. Moreover, "not only are the metaphysics, such as they are, evidently for show in a brilliant simulacrum of analogical illustration or 'proof,' but the argument they elaborate was not new when Donne used it" (177).[27] "It is not, then," he continues, "the novelty of its attitudes or insights that makes the poem worthwhile" (178). Nor is it the expression of emotion, since it conveys the "flimsy minimal element of the common love situation" (178). However, because of its diction, its rhythm, its phrasing, and its elegance, "Aire and Angels" is "perhaps as fine poetry as anything Donne offers" (178)—a statement that is itself rather ambiguous praise. Helen Gardner is not willing to go this far. Commenting on Smith's essay, she writes: "I cannot believe that Donne's poetry had no relation to the development of his moral, intellectual, and emotional life, and that his readers in our century were wholly astray in finding in his poetry the revelation of a very powerful individual" (1962, 12). Smith does, of course, praise Donne's poetry, but, in order to minimize the New Criticism's worth, he had first to minimize those elements of Donne's work the New Critics praised.

Tuve, Gardner, and Smith have all certainly made valuable contributions to the study of Donne's poetry. They corrected the idolatry of the New Critics and rescued Donne from the twentieth century by returning him to his historical place. However, in doing so—and it was a position they were forced to take—they sometimes undervalued his unique style. If

Donne did use stock situations and Neoplatonism, he did so in a new way, and, despite Smith's protestation, this is what gets lost in historical studies of his poetry. Patrick Cruttwell, whose identification with the " 'thirties generation' " (1970, 28) may prejudice his point slightly, states the problem succinctly: "No amount of evidence that Donne took over from his predecessors many themes, poses, conventions, etc., and that he, like everyone then, had been well grounded in the poetic and rhetorical theories of the Renaissance, makes a poem by Spenser in the smallest degree less unlike a poem by Donne" (30–31). In the fifties, because of reactions to New Criticism, scholars and critics could not reach a consensus about the relationship between Donne's inventiveness and his sources in Renaissance tradition.

A word or two remains to be said about the boost the New Criticism gave to the study of Donne through adoption of certain techniques rather than through reaction against them. Perhaps the greatest benefit of New Critical methods was that Donne's poetry was removed, at least temporarily, from biographical studies. For a time, "The Canonization," for example, was discussed as a poem rather than as a document of Donne's feelings toward the world after his marriage. The *Holy Sonnets* were artifacts rather than personal testimonies of religious doubt or faith. This change in focus was especially important for Donne, since his life is more apt than the lives of most poets to provoke the critic's dismay. Even though biographical interpretations of the poems continued, another option for study became available, and it was possible to react to the work of art rather than to the man who wrote it.

However, the New Criticism had more than a prohibitory effect. With their emphasis on reading a poem apart from its historical, philosophical, and biographical context, the New Critics and those who adopted their methods demonstrated the art and skill of Donne's poems. Most obviously, what had once been thought of as extravagant, tortured figures became the objects of close study. Robert Sharp, for example, was anxious to show that Donne's obscurity arose directly from his subtlety of mind and his desire for psychological realism (1934, 503). Although this sounds in many ways like the pre–1920 writers on Donne, Sharp's emphasis is clearly laudatory and analytical: "Donne's obscurity, rising from his thought and his images, is the result of a poetic ambition which sought expression not for the inexpressible but for the untraditional." To do this he used the conceit, which was for him "both intellectual and emotive" (503). Allen Tate, by examining conceits, provided a subtler, deeper meaning for "A Valediction: forbidding mourning" than had previously been attempted when the poem was admired primarily for its sincerity and its relation to Donne's life ([1953] 1953, 171–76). In addition, attempts were made to remove what some saw as pejoratively connotative terms from the study of Donne's metaphors so that the figures could be studied more objectively. John Douds rejected Johnson's "*discordia concors*" as a description of Donne's conceits because "discordant imagery is only one part of a general method which involves many other elements in his poetic style, and which is responsible to a considerable degree for his most striking and individual effects." Thus he chooses the term "dissonance" to describe Donne's poetry because it has fewer negative connotations than "discord" and will not prejudice the reader against the poetry (1937, 1051). George Reuben Potter, tracing the connotative meanings of the term "conceit," concludes that the term has been used too loosely by most critics, especially when it is applied to Donne's poetry, and that it has often been given negative meanings by those who wish to make poetry like Donne's seem "pathological" (1941, 282–91). Similarly, Donne's images were studied with a greater depth and carefulness than previously,[28] and if scholars were overly enthusiastic and generous about Donne's sometimes-too-ingenious images, they were merely balancing the negative comments before 1920. Furthermore, they were at least taking the images seriously.

The structure and function of Donne's poems, the way they "work," came under the close scrutiny of such critics as Brooks, James Smith, Unger, and Williamson, who recognized in the poems a seriousness and artistic integrity not previously accorded them. In short, although the idolization of Donne to the disparagement of others and the idealization of him as a "modern" poet produced a number of harmful consequences, the New Critics also provided the needed impetus to raise Donne from an idiosyncratic pagan turned priest to a poet worthy to be studied.

# 4

# Donne and Literary Tradition

In 1913, Felix Schelling said that Donne "rejects most of the poetical furniture . . . in the houses of the poets" (68). Yet twenty-one years later Merritt Hughes called him more "appreciative of tradition" than Milton ([1934] 1975, 52). As I have suggested, reactions against New Criticism even while it was at its height did much to change early twentieth-century perceptions of Donne as a rebellious innovator and to place him within literary traditions. These reactions caused their own peculiarities in Donne scholarship, but attempts to determine his traditional lineage are noteworthy for another reason too: his poetry and prose can fit, or can be made to fit, into a large number of varied, often contradictory traditions. I do not mean that scholars attempt to insert the *Songs and Sonets,* for example, into the tradition of the *Sermons.* Rather, they usually attempt to define the tradition of one group of works or even of one poem or piece of prose. Even so, different scholars can see one poem as having several different analogues or one group of poems as developing from several different traditions. Furthermore, when those studying Donne's work in the context of a tradition find a lyric, an elegy, an epithalamion that does not fit, they sometimes follow one of two dangerous routes. They may either wrench the meaning to make the poem fit the tradition or pronounce the anomalous poem to be flawed. Finally, some scholars, concentrating on Donne's modification of a tradition, return to Donne the revolutionary. To explore some of the advantages and problems of placing Donne within a literary tradition, I will look at attempts to place him in each of nine such traditions: the Petrarchan, anti-Petrarchan, Spenserian, Neoplatonic, meditative, baroque, mannerist, plain style, and classical traditions. However, I will first examine a few early representative treatments of him as a revolutionary poet, since reactions against these form the basis for the later treatments of him.

Scholars before 1921 had no doubts about Donne's place in English literary tradition. With few exceptions,[1] they believed he had rebelled against his contemporaries' Petrarchan conventions to write a new kind of poetry. Although Donne was often discussed with late Elizabethans like Drayton and Daniel, he was "hyperbolically Elizabethan" (Eaton 1914, 53). He carried Petrarchan conceits to new heights of extravagance. Depending on the writer's taste for sixteenth- and seventeenth-century lyrics, this rebellion was seen as either a positive or a negative influence on English poetry. Felix Schelling, for example, praised Donne for overturning Petrarchan conventions because "his total break with the past, his mannerisms, ingenious similitudes, even, to some extent his cynicism . . . were genuine and innate qualities of his genius" (1913, 69). For George Saintsbury, Donne was "born to combine all the elements of the Renaissance spirit" and to add to these his own "peculiar mystical charm" (1908, 366). He praises Donne so much that he feels he must apologize: "If this language seem more highflown than is generally used in this book or than is appropriate to it, the excuse must be that every reader of Donne is either an adept or an outsider born, and that it is impossible for the former to speak in words understanded of the latter" (368).

Richard Garnett and Edmund Gosse present the opposite extreme. In their view, Donne "conceived nothing less daring than a complete revolution of style, and the dethronement of the whole dynasty of modern verse" ([1903] 1904, 2:291–92). Unfortunately, he was not great enough for this revolution and, as a consequence, injured English verse more than did any other poet (2:292).

Between these two extremes are scholars, like Grierson (1909, 4:197–98), Carpenter (1909, lvii–lviii), and Reed (1912, 235–37), who saw Donne as, in Grierson's words, "the poet who challenged and broke the supremacy of the Petrarchan tradition," beginning "a new era in the history of the English love lyric." His influence, however, was both good and ill—a middle position held by the majority of pre-1921 scholars. Donne had rebelled against poetic convention; his turning away from or modifying of Elizabethan conventions was a worthwhile endeavor, but too frequently the extravagant wit accompanying this break with tradition corrupted his and his followers' poetry.

Although the New Criticism hindered biographical readings of Donne, it did not reverse the trend of seeing him as a poetic revolutionary but instead encouraged it. Oddly enough, Eliot's comments on Donne, enthusiastically received during the twenties and thirties, should have changed the view of Donne as a revolutionary. In his famous 1921 essay, Eliot remarked that "the poets of the seventeenth century (up to the [English] Revolution) were the direct and normal development of the precedent age" (669). Thus Donne and his followers did not change the course of English literary history but rather culminated the achievements of their predecessors. Unfortunately, however, Eliot wrote little about the Elizabethan lyricists who preceded Donne, concentrating, instead, on the dramatists and on Donne's contemporaries, Chapman and Jonson. Donne's achievement was using the language, style, and conceits of the sixteenth-century dramatists in lyric poetry. In doing so, he was, according to Eliot, involved in "the direct and normal development of the precedent age," but in lyric poetry he was also beginning a new trend (670). Nine years later, Eliot explained this theory more explicitly: although they were "the successors of the dramatists of the sixteenth" century (1921, 669), seventeenth-century poets differ from sixteenth-century lyricists in that the latter "*sing* in verse," whereas the former "*think* in verse" (1930, 441). Eliot never stated his preference, but since his definition of metaphysical verse rests on the poet's ability to translate feeling into thought, his preference is, nonetheless, clear. Even though Eliot continued to insist that Donne's poetry derived from the sixteenth-century dramatists, the fact that Donne was not a dramatist but a lyric poet encouraged Eliot's followers to see Donne as the revolutionary who "sounded the death-knell of the son-neteering vogue" and did away with Spenser's smoothness and ease (Bald [1932] 1965, 11–12).

George Williamson's studies from the twenties and early thirties pressed this comparison most forcefully. In 1927, he wrote: "Eliot stands to his age as Donne to his, in opposition to the merely pretty and conventional, to the facile and copious, and to the shallow and affectedly simple. He abhors the commonplace and delights in the subtle" (294).[2] However, even non-scholarly writers noted the supposed similarity in positions. The pseudonymous Affable Hawk, for example, praised Donne as an inno-vative rebel against Petrarchan traditions; he is to the seventeenth century as the poets of the 1920s are to their generation (1923, 660).

Thus, when New Criticism was at its height, Donne's position in English literary tradition remained much the same as it had been in the first two decades of the century—with one difference. Between 1921 and 1934,[3] his presumed originality and rebelliousness were, almost without exception, viewed positively. Grierson in 1929 called Donne "the great rebel against the tradition of Petrarchan idealism" (143). Williamson in 1928 said there is "little doubt of the revolt and experiment in Donne" (429). For Ralph Crum in 1931, Donne rebelled against "the classical ideals of poetry, especially the pseudo-classic concept of slavish imitation" ([1931] 1966, 44). And Mario Praz, while noting that Donne was "himself a Petrarchist, thanks to his mediaevally trained mind," added that he must have "actu-ally felt in opposition to the poetry of his day, and if he still remained a Petrarchist to some extent, this is due to the fact that, no matter how strong is one's personal reaction, one cannot avoid belonging to a definite historical climate" (1931, 66). Even Gosse modified his negative judgment (in 1904) of Donne's originality. In 1923, he claimed Donne should be praised because the sonnets of the other Elizabethans were mere imita-tions or translations (311). As in the previous two decades, some tried to put Donne into a literary tradition,[4] but for the most part, his position as a revolutionary seemed assured.

In 1934, Merritt Hughes wrote: "Like Milton in the *Areopagitica,* Donne thought of truth as a power in the realms of both knowledge and behavior, of which men had been in possession in the past and to which they must win their way back. . . . Of the two men Donne was immeasurably the more conservative, the more appreciative of tradition" (52). His "Kidnapping Donne" was the first scholarly, measured objection to what the New Critics had done to the poet. For Hughes, Donne was neither the revolutionary holding the "master key to literary history" (41) nor the modern skeptic New Critics adored but rather a man of his time. His essay thus marks a turning point in scholarship on the poet, no less important than Eliot's essay "The Metaphysical Poets," because, from the mid-thirties on, there was a concerted effort to place Donne's poetry into classical, Medieval, and Renaissance literary traditions.

The picture of Donne as an outlaw, intent on overturning all the poetic conventions of his time, standing in gigantic but solitary splendor among mere imitators and sweet-singing sonneteers,[5] is indeed an odd—and inaccurate—one. Donne did live in a historical period, even if he may not always have been in complete sympathy with that time, and had received the same kind of education as Sidney or Daniel or Marlowe.[6] He read the works of his contemporaries and predecessors; he attended plays; he conversed with fellow scholars and men of letters. Thus the attempts to find Donne's sources or to study the *Songs and Sonets,* the *Anniversaries,* or the *Elegies* in the context of other Renaissance works of a similar nature give us not only a better picture of the historical man but also a clearer understanding of his poetry.

The most important and widespread reservation to Donne the revolutionary began in the forties and fifties and gained ground in the sixties and seventies. It sought to explore his lyrics' possibly Petrarchan origins.[7] In two cases, both in the fifties, this approach depended mainly on reactions against New Criticism's touting of Donne's originality and complexity (Louthan 1951, 128–38; Clay Hunt 1954, 8–11). This kind of treatment, however, was more infrequent than those seeking simply to examine Donne's relationship to Petrarchan conventions.

The two who have written most convincingly on Donne's Petrarchism are Donald Guss and Silvia Ruffo-Fiore. Both scholars emphasize the difficulties modern readers have encountered in trying to place Donne in a tradition. For Guss, the problem is that, "in becoming contemporary, Donne's poetry has become puzzling" because individual poems can be interpreted in contradictory ways and because Donne's sources can be traced "to the most diverse aspects of Western culture, and the least reconcilable elements of the human mind" (1966, 11). In his view, the solution to this problem is Donne's Petrarchism—not the "humanistic Petrarchism" informing the English lyric before Donne, but that "characterized by fantastic arguments, emotional extravagance, and peregrine comparisons." That is, Donne used the Petrarchan style popularized by Serafino, Tasso, and Guarini (18). Through extensive comparisons of witty-Petrarchist poetry and Donne's, Guss shows Donne to have worked in this Italian mode, using the same kinds of extravagant conceits.

Scholarly and convincing, Guss's work still reveals some interesting problems in Donne criticism, which even so illuminating a work cannot solve.

First, even if one considers only Donne's *Songs and Sonets,* the poems are not of a piece. Guss can find Italian analogues for most, but not all, of Donne's lyrics. Thus, he must make exceptions for six—"Womans constancy," "The Indifferent," "Goe, and catche a falling starre," "Confined Love," "Communitie," and "The Flea." These are, instead, "(un-Petrarchan), epigrammatic poem[s]" (113).[8]

Guss's characterization of these poems raises the second problem: those poems not fitting the pattern are too often dismissed as inferior. The six poems Guss names do not fit the "extravagant Petrarchan mode" (18) and so lack "the veneer of a rich civilization" imparted to Donne's other lyrics through Petrarchism (113). In these poems, Donne's stance as a lover who knows women to be unfaithful and who enjoys promiscuity himself offers him only "limited possibilities" (113). "The Indifferent" is "stilted, paradoxical, and consciously knowing" (113); " 'The Flea' . . . invites the reader to apply his own standards of propriety, and probably find its cleverness either vulgar or, at best, academic" (60). All these poems, even "Womans constancy," which Guss admires for its "delightful display of logical agility" (114), reveal a "pose that shows no complex consciousness behind it" (115). Although these six poems are not necessarily among Donne's best, I would venture to say it is possible to find "The Flea" to be something other than vulgar or academic if one does not approach it from a Petrarchan perspective. Donne's relationship to Petrarchism in certain poems can thus become a criterion for taste.

A third interesting feature of Guss's argument is that despite his evidence of Donne's indebtedness, he still draws a picture of a revolutionary poet. Having insisted that Donne is not poetically related to Spenser by his use either of Ramist logic or of "universal analogy," Guss asserts that "Donne's stylistic departure from the Spenserians results largely from his being the first great English lyricist to write in the extravagant Petrarchan mode" (18). That is, although Donne is related to the Italian Petrarchists, his poetry was a definite departure from that of his English contemporaries.

Fourth, proponents of Donne's Petrarchism disagree among themselves about the specific origins of his poetry. Ruffo-Fiore contends that "Donne's relationship to Petrarch is more complex than either Petrarchist imitator or revolutionary innovator will allow" (1976, 22). Differing with Guss, she wants to show Donne's direct relationship to Petrarch rather than to Petrarch's imitators (122, n. 2) and observes that in changing Petrarchan conceits, in making these conceits the starting point for probing his own love (84), Donne gives "a fresh interpretation of conventions by juxtaposing the excellencies of the ideal to the disenchantments of the real" (11). Because of these changes, he makes "an original contribution to the mode and, thus, can be rightly called as much an innovator as Petrarch was in his day" (22).

In addition, when critics or scholars are too set in exploring Donne's Petrarchism, they sometimes misread some of the *Songs and Sonets*. The most blatant examples of this occur in N. J. C. Andreasen's *John Donne: Conservative Revolutionary* (1967). Classifying "The Extasie" and "The Canonization" as Petrarchan poems, she concentrates on their "satiric comedy which makes fun of lovers who deceive themselves into believing that their profane love is not profane" (168). In "The Canonization," Donne mocks a lover who takes Petrarchan imagery too literally. In proving "that his love does not injure anyone else, he shows it to be violent and grief-ridden and therefore injurious to himself" (164). The poem embodies the "set Petrarchan themes, the answer of a lover to the criticism of a friend," but the first line of the poem is a violent overreaction that sets the tone for the following stanzas (163). Furthermore, this lover is so vain that he has "counted the precise number of his gray hairs" (163). Therefore, she concludes, "Donne is dramatizing the stock comic situation of an extramarital love affair between an aging man of the world and a youthful mistress, an affair which further injures the debilitated rake's already-ruined fortune" (164). However, by concentrating on the speaker as "a typical profane Petrarchan lover," interested only in lust (164–65), she ignores the speaker's tone of self-mockery. Anyone who would admit in such outrageous tones to having counted his gray hairs surely has some talent for self-ridicule. Andreasen's reading may be as tenable as those, like Bald's, connecting it with Donne's marriage (1970, 146–47) or at least with other "mutual love" lyrics (Gardner 1965, xxx; 1982b, 184). However, I suspect, approaching it from a Petrarchan perspective has caused her to overlook the possibility either that Donne believed emotional and physical love could work "together" to create a "pattern" for love or that he realized lovers can sometimes foolishly overreact to their situation without being—as Andreasen terms them—profane.[9]

Andreasen's thesis also leads her to underemphasize what she implies is a positive ending for another Petrarchan poem, "The Blossome": "The woman in London . . . will return whole love for whole love" (185)—a seemingly desirable outcome; still the lover "speaks with undertones of Ovidian libertinism. He . . . substitutes lust for silent worship, harsh

naturalism for hazy romanticism" (185–86). In the same way, her treatment of "A Nocturnall" as the "reaction of a lover who has loved a mortal
woman inordinately, so inordinately that he is overwhelmed with grief and
despair when her death reveals to him that she was only mortal" (152),
neglects any sympathy the reader feels for the speaker. Donne is mocking
this profane Petrarchan lover who has not transformed his love, as Petrarch does, into *caritas* (152) and who, consequently, is damned (158).
Her emphasis on the idolatrous Petrarchan lover prevents her from noticing what Helen Gardner calls Donne's "sense of dedication for another
life" in this poem (1982b, 197). In a way, Andreasen falls into the biographical fallacy in reverse: she begins with the fact of Petrarchism in England
in the sixteenth and early seventeenth centuries and reads Donne's poems
only in that context, with little regard for the changes a poet might work on
those themes.

Both Guss (1966, 15–16) and Ruffo-Fiore (1976, 26–27, 31ff.) deny that
Donne's poems mock Petrarchan conventions. Others, however, while
placing Donne in the Petrarchan tradition, argue that one stance in the
*Songs and Sonets* is that of a parodist of Petrarchan language and conceits.[10] Others use an assumption of Donne's un-Petrarchan sentiments—
his seeming approval of women's inconstancy, his refusal to idolize
women, his frankly sexual language—or poetic form to place him in other
traditions. Still others continue to insist on Donne's rebelliousness, often
by denying his relationship to Petrarchism (Webber 1963, 4; Peterson
1967, 285–88).

When writers before the 1930s labeled Donne an anti-Petrarchan, they
often used the term loosely to designate one who had broken away from
what they saw as the slavish imitations of Elizabethan sonneteers. Thus
"anti-Petrarchan" and "poetic revolutionary" became synonymous terms.
Although "anti-Petrarchan" came to be more precisely defined in the
decades after 1930, it was still often used simply to reinforce the scholar's
belief in Donne's rebelliousness. For example, in 1935, F. R. Leavis declared that after reading Greville, Chapman, and Drayton, "respectable
figures who, if one works through their allotments, serve at any rate to set
up a critically useful background," we come upon Donne and we stop
reading "as students . . . and read on as we read the living" because
Donne's originality makes him seem contemporaneous with us moderns
([1935] 1936, 10–11). In 1964, J. B. Broadbent, using Shakespeare's sonnet
"My mistress' eyes are nothing like the sun" as an example of anti-
Petrarchism, conceded that Donne's poems, "often Petrarchan in form,"
are "anti-Petrarchan in sentiment" (233). By acknowledging that anti-
Petrarchan poems were not new in Donne's time (233), he places the poet
historically: that is, Donne's poetry was not, as some scholars before 1930
supposed, a complete break with tradition. Nevertheless, Broadbent still

implies Donne's poetic rebelliousness: unlike Shakespeare's, "Donne's antagonism [toward Petrarchism] isn't just literary; it is psychological" (233). Similarly, in 1970, four years after Guss's *John Donne, Petrarchist,* Patrick Cruttwell, allowing a few of Donne's poems to be in the Platonic-Petrarchan tradition (25–26), called his poetry "a real revolution, a genuine shock to established habits, when it first appeared in the fifteen nineties" (29). In 1972, John Bernard denied the "myth" of Donne the Petrarchist and argued that in Donne's poetry "the very ground underlying Petrarchan poetry is cut away" (388). Brian Vickers in the same year contended that "Donne broke through this barrier of unattainable desire" of the Elizabethan sonneteers (1972, 135). Three years later Anne Ferry showed the difference between Petrarchan lovers and the lovers of "A Valediction: forbidding mourning" (1975, 98–101)—a poem Guss believed validated "the sentimental conceits of madrigalesque Petrarchism" (1966, 75). Thus, even though "anti-Petrarchism" was itself a literary convention, it often enforces, when applied to Donne in a loose sense, his rebellion against Elizabethan poetry rather than his place in poetic tradition.

The difficulties with making Donne either a Petrarchist or an anti-Petrarchist should be obvious. Some poems fit both modes (as do some of Shakespeare's). But with Donne, an early critical insistence on his rebelliousness has occasionally led to a later, often willful, insistence on his Petrarchism. Certain poems, then, are judged inadequate because they are not of the same Petrarchan stamp as others, while certain other poems are misread to make them Petrarchan.

Like the question of his Petrarchism, the notion of Donne as a follower of Spenser has caused irreconcilable readings of certain poems. Although it would be difficult to label all Donne's poetry "Spenserian," disputes about individual poems sometimes arise. The minor controversy surrounding the "Epithalamion made at Lincolnes Inne" is a representative example. In 1955, Bernard Groom noted Donne's anomalous position in English poetic tradition: although Donne appeals to the "present century . . . the general consensus of opinion for centuries was that his methods were opposed to the true genius of the language" (64). In this Lincoln's Inn wedding poems, however, "Donne is actually a Spenserian" (65). One year later, David Novarr, pointing to the incongruous elements in this epithalamion and especially to the refrain, "To day put on perfection, and a womans name" (Donne 1967a, 171–73),[11] argued that Donne wrote the poem not for a real but for a mock wedding between two of his fellow students at Lincoln's Inn ([1956] 1980, 73). Thus the poem parodies Spenser's "Epithalamion" (78–79).

Heather Dubrow Ousby, twenty years later, assayed a rebuttal by showing some elements Novarr termed "parodic" to be the result of Donne's early and "somewhat unsuccessful experiments in metaphysical word-play," his "idiosyncratic interests and fears," his preoccupation with death, and his "insecurity about his own social status" (1976, 133–35). She concluded that Donne was trying to imitate Spenser's sensuous language in this early poem but lacked the necessary skill and grace (138–39).

Both Ousby and Novarr are thorough and scholarly in their assessments, but both argue from different perceptions of Donne. For Novarr, Donne even in his youth was a poetic innovator; for Ousby, he was indebted to other poets. His innovativeness, she asserts, grew out of his imitation and subsequent rejection of them (143). As do so many of Donne's poems, this epithalamion answers both interpretations, preventing a conclusive assessment of Donne's traditionally accepted rebelliousness.

Whether Donne was directly inspired by Petrarch, Petrarch's followers, or Spenser or instead parodied them, he was certainly cognizant of the Neoplatonic theories informing the poetry of his predecessors and contemporaries. As early as 1903, J. S. Harrison suggested that certain of Donne's poems are Platonic (141–54).[12] The 1930s and the following decades, however, generated the most assiduous studies of this relationship. Scholars have found Neoplatonic elements in, among others, "The Anagram," "Lecture upon the Shadow," and the *Anniversaries* (Ure 1948, 269; Goldberg 1956; Benson 1971, 340–56). Others have noted a general strain of Neoplatonic thought in the best of the *Songs and Sonets* (Gardner 1965, lvii–lix; Martz 1969, 38; Doebler 1972, 504–12; Sharrock 1972, 46–52), although others have denied that his poetry embodies Neoplatonism at all.[13]

The two poems to cause the most dispute in this area are "Aire and Angels" and "The Extasie." The former is the easier with which to begin, since the body of criticism is not quite as large as that for "The Extasie." Two, sometimes-overlapping, difficulties arise in applying Neoplatonic doctrine to "Aire and Angels."

First, Neoplatonism as modified by the Renaissance allowed for physical, sexual love on the lowest rung of the Neoplatonic ladder of love. To some, though, the poem not only argues for physical consummation but also is almost pornographic. John Dean, for example, finds Donne's language in the poem heavily fraught with double entendres and concludes that Helen Gardner's difficulty with the poem (as noted in Chapter 3) arises because the two strains of Neoplatonic spirituality and sexuality are never resolved; therefore "the poem ends half finished and half complete" (1972, 88). Katharine Mauch more overtly confronts the issue of Neoplatonism and sexuality. By exploring Donne's pun on "angel" and on "pinnace" ("prostitute" but also vocally suggestive of "penis") and by using Neoplatonic doctrine, she argues that the speaker of the poem descends from the highest level on Bembo's Neoplatonic ladder of love in the first six lines to the lowest in the next fifteen (lines 7–22), skipping the middle level. At the end of the poem, he returns to the highest level while recognizing that, of necessity, his beloved must remain on the middle level. The last three lines, thus, are not derogatory but bittersweet (1977, 108–11).

As even brief summaries of these two arguments show, the most perplexing part of the poem is the final three lines:

> Just such disparitie
> As is twixt Aire and Angells puritie,
> 'Twixt womens love, and mens will ever bee.

These concluding lines have troubled more readers than Helen Gardner by their seeming underrating of women's love (1959b, 62–75). Far from being demeaning, however, these lines, according to Martz, wittily express the old Petrarchan compliment—her love is inferior only because she is loving an inferior being (1969, 38).

A. J. Smith in 1957 also concentrated on the wit of the poem yet showed how it relies on the stock Neoplatonic situations common to Donne's time (1957b, 186–89). Wesley Milgate most explicitly delineated the poem's problems for readers. Beginning the poem with a Neoplatonic "shorthand" (1972, 155–56), Donne then proceeds, "with characteristic perceptiveness and imaginative daring . . . to show that the exalted conception of spiritual love on the exposition of which the Neo-Platonists labored with such ingenious care is only a stage in the development of true love" (157). At the end of the poem, Donne minimizes the difference his contemporaries saw between men's and women's love (168). "The main point of the poem, in fact, is a refined statement of what is still a popular truism—that love can exist only as it is returned" (170). The problem at the end of the poem arises because Donne has tried to do too much; too many ideas are pushed into too few lines. Milgate is correct: the poem can be perplexing. It seems akin to the "mutual love" lyrics and yet, to some, the last three lines violate the spirit of the preceding ones. Relating the thought in "Aire and Angels" to Neoplatonism may illuminate much of the poem, but it fails to solve what many regard as a puzzling conclusion.

Arthur Marotti has most recently attempted to unify the troublesome concluding lines with the rest of the poem. In "Aire and Angels" and several other poems that Donne, according to Marotti, wrote to Lady Bedford, Donne assumes the stance of an encomiastic poet-suitor, employing the arguments and terms of Neoplatonism. At the end of the poem, however, Donne wittily shifts from his original role: "As the lines return to the Platonic valuation of male love as superior to female love (and homosexual affection to heterosexual intercourse), they engage in some witty antifeminist teasing, demand the reciprocity that enables love to exist, and daringly, but entertainingly, threaten the decorum of the complimentary situation" (1986, 220). Although this is not Marotti's expressed intent, his analysis of Donne's actions brings together the rebel Donne and the Neoplatonist and may indeed be the path of moderation in dealing with Donne's roots in tradition.

In "The Extasie," the problem of Donne's relationship to Neoplatonism is even more pronounced. In 1928, Pierre Legouis, rather cavalierly, proclaimed it a seduction poem (66–68). Rebuttals produced a flood of Neoplatonic interpretations of the poem. Predictably enough, however, these readings are themselves at variance. Merritt Hughes in 1932 was the first prominent scholar to take issue with Legouis's reading of the poem, and it is significant that he disagreed in terms of Neoplatonism. Rather than the "original dramatic impulse" Legouis saw in the poem, Hughes found "merely the dramatisation of a conflict and reconciliation of ideas which had long been familiar in Italy and France, if not in England" (2). Contending that Donne followed French and Italian Neoplatonists in admitting the body into Platonic love (2–4), Hughes, nevertheless, denies that "*The Extasie* is a profession of faith or in any sense an expression of sympathy with neo-Platonism on Donne's part" (5).

Others, however, have aligned "The Extasie" with a number of varying strains of Neoplatonism. Frank Doggett (1934, 290) and George Williamson (1960, 76) wanted Bembo's speech in the *Courtier* to be the starting point for understanding "The Extasie," even though Donne accorded physical passion a higher place than did Bembo. René Graziani believes Donne's representation of the body and soul combining in love has a precedent in one of the continuations of the *Amadis de Gaula* (1968, 123), whereas Elizabeth McLaughlin, stressing the poem's affinities with Plotinus, can also demonstrate that the two lovers exhibit schizophrenic traits (1970, 59–63). Underplaying the poem's Neoplatonism even more than McLaughlin, Raman Selden argues that "despite his frequent flirtations with Platonism in the *Songs and Sonets* Donne rarely adopts an unqualified Platonic Stance. His affinities are with the Aristotelian 'Word-Man' type of Christianity which refuses to recognize a substantive dualism in the two-natured Christ" (1975, 60). He analyzes "The Extasie" to show that "the poem's thesis and antithesis are finally synthesized in the metaphor of incarnation. The incarnational conviction cannot accept a simplistic body-soul opposition. 'The Extasie' cannot be labelled unequivocally 'Neoplatonic' or 'Christian' without being grossly oversimplified" (64). As these sentences show, Selden is never himself in danger of oversimplifying the poem; in fact, in denying its affinities with Neoplatonism, he complicates an already-difficult poem even further. For Andreasen, "The Extasie" is a story of self-deluding lovers, who use

Neoplatonism for their own ends (1967, 174–75); for John Huntington, it is a "philosophical seduction" (1977, 40–59); and, for David Novarr, its overtones of the Song of Solomon produce more argument and philosophy than feeling (1980, 38–39). Although Arthur Marotti has his own theories about the poem (it was written as an "artistic publicizing of Donne's own marriage" rather than as an argument for "Neoplatonic soul-union" [1974, 158]), his analysis of its modern critical history is an apt one: "What is usually at stake . . . is the individual critic's conception of Donne and his art; so the debate has been a heated one" (142–43).

Helen Gardner's "The Argument about 'The Extasy' " illustrates what can happen when scholars approach a Donne poem with their own ideas of what that poem means and what traditions—in this case Neo-platonism—helped shape it. Denying sexual union in the poem, Gardner argues that "the only 'proposal' which is made in these lines [49–76] is the perfectly modest one that the lovers' souls, having enjoyed the rare priv-ilege of union outside the body, should now resume possession of their separate bodies and reanimate these virtual corpses" (1959a, 283). Thor-oughly and lucidly, she demonstrates the very close similarities between Donne's poem and Leone Ebreo's *Dialoghi d'Amore* (287–95). However, her insistence that the poem does not include a justification of physical love[14] leads her, when she reaches Ebreo's encouragement of physical union, to argue that here Donne departed from this specific passage and instead concentrated on Ebreo's description of the "semi-death of ecstasy . . . the force of ecstasy might be so strong that it would break the bond between soul and body and lead to the death of rapture. This death in ecstasy his [Donne's] lovers withdraw from, to return to life in the body" (295). It may be that she is correct. But since she has on occasion scorned sexual interpretations of Donne's poems,[15] it may also be that with "The Extasie" she has neglected the obvious and discovered another "source." Similarly, the solution to Donne's "Extasie" may lie in Neoplatonic doc-trine, but insisting on one source to the exclusion of others or demanding that the poem be only Christian, only Neoplatonic, or only seductive denies the richness of a poem that may be all these and more.

Not at variance with, but still different from, attempts to place Donne in the Neoplatonic tradition are those placing him in the meditative tradition of Ignatius Loyola. In the late forties and early fifties, Louis Martz (1947, 247–73) and Helen Gardner (1952, l–lv) both discovered the relationship between Loyola's *Spiritual Exercises* and the structure of Donne's *Anni-versaries* and *Holy Sonnets,* respectively. Although discussions of both play a major part in determining Donne's traditional background, I will limit my discussion to the meditative structure of the *Anniversaries,* both because this has provoked slightly more interesting critical commentary than has the meditative structure of the *Holy Sonnets*[16] and because affirming or denying the meditative structure follows essentially the same lines for both.

Martz was the first critic to examine the unique structure of the *Anniversaries* and to object to Donne's praise of Elizabeth Drury not because of its excessiveness—Petrarch and Dante described Laura and Beatrice in the same hyperbolic and even religious terms—but because Elizabeth was irrelevant to Donne's true subject, a religious meditation on the world's decay in the manner of Loyola (1954, 28–29). After examining in detail the form of various religious devotions, Martz concludes that the *First Anniversarie* is divided, in accord with the meditative tradition, into five sections plus an introduction and a conclusion. Each of these sections is further subdivided into three parts—a meditation on some aspect of the frailty of the world, a eulogy of Elizabeth Drury, and a refrain to introduce a moral (1947, 248). The *First Anniversarie* fails, however, because it tries to be both a meditation and a eulogy. Its first meditation (lines 91–170) strictly follows the tradition, but Donne "clumsily and evasively" comes back to Elizabeth's connection with the world's death; soon the "difficulty of including this hyperbole . . . becomes embarrassingly obvious" (1947, 256–57). The *Second Anniversarie* drops the mechanical inclusion of Elizabeth and thus is far more successful structurally (1947, 264).

Martz is certainly correct in insisting that Donne had firsthand knowledge of Ignatian meditation and meditative poetry. However, his remarks about the *First Anniversarie* point once again to the difficulty of explaining Donne's poetry in terms of a tradition. There is always an exception, and for Martz this exception illustrates Donne's flawed artistry.

More troublesome than what Martz argued is what he failed to recognize. First, the *Anatomy,* perhaps because it is less than perfect, has excited more critical discussion than the *Progress.* Martz did not, of course, simply dismiss the entire *First Anniversarie,* but, rather than try to explain the tension created by the opposition of Elizabeth and the decay of the world, he assumed the latter was Donne's main subject of interest and the former merely a necessary but irrelevant occasion—a problem arising from Donne's attempt to combine eulogy and meditation. But Donne, in 1611, was too accomplished a poet to use Elizabeth as mere decoration. He had already written, according to Shawcross, the majority of the *Songs and Sonets,* a substantial number of the *Holy Sonnets,* and all the *Elegies* and *Satyres* (Donne 1967a, 411–16). Why not have written a traditional eulogy for Elizabeth Drury (he had already done that on more than one occasion) and then a perfect devotional meditation without the obligation of including Elizabeth? Second, Martz underplayed the poems as companion pieces. Several critics have noted that the falling action of the *First Anniversarie* is countered by the rising action of the *Second* and that the *Second* answers the doubts raised in the *First.*[17] Donne apparently structured the poems to work together on other levels besides that of meditation, a possibility Martz neglected.

Nevertheless, Martz's argument is clearly developed and supported, and he has been referred to and acclaimed by virtually every other scholar discussing the structure of the *Anniversaries*. Even those who disagree with him can do so only by proposing their own system of divisions. O. B. Hardison claims, contrary to Martz's theory, that the *First Anniversarie* consists of three parts representing the physical, aesthetic, and spiritual aspects of the world (1962, 171–72). Furthermore, in structuring the *Anatomy* as he did, Donne created a more emotionally logical eulogy than does a traditional eulogy. By reversing the lament and eulogy sections of the typical eulogy-lament-consolation pattern, he indicates that, after a death, one grieves before praising the dead (178–79).

George Williamson objected to Martz's whole theory because the definition of meditative verse is too vague and could be applied to "any poem that works from a situation to a solution" (1963, 183). Although Martz's argument is more complex and specific than Williamson suggests, he is in later parts of his discussion raising a well-founded objection to Martz: Elizabeth is related in Donne's poems to man (the microcosm), to the world (the macrocosm), and to the past (the Golden Age) (188), a relationship Martz did not acknowledge.

Harold Love disagrees strongly with Martz and, like Williamson, he objects to his treatment of Elizabeth: "That Martz is basically wrong about the poem I take to be self-evident" (1966, 126) because he has failed to recognize "the full complexity of the role played in the poem by the figure of Elizabeth Drury" (127). Patrick Mahoney also rejects Martz's thesis of the flawed structure of the *Anatomy*. He sees the *Anniversaries* as two structurally related, complementary companion poems. The *First* relates man's fall; the *Second* takes a positive spiritual direction (235). He also notes that sections within each poem correspond structurally to other sections in that poem and to sections in the other; for example, the introduction to the *Progress* corresponds to and reverses the thesis of the *Anatomy* (236). This is, of course, another aspect of the poems Martz overlooked in his enthusiasm for meditation.

Like other poems of Donne, the *Anniversaries* do not fit neatly into a tradition. Although some of the proposed traditions are, or can be seen as, overlapping,[18] the *Anniversaries* can also be related to conflicting traditions. This is what happens in Barbara Lewalski's *Donne's "Anniversaries" and the Poetry of Praise*. While not denying the usefulness of Martz's study, Lewalski calls attention to his failure to "resolve the central problem of the *Anniversary* poems" (1973a, 73): finding a fit subject for what seems to many readers Donne's excessive eulogizing. A "more promising approach" is to see these poems as "informed by a conception of meditation strikingly different from the Ignatian method" (74)—that is, the "contemporary English Protestant theory and practice of meditation" (74). Lewalski's study is no less scholarly than Martz's, yet, as might be supposed, the conclusions she reaches are quite different from his, since she takes as Donne's starting point a "strikingly different" tradition. The *Anniversaries* are neither private meditations nor public celebrations; rather they are a conflation—in the Protestant tradition—of sermon and meditation (90–91).

Whichever tradition one proposes, Donne as a meditative poet can still be labeled unique. Lewalski sees the *Devotions* as "innovative" because Donne "fuses the methods of occasional and deliberate meditation" (100). In fact, the *Devotions* "may well be the first significant example of the fusion of these two forms of Protestant meditation, and of both with sermon techniques" (101). W. M. Lebans sees the meditative structure and the classical tradition of funeral elegy working together in the *Anniversaries* but concludes that these poems are also different from traditional elegies (1972, 555). Reinhard Friedrich recognizes the meditative tradition in the *Devotions* but argues that the immediacy of place and the "work's startling sense of presence" differentiate it from any other meditation on death (1978, 18), whereas Richard Hughes in 1968 and John Carey in 1981 rejected altogether the meditative tradition as a basis for the *Anniversaries*. For Hughes, Donne hesitated "to accept all the demands of the Ignatian meditation" because he felt himself incapable at the time they were written of achieving regeneration and transformation (1968, 175). For Carey, the *Anniversaries* exemplify Donne's extreme ambitiousness. Rejecting all other studies of these poems because they seek to find an important enough subject for Donne's extravagance, Carey maintains their true subject is Donne's expanding imagination. Through the poems he finds a new patron and renounces the world that had rejected him (1981, 100–105). Marotti also has doubts about the meditative origins of the *Anniversaries:* "By now the emphasis on the importance of Ignatian meditation for Donne's religious poetry found in Martz's *Poetry of Meditation . . .* has been corrected by a counteremphasis on Augustinian Protestantism" (1986, 345, n. 262).

In sum, Donne's debt to the Ignatian meditative tradition has become a commonplace in literary scholarship; however, to many, his place in this tradition is not as clear as others believe, and for some he is indebted to the Protestant tradition or responsible for molding a unique work from these traditions.

Treatments of Donne as a baroque or a mannerist poet are exceptions to the general thesis of this chapter because these approaches are complicated more by the terms themselves than by a scholar's particular interest or by the nature of Donne's poetry. As many have noted, the transferral of these art-historical terms to literary criticism has caused both terms to be somewhat ambiguous when used to describe Donne's poetry—or Milton's or Crashaw's. Particularly before the sixties, it was the poetry that helped illustrate the usefulness of the terms for literary scholarship rather than the terms that defined the poetry. That is, Martz can relate the *Anniversary* poems to Ignatius Loyola, and even if one disagrees that Donne drew upon the *Spiritual Exercises,* they provide a specific source with which to disagree. The same is true for Neoplatonic readings of Donne. Although the Neoplatonic tradition is more varied than the meditative tradition, scholars of Donne are generally interested in whether the poet followed Ebreo or Bembo rather than in defining Neoplatonism. Labeling Donne's poetry "baroque," however, often illuminates the term more than the poetry. Thus, the problems arising from the uses of "baroque" and "mannerist" reside more with the terms themselves than with critical interpretations of Donne's poems.

Mario Praz noted in his 1964 essay, "Baroque in England," the historical difficulties with the two terms. When Donne was rediscovered in the 1920s, he says, art history had only two designations for this time period at its disposal—Renaissance and baroque (172). Donne, as Eliot read him, seemed to fit conceptions of baroque art (Praz 1964, 173), but, in fact, this baroque aspect is seen almost exclusively in the *Sermons* and religious poems. On the other hand, "the tortuous pattern of his lyrics . . . is akin to the *linea serpentinata* of the Mannerists" (175). Thus, before mid-century, many scholars saw Donne as baroque but believed him to be essentially different from Richard Crashaw, the only generally recognized English baroque poet, or even from Milton in his baroque poems. For example, Joan Webber, whose main subject in *Contrary Music* is Donne's prose, notes the difference between metaphysical poetry (that of Herbert and Vaughan) and baroque (that of Crashaw and Giles Fletcher): "Donne's poetry stands somewhere between the two" (1963, 25–26). Even in Donne's prose, which she pronounces baroque in sentence structure and metaphors (26–28), his uniqueness is evident: "But from all the kinds of images that were available, Donne chose *these,* and he chose to use them always in certain peculiar ways" (89).[19]

In 1953, Elbert B. O. Borgerhoff was the first to classify Donne as a mannerist poet and one of the first to distinguish between mannerism and baroque (323–31). Since then, the cases for Donne as a mannerist or a baroque poet have become increasingly confusing as have the "meanings" of the two terms themselves. Sypher, in 1955, applauded the use of "mannerist" as a label for that "period when the renaissance optimism is shaken, when proportion breaks down and experiment takes the form of morbid ingenuity or scalding wit" (102). Unfortunately, as Sypher's words aptly illustrate, mannerism entered literary criticism burdened with heavily negative connotations.

Since 1955, of course, these connotations have been modified, at times only in part, at others drastically. Murray Roston, for example, writing in 1974, saw mannerism as Donne's way of "responding to the problems and challenges of his day" (20). Furthermore, he continues, "the traditional condemnation of mannerism rests upon an outmoded critical assumption—the idea that art flourishes only in eras confident of their ideals and secure in their political and social institutions" (22). This assumption has led, in the case of Donne, to explaining the weaknesses of his poetry by labeling it "mannerist" (24). After distinguishing between mannerism and the baroque,[20] Roston proceeds to analyze Donne's poetry in terms of mannerist art in order to add to "our critical understanding of his poetry" (66). A. D. Cousins looks at Donne's mannerism in a similarly illuminating way (1979, 86–107), while Robert Jackson sees mannerism as a whole way of life (1970, 50–52). Jackson is perhaps overeager in his willingness to regard Donne's whole life as mannerist (he states in his introductory chapter that "in a sense . . . my own book is a mannerist book, since it expresses a strained communication between myself and John Donne, in which I adopt now a critical stance toward him and now an uncritical one, now see him as though he were far off from me and now as though he were nearly myself" [7]). But his enthusiastic identification with the poet aside, he does show that "mannerism" need not imply "bad" or "tortured."

Even after the application of this new term, however, Donne's baroque characteristics continue to be discussed,[21] proving perhaps that Donne's work at times is both baroque and mannerist. Given the complexities cited, the following statement on the problems with "mannerism" is an apt summary: "In one sense, everything is mannerist or possibly baroque. In another, equally disturbing sense, only good works are mannerist, or only bad ones are. Is mannerism anticlassical, or is it the ultimate refinement of classicism? Silver rather than Golden Age? Is Tasso mannerist or baroque?" (Mirollo 1972, 14). Since Donne's poetry can be linked to numerous other traditions, the disputes about his mannerist and baroque art intensify the questions.

One other important reason Donne's baroque and mannerist qualities are problematic is their relationship to his poetic style.[22] When Robert Jackson discussed Donne's mannerism, he was not writing simply about Donne's style but about his world view, his way of looking at life. The same is often true of discussions of Donne's baroque sensibility; they do not depend so much on the way Donne writes as on the way he sees the world. Naturally, the two are closely related, often inseparable, yet discussions or categorizations of Donne's style are complicated by more than this. Since a writer's style is in part determined by the kinds of images and metaphors he uses as well as by the kinds of subjects he writes about, classifications of Donne's style vary, depending on whether a scholar believes him to be Neoplatonic, Petrarchan, anti-Petrarchan, or mannerist. Obviously then, there must be more agreement on Donne's beliefs before his poetic style can be defined. In addition, the number of styles Donne can be shown to use complicates the matter of tradition, especially since the terms overlap. Stylistically, Donne can be termed a Senecan, Augustinian, metaphysical, baroque, or plain stylist. The last three are particularly relevant to his poetry.

Primarily in the thirties and forties, some scholars were interested in justifying or explaining Donne's metaphysical style, at times by showing his affinities with other "metaphysicians" but more frequently by showing the differences between their style and Donne's. James Smith, for example, writing in 1933, believed Donne's "turbulence and obscurity" make him closer to St. Thomas Aquinas than to Dante and Lucretius, both of whom he terms "disciples of metaphysicians" (225). Both Thomas and Donne have an "air of being puzzled" (226–27). But, Smith adds, in this way and no other are they alike (227). Furthermore, not only is Donne's poetry different from that of Dante, but it also differs from that of Donne's contemporaries—Chapman and Marvell, for example. Marvell wrote metaphysical poems using conceits; that is, his conceits depend on an "association of things on account of a similarity due to an accident as that a canoe for a moment rested upon a head" (235). Donne, on the other hand, wrote poems using metaphysical conceits: these compare "things that, though hostile, in reality cry out for association with each other" (235). Thus what seems a desire to place Donne in a historical tradition is actually an attempt to differentiate Donne from both his predecessors and his contemporaries. Smith's definition of Donne's metaphysical style as unique ignores the scholastic affinities between Thomas and Donne. His differentiation of Marvell's style and Donne's assumes that Marvell merely played with comparisons whereas Donne saw into the deeper nature of things.

Robert L. Sharp, in an article published one year later, also wanted to define Donne's metaphysical style and to show how unique this style was. Depending on obscurity and roughness, Donne's style can be explained not "in terms of literary tradition but of Donne's own type of mind and his attitude toward the poetry of the Petrarchans and Spenserians" (1934, 502). This attitude, according to Sharp, was one of rebellion against the traditional (503). Thus, "metaphysical" as applied to Donne's style, like the term "anti-Petrarchan," is for some a way of placing him historically while still maintaining his individuality.

George Williamson, certainly one of the greatest advocates of Donne's rebelliousness, followed a similar procedure in his 1936 essay "Strong Lines." Contending that the "epithet 'strong-lined' " is more inclusive than "metaphysical" (158), Williamson concentrates on the Jacobeans' kinship with the "Silver Latin poets" (roughly equivalent to the anti-Ciceronians). The seventeenth-century poets "cultivated the obscurity and asperity of style that, with a wit of their own, produced strong lines" (153–54). Although Williamson's essay has been greatly influential in Donne studies and although no one has argued to the contrary that Donne's style is Ciceronian, still Williamson's essay has not precluded other—sometimes related—classifications of Donne's style.

It is in this context that the baroque elements of Donne's style become important. In 1953, Odette de Mourgues noted the confusion often existing between "baroque" and "metaphysical." Some, she contends, believe they describe the same poetry in Europe and England respectively (71). However, for her, the difference is clear:

> In metaphysical poetry we judge a poem by the art with which the poet achieves the reconciliation of clashing opposites. In baroque poetry we should judge a poem by the art with which the poet expresses the experience of a sensibility determined to go, unchecked, to the bitter end of its reactions to the problems of the age. (74)

Thus Donne is mainly metaphysical, although she admits that more study is needed to determine "to what extent Donne wrote baroque poetry, and to what extent purely metaphysical" (102).

For others, however, Donne's style clearly displays baroque features. Lowry Nelson, for example, in *Baroque Lyric Poetry* attempted to bring Donne "into a general scheme of European Baroque style in poetry" (1961, 121). Like other baroque poets, Donne used dramatic devices—the evolution of various attitudes within poems, the developing rhetorical situation between speaker, listener, and audience, and exclamations and questions (121–37). Although some of these dramatic elements appear also in the poetry of Ronsard, Wyatt, and Petrarch, "Donne is one of the first to make use of the rhetorical situation in the lyric in such a way as to present a complex change, an evolution, in the speaker's attitude" (136–37). In doing so, he prepared the way for later baroque poets like Milton, Crashaw, Vaughan, and Marvell (136).

Perhaps because of its association with art, poetry labeled "baroque" would seem only with great difficulty to have any affinities with poetry written in the "plain style." C. Hugh Holman defines "baroque" style in part as "efforts to avoid the effects of repose, tranquility, and complacency . . . [which] sought to startle by the use of the unusual and unexpected. This led sometimes to grotesqueness, obscurity, and contortion" (1980, 4th ed., 45). He defines "plain style" as "free, natural, untrammeled by

contrived cadence. Its fundamental characteristic is an artful simplicity"
(333). C. S. Lewis in 1954, less objectively, characterized "Drab Age"
poetry as that with "little richness either of sound or images" (64). Although Lewis insists he uses the term descriptively rather than pejoratively, his preference for Golden Age verse is clear. Five years earlier,
however, Yvor Winters had not hesitated to admit his preference for the
plain stylists, roughly equivalent to Lewis's Drab Age writers.[23] For Winters, Shakespeare, Jonson, and Donne "combined the essential qualities"
of the school of Sidney, Spenser, and Daniel and also that of Gascoigne,
bringing "the fusion of these qualities to a high level of achievement"
([1939] 1967, 116).

More important for categorizing Donne as a plain stylist is Douglas
Peterson's *The English Lyric from Wyatt to Donne,* which, the author
admits, is heavily indebted to Winters's studies (1967, 4). There are two
interesting aspects of Peterson's treatment of Donne as a plain stylist.
First, he names as indicators of Donne's plain style many of the same
elements Nelson found indicative of his baroque style: "Donne's [style],
as has been often remarked, is often colloquial and conversational in its
idioms." This leads to "an intentional harshness" in rhythm that is far
from the melodious smoothness of Elizabethan lyrics (Peterson, 286). In
his *Holy Sonnets,* Donne, in the tradition of Skelton's "penitential
lyric[s]," relies "upon strategies which most effectively dramatize the
penitent's position. He must see and feel death's imminence" (331). To do
so, he "relies upon the resources of the plain style" (331). The drama of
Donne's verse can thus show him to be either a baroque or plain stylist,
and the issue here is not which classification is right, but simply that
Donne can illustrate both seemingly mutually exclusive categories.

The second interesting feature of Peterson's argument is the main focus
of his chapter on Donne: Donne assumes "the conventions of the plain
style to express opposition to the Court as legislator of social and literary
norms" (285–86). That is, Donne is both anti-Petrarchan and anti-Platonic
(296). So then, accepting Peterson's view of Donne's style means rejecting
not only other classifications of his style but also the most commonly
accepted readings of "Aire and Angels" and "The Extasie" along with a
substantial body of recent scholarship on Donne's overall relationship to
Petrarch and Neoplatonism.

What finally can be said, then, of Donne's poetic style? It is stong-lined,
but that designation rules out neither baroque nor plain style. It is colloquial; its images are often extravagant and far-fetched; its language at once
informal and scientific. In some cases—metaphysical and baroque, for
example—the terms themselves are sufficiently flexible or ill-defined to
permit Donne's inclusion. But more important, his poetry itself is sufficiently textured to allow various classifications. Although these features

do not distinguish Donne from any other major poet, the treatment of him by his critics does. Too many are intent on exploring Donne's relationship to only one tradition to the exclusion of others. Peterson is a good example of this tendency. Because Donne has often been tied to the Petrarchan tradition—a tradition more often associated with the aureate stylists—Peterson must first deny Donne's Petrarchism and also his Neoplatonism before he can classify him as a plain stylist. The three traditions do not necessarily conflict, but for Peterson, as for a number of others, it seems essential to disavow one style or tradition before placing Donne in another. Perhaps because Donne was seen for so many years as a rebellious poet without ties to Renaissance traditions, scholars have felt impelled to place him in one tradition absolutely.

Finally, the poet who once was thought to have eschewed classical allusions and sources has been found actually to have drawn on many differing Greek and Roman authors. Beatrice Johnson in 1928 examined the allusions to Greek mythology in Donne's poetry to show that although he uses these with "characteristic independence and originality," he "had part in the all-but-universal interest of the Elizabethans in classical material" (1098). In 1941, however, D. C. Allen could still insist that "Donne was probably not so great a classical student as some modern scholars would have him be" because he relied on his contemporaries' renditions of classical authors rather than on primary sources (132–33). Three years later, Arnold Stein concluded: "There is no important evidence to indicate that Donne's literary attitude is in any material way directly influenced by classical sources" (1944, 267).

Nevertheless, in the last forty years, Donne has been linked to a wide variety of classical authors ranging from Aesop, Aristotle, Catullus, and Cicero to Pliny, Propertius, Seneca, and Tibullus. In the next few pages, I would like very briefly to point to the number of classical sources from which Donne may have drawn his material. Doing so will both emphasize the number and range of these sources and indicate a few of the problems that can arise from such studies. Although individual poems from the *Songs and Sonets,* verse letters, and epicedes can be traced to Greek and Roman poems and images, Donne's *Satyres* and *Elegies* have attracted the most scholarship on classical sources. However, some disagree on what those sources were. For Hallett Smith, the fourth satire is based on "Horace's encounter with a bore," but the others are not so clearly inspired by a classical model (1952, 225–26). For John Peter, the *Satyres* are not Horatian but rather are related to Martial and Juvenal (1956, 134–36), whereas for Heather Dubrow they are a blend of Horace and Juvenal (1979, 71). Emory Elliott traces the English and classical satiric tradition to show Donne's use of a "narrative and formal structure" in his satires, but Elliott concentrates more on Donne's use of Scripture in these poems

(1976, 106). Milgate sees a "consistent adoption of the technique and tones of Roman satire" (1967, xvii). Nevertheless, whether Donne's *Satyres* follow Horace, Juvenal, Martial, or all three, most agree that, to paraphrase Milgate, he makes them his own (xviii).[24] Donne's innovations in satire, dependent as he undoubtedly was on classical works, are what prevented recognition of those sources for so many years and what make disagreements on his borrowings as common as they are.

The problems that can arise from tracing Donne's classical sources are more evident in studies of the *Songs and Sonets* and *Elegies* as Ovidian than of the *Satyres* as Horatian or Juvenalian. One problem for those who stress Ovid's influence on Donne is deciding which poems show this influence.[25] Richard Hughes says only the *Elegies* and early *Songs and Sonets* do. But his proof raises another problem. He maintains that in these, especially in nine from the latter group,[26] Donne relies on Ovid, Horace, and Petrarch because he was "protecting himself from exposure"—that is, from biographical interpretations (1968, 38–39). Despite these sources, Hughes is more interested in positing a young Donne who is "still . . . too egotistic, too aware of the solipsistic *I* to submit himself to anything, let alone his own creations" (37). Ovid and the rest thus become primarily a tool in Hughes's hands for a new kind of biographical reading of Donne's "interior career."

N. J. C. Andreasen's Ovidian readings present a similar problem. Following Ovid but also attempting to "outdo" him, Donne presents in "The Sunnes Rising," "Breake of Day," "Loves Alchemie," "Farewell to Love," and Elegies XVII and XIX a lover disillusioned with lust (1967, 115–29). Because she treats these poems as Ovidian condemnations of lust, she sees the same *persona* speaking in all of them, thus ignoring the many different moods and tones present in even these few poems.

Furthermore, the sheer number and contrariety of classical and medieval traditions into which scholars have placed Donne illustrate the elusiveness of his sources. The *Anniversaries*, for example, follow the stoical tradition, have a Horatian character, or depend on classical funeral elegies.[27] His rhetoric is Aristotelian or non-Aristotelian, Ramist or not Ramist;[28] it depends on the rhetorical figure of repetition or of "dilemma";[29] it is based on the "formal logic" of the Scholastics or is intentionally fallacious or is both.[30] Add to these Ignatian and Protestant meditation, Petrarchism, Neoplatonism, baroque and mannerist characteristics, and the difficulties of placing Donne within a tradition become obvious.

Although taken individually, such attempts would not distinguish scholarship on Donne from that on any of his contemporaries, the range and number of these disputes point to the unusual nature of Donne criticism. Nevertheless, scholarship of this kind, while sometimes leading to idiosyncratic interpretations of certain poems, on the whole treats Donne more objectively, with less unsubstantiated speculation than biographical studies and with fewer in-house literary quarrels than those influenced by Eliot and the New Critics. It is plagued less by Donne's personality or by his relationship to modern criticism. For example, Thomas Hester in *Kinde Pitty and Brave Scorn* (1982) argues that Donne used techniques of Roman satirists but used them for his own purposes: while imitating the classical satirists, "Donne has replaced the spokesman of Horace, Juvenal, and Persius with a speaker of Christian zeal" (15). Thus Donne is in a historical period and uses ideas both from his present and from the past the Elizabethans so admired to create his own poetry. However, this originality and Donne's innovations in using these traditions along with the many possible "sources" cited for his works point to the difficulty of placing his works in the standard literary traditions.

# 5
# Donne's Views on Women, Religion, and Science

To explore interpretations of Donne's attitudes and beliefs is to return to biographical considerations of the poet, since opinions on Donne's beliefs often depend on interpretations of his life and vice versa. A scholar's position on Donne's Catholic sympathies and his tolerance of other religious beliefs as an Anglican preacher depends, at least partially, on that scholar's interpretation of Donne's early life, religious conversion, and ministry. Likewise, the poet's youthful libertinism, attitudes toward women, preoccupations with death, and acceptance or rejection of the "New Science" are closely connected to his youth and marriage, death pose, and education. For example, if a scholar believes Donne's Mitcham letters reveal marital unhappiness, then he or she will probably also concentrate on Donne's cynicism and distrust of women in general.

However, scholarship attempting to elucidate Donne's thought also departs from avowedly biographical studies, first by its ability to depend more legitimately than can biographical studies on Donne's literary works and second by its interest in the origin and progress of his beliefs. That is, some scholars interested in Donne's religious beliefs may assume his conversion to Anglicanism was insincere, prompted by ambitious, materialistic motives, but focus on the latent Catholicism revealed in his sermons and religious poetry. Others may assume Donne in youth was a rake but focus on his philosophical and religious libertinism in relation to Montaigne's.

The problem with determining Donne's thoughts, attitudes, and beliefs is similar to the problem in other areas of Donne scholarship: it is difficult to decide how committed Donne was to the ideas that appear in his works, how often he believed in a theological or philosophical idea, and how often he merely played with that idea. Thus scholars who believe Donne was an advocate of the New Science must explain why he pilloried Copernicus along with Loyola in *Ignatius his Conclave* and wrote that "the New Philosophy calls all in doubt." Alternatively, those who believe he distrusted the New Science must explain why he used its images with such imagination and energy. There are reasonable answers to these and similar

136

questions, but, more important, the answer lies in Donne's divided mind. Only a mind so divided could write both "The Good-morrow" and "Loves Alchemy," favor and disapprove of the New Science, believe in tolerance and lash out at Jesuits, fear death and welcome it.

It stands to reason, then, that scholarship on Donne's thought is similarly divided about his amatory, religious, and scientific beliefs. Examining such studies not only illuminates the major controversies but also epitomizes Donne studies as a whole, showing why and how some scholars look at only one half of that divided mind, what helpful studies result from trying to piece that mind together, and why Donne is so recalcitrant and so rich a subject for literary criticism.

Since Donne is still known primarily as a love poet, discovering how he regarded women is the most obvious starting point for exploring his system of beliefs. However, scholars can find in his poetry evidence for diametrically opposite views, as the following two statements, written by Arthur Symons and Evelyn Simpson, respectively, aptly illustrate.

It may be, though I doubt it, that other poets who have written personal verse in English have known as much of women's hearts and the senses of men. . . . If women most conscious of their sex were ever to read Donne, they would say, He was a great lover; he understood. (Symons [1899] 1916, 100–102)

Donne's attitude towards women is characteristic of the man in its superficial inconsistency and its underlying fixity. He is a sensualist and an idealist. . . . He has passion in abundance but little tenderness. . . . Few great writers have shown so little insight into the secrets of a woman's heart. (Simpson [1924] 1948, 71)

Quite obviously, there is profound disagreement here—disagreement that depends not on the interpretation of a single poem or of the events in Donne's life. Simpson, for example, believes his marriage, while teaching him "reverence for the spiritual qualities of womanhood," did not change these attitudes ([1924] 1948, 71). Rather, the disagreement evolves from perceiving differently the underlying attitude present in the love poems as a whole. Perhaps, though, the twenty-five years separating the first writer from the second or the gender difference accounts for the different perceptions. How well could Arthur Symons himself know "women's hearts"? Is not Evelyn Simpson a better judge? The hypothesis that Donne's treatment of women appeals more to his own sex than to women would be an interesting one—if it were true. In fact, it is not. Douglas Bush in 1952 contended that Donne "has little interest in women's feelings except as they affect his" (58), whereas Lu Emily Pearson in 1933 believed "he would examine, not only his own soul, but also that of the woman who was partner to his experience" ([1933] 1966, 223), and Ilona Bell, in 1983, wrote: "I think Donne's *Songs and Sonets* are the first Renaissance love poems written for adults, loving and empathetic enough to grant the man's and the woman's point of view equal credence" (129).

What lies behind Bush's statement (and perhaps Simpsons's too) is a revulsion from Donne's egocentricity. "Let me love," Donne says. "I had rather owner bee / Of thee one houre," "Since that I / Must dye at last," "She'is all States, and all Princes, I"—Donne does seem in his love poems greatly concerned with himself, his love, his reactions.[1] And so, perhaps, in fact, he had no attitudes about women themselves but only about how they affected him.

Several critics, in fact, see it that way. Wilbur Sanders, for example, dislikes "The Extasie" and "The Canonization" because "the lover finds it necessary to exhibit himself and his love for the admiration of mankind at large" (1971, 56). Similarly, Richard Hughes finds "The Sunnes Rising" a piece of "raucous male chest-pounding" (1968, 115) and thus sees little regard for the woman who encompasses "the'India's of spice and Myne." Clay Hunt also accuses Donne of egotism (1954, 176–77), whereas Tillyard, discussing "Since she whome I lovd," thinks it odd for Donne to concentrate so much on himself in a sonnet presumably written to his dead wife (1956, 12). John Carey takes this assertion of Donne's egotism the farthest when he says that "the *Songs and Sonnets,* which look like a collection of love lyrics, turn out to be largely about the instability of the self" (1981, 190). Furthermore, Donne's ambition and his egocentricity provoke him not simply to ignore but to abuse women: in " 'To his Mistress, Going to Bed' the lust for power takes the form of a wish to insult, humiliate and punish." Donne's "sadism" in this poem is "turned loose . . . against one wretched, half-naked girl" (124). Carey has been severely censured for this distorted reading of a poem most find delightfully erotic,[2] but the point here is that he has merely carried to extremes the kind of treatment possible when only one side of Donne's mind is emphasized and, incidentally, when little or no distinction is made between *persona* and poet. Egocentric in concentrating on his own feelings in love he may be (although he is not in this so much unlike other lovers), but dwelling on that aspect of his view of women has blinded too many critics to his more tender moments and to his obvious respect for at least one woman in such poems as "A Valediction: forbidding mourning" and "Sweetest love."

Scholars who do concentrate on these tender moments paint quite a different picture of Donne. Although centering his discussion on just one poem, Novarr demonstrates not Donne's egocentricity but just the opposite: the lover in "A Valediction: forbidding mourning," he argues, creates an argument that is illogical but quiet. Wanting to calm his lover's grief, he shows through his argument-poem his awareness of the humanness of grief and his concern and love for her (1980, chap. 2). A. J. Smith, more inclusively, says that "for Donne, it seems, love is an active state of mutual concern" (1972a, 129). Despite this century's rapidly evolving attitudes toward women, two female scholars, writing forty-five years apart, agree that Donne clearly reveals great sympathy for and understanding of women. Joan Bennett in 1938 used Donne's rhythms and the plain sense of his poetic lines to reveal a poet and man who loved and sympathized with women ([1938] 1962, 123–24). Ilona Bell insisted that "what Donne *and* his speaker expressed most intensely was not egocentricity or intellectuality but empathy" for the woman (1983, 115).

This may seem a conventional enough literary dispute, but, in fact, scholars do not so vehemently disagree about how any other Renaissance love poet felt toward women. The closest parallel is the controversy over Milton's antifeminism, but since the main subject of Milton's major poems is not the love between a woman and man, this dispute does not determine the central meaning of Milton's major poems as it does of Donne's *Songs and Sonets*. Although Eve and Dalila may be presented unsympathetically, Milton's main themes are not undermined. That is, if one believes Milton's works express antifeminist leanings, the poet may become a less attractive figure, but since human, romantic love of the kind Bennett finds in Donne's poetry plays a limited part in Milton's major poems, believing in his antifeminism does not influence the overall interpretation of *Paradise Lost* or *Samson Agonistes*. However, since Donne's major theme is love, insisting on his egocentricity with regard to women can remove the *Songs and Sonets* completely from the realm of what many expect from love poetry: devotion, tenderness, passion, and appreciation for women. If, for example, Sanders is justified in calling "The Canonization" "a sad kind of intellectual hypochondria, a state of self-absorption so acute that the sufferer can enter into relation with nothing external to himself" (1971, 23), or if C. S. Lewis's more generalized statement that Donne "is perpetually excited and therefore perpetually cut off from the deeper and more permanent springs of his own excitement" ([1938] 1962, 95–96) is accurate, then can Donne's poetry rightfully be called love poetry? If Wyatt's speaker is cynical about women, he at least professes to having been at one time enough in love to appreciate and react to his lady's responses and actions in the game of love: "And she me caught in her arms long and small, / Therewithal sweetly did me kiss" (1975, 11, 12–13). If Donne, however, has the extreme egocentricity some of these critics believe him to have, then he far surpassed Wyatt in his cynicism toward women. This kind of interpretation of Donne's attitudes leads to Carey's statement that in some sense, Donne was not a love poet at all: "The physical characteristics of the girl he's supposed to be talking to don't concern him. Nor does her personality: it is completely obliterated by Donne's. He doesn't even seem to feel sexually excited. . . . Donne never rises to single-minded lust" (1981, 9–10).

Yet it must be conceded that readers like Lewis, Sanders, and Carey are not pulling their conclusions about Donne's relationship to women from thin air. Even if some readers are not inclined to censure Donne for his supposed egocentricity, the strain of cynicism in his love poetry has rarely escaped notice in the twentieth century. Different from an egotistical stance, which ignores the feelings of women, this cynical strain is usually seen as an active sneering at women. Egotism believes only the self exists; cynicism accounts for others but smirks at their foibles.

The scholarly controversies about Donne's cynical attitude are not as much at variance as those about his egotism; rather, the former diverge into shades of interpretation, not into opposites. The most widely circulated view of Donne's cynicism is, of course, that his early poems express a cynical attitude toward women, which allegedly changed after he met and married Anne More. Especially common before 1921, this view often dwelt on Donne's disgust with his own sensuality while ignoring the possibility that he was wittily showing off for his friends. Andrew Lang's is a representative treatment: "Donne in youth was not at ease with himself: he speculates too curiously. He may try to play the sensualist, but there is a dark backward in his genius; there are chords not in tune with mirth and pleasure. . . . If his Elegies contain . . . the story of a love affair, it was of a nature to make him uneasy" (1912, 286). Obviously, this statement, like those propounding Donne's egotism, concentrates more on his view of himself than on his attitude toward women but the two are inextricably linked. Donne treats women and the nature of love cynically because he is (to the ego-critics) self-involved or (to the biographical critics) disgusted by sex.

Although the New Critics modified this view, such interpretations of Donne's cynical attitude have persisted. Leishman in 1934 contended:

> At one time . . . he really thought that there was such a thing as true love and faithfulness in woman, that there was something in the chivalrous devotion of Spenser and the sonneteers. Then he was deceived, was for a time inflamed with hatred and bitterness, but gradually developed a cynical philosophy of love; resolved to get what enjoyment out of it he could, but not to let it unduly disturb his peace of mind. (19)

For Leishman and a number of others, this cynicism dissolved when Donne married.[3] D. W. Harding, however, maintains that Donne constantly feared betrayal by women because of an "unwilling and protesting separation from the fantasy-perfect mother of infancy" (1951, 432).[4] Thus his cynical poems express a "divided feeling . . . towards ordinary women," and even his mutual love lyrics express suspicion of betrayal

(433–38). Donne, then, according to Harding and Leishman, was cynical and distrustful of women and spent at least his youthful love poetry detailing that distrust.

Other commentators on Donne's cynicism, some of whom apply their discussions to the "speaker" of the poems, discover several variations on the theme of cynical youth and later amatory conversion, redefining and sometimes rejecting his supposed misogynous cynicism.

Writing in 1972, Roger Sharrock exemplified a middle position in studies of Donne's attitudes toward women. Although interested in biographical readings of the *Songs and Sonets,* he is more concerned to show that these lyrics are not mere "exercises in wit" but rather expositions of the states of love (46). Thus the cynical love poems are so only because the "balanced love" of the mutual love poems "is invoked theoretically as a standard by which to measure the inequality of desires devouring the lover" (52). That is, the lover's attitude toward women changes only as his attitude toward himself in love changes; as he relinquishes his ego-centricity, he can regard the woman more positively than he had pre-viously. John Bernard also believes Donne's cynicism arises from his feelings about himself and love. Couched in the language of New Crit-icism, his essay presents a Donne "venting a thirst for the infinite and then imposing rational limits on it" even in his less cynical love poems like "The Good-morrow," "The Canonization," and "The Anniversarie" (1972, 380–84). In his more cynical love poems, Donne "poses" as a libertine because of the tension between the speaker's "almost frantic desire for some sort of infinity in love" and the poet's desire to "check and deny" the purely physical nature of the poems (380). Writers who follow the route taken by Sharrock and Bernard,[5] then, are not much concerned with Donne's attitudes toward the woman addressed, or toward women at all. Instead, seduced by the dominant "I" in the *Songs and Sonets,* they see only Donne's—or the speaker's—doubts and uncertainties about his own ability to love.

Another variation on Donne's cynicism sees it as a creative force in the poems. Since hate is part of love, Donne in his loving poems shows a recognition of its destructive power, and, in his cynical poems, he "cre-ates" cynicism to show "the other side of love" (Barbara Hardy 1977, 20–25). Working in this mode, Rosalie Colie sees Donne's cynicism as only one part of his creative paradoxality: "Donne does not seek . . . to describe the frustration induced by the mixed emotion of love; he at-tempts its evocation" (1966, 111). Even as early as the *Paradoxes and Problems,* Donne's double view of women emerges because "he manages to exploit both the tradition of derogation and the tradition of praise" (103).

The final treatment of Donne's cynicism wishes to deny it is there at all, usually by emphasizing his acceptance of or rebellion against literary tradition. Proposing the latter theory, Douglas Peterson contends that the apparent inconsistency in attitude between the cynical and mutual love poems need not depend on biographical developments; rather, the cynical poems are directed not at women, but at the current attitudes toward women (1967, 301). Donne is attacking "neo-Platonic truisms by affirming their dialectical contraries" (297). Donne's own attitudes toward "women and love are founded . . . upon a psychology which provides for a resolution of the attitudes set in opposition in the mocking poems" (301). Ruffo-Fiore also denies Donne's cynicism about women but for a directly opposite reason: "Donne's ruse of the cynical mask, perhaps one of his unique contributions to the evolvement of the Petrarchan tradition, should not be mistaken for a negation of the ideal" (1976, 28). Donne's speaker wishes to believe in Petrarchan ideals but overturns his own arguments through faulty logic (28–38). The differing conclusions reached by Peterson and Ruffo-Fiore, who begin with the same assumption about Donne's perception of women, point to the difficulty of ascribing to Donne one certain attitude or position.

One final twist to this denial of Donne's cynicism is presented by George Nitchie in a unique biographical interpretation of "Loves Alchemie." This poem, he argues, does not reveal a cynical attitude toward women but rather "intellectual disgust at a stupid idea ('Love's centric happiness, indeed!')" (1979, 18). Donne, he says, is mocking his own perceptions when he and Anne married: "Had Donne at one time sworn that it was not the bodies but the minds that married? Was it perhaps what a thirty-year-old husband told his sixteen-year-old wife?" (21). If Nitchie's argument appears farfetched, it is no more so than the argument that sees Donne as holding "himself intact, refusing to give away anything. . . . build[ing] a fortress around his own ego" in the cynical poems (Richard Hughes 1968, 44). Nor is Nitchie's treatment of this poem any more strained than those seeing jealousy and contempt in "The Sunnes Rising" (Carey 1981, 109) or seeing the speaker of "The Good-morrow" as asserting "a truth [about love] he knows has no general assent and no general support in experience" (Cathcart 1975, 66). Nitchie simply emphasizes the tender side of Donne to the exclusion of the cynical, whereas others emphasize the cynical to the exclusion of the tender. Both emphases seek to unite the poet of "A Valediction: forbidding mourning" with the poet of "Loves Alchemie."

However, in these attempts to unify Donne's attitudes toward women, the cynical emphasis usually triumphs, if not by its logical reasoning, then at least by the sheer number of such responses. It is, I would suggest, easier and more interesting to find in Donne (and his speaker) this cynical, mocking, distrustful attitude toward women than a loving, trustful one. In the seventies and eighties, the old biographical progression (cynicism dissolved by marriage) has seemed too outdated, and also too simply a means of uniting these attitudes. To dismiss Donne's cynicism as Peterson and Ruffo-Fiore do, thus proposing a gentler, more tender attitude toward women in youth than has generally been supposed for Donne, annihilates the rakish Donne that textbooks still propose and that students (and critics?) still find so interesting. Thus proposing cynicism or at least distrust for all the *Songs and Sonets* allows us to retain the exciting, complex Donne, the cynic and libertine.

Although exploring Donne's libertinism raises some provocative questions, doing so provides yet another way to unify the many dimensions of Donne's beliefs, not this time the cynical with the tender lover, but instead the lover with the priest.[6] Toby Mathew, son of the archbishop of York and convert to Catholicism, is primarily responsible for attaching the label "libertine" to Donne. In 1607, he wrote from the Fleet, where he was imprisoned for remaining obdurate in his Catholicism, that Donne and Richard Martin were "mere libertines in themselves; and that the thing for which they could not long endure me was because they thought me too saucy, for presuming to show them the right way, in which they liked not then to go" (in Bald 1970, 188). Since Mathew, much against the wishes of his father, had converted to Catholicism in 1606 (Bald, 187), he had his own reasons for using the term: Donne by 1607 had probably renounced his own early Catholicism. Therefore, as Ernest Sprott showed in 1950, Mathew was using "libertine" in a very specialized sense. Donne was a libertine for Mathew, Sprott says, only because he had changed religions, not because he was a profligate or a skeptic (339–41). However, for many exploring Donne's morality and religious development, the term has taken on wider meanings. Robert Ornstein's definition comes closest to encompassing these broader connotations: a libertine is one who "condemns *all* moral restraints on appetite as the artificial chains of custom" (1956, 214). This definition provides a connecting link between the Donne who wrote "Chang'd loves are but chang'd sorts of meat" ("Communitie," line 22) and the Donne who, while not doubting God, did question the efficacy of man's churches.

In discussions of Donne's alleged libertinism, belief in his early sexual promiscuity plays, however, only a minor role. Many writers simply took for granted that Donne was a rake, with libertinism providing a philosophical motive for that rakishness. Rather, it is his attitude toward established religion that most interested writers of the thirties, forties, and fifties. To support the view of Donne as both a sexual and a religious libertine, there is some sketchy evidence from Donne and his contemporaries. Besides Mathew, Richard Baker said that Donne lived "not dissolute, but very neat; a great visiter of Ladies, a great frequenter of Playes, a great writer of conceited *Verses*" (1643, 156). Donne himself wrote of being "delivered . . . from the Egypt of lust" (Donne 1967b, 79) and preached about his own sins of the flesh. Izaak Walton wrote in his life of Donne that when the poet was eighteen years old he had "betrothed himself to no Religion that might give him any other denomination than *a Christian*. And Reason, and Piety had both perswaded him, that there could be no such sin as *Schism*, if an adherence to some visible Church were not necessary" ([1970] 1927, 25).

From these bits of information, which, taken in conjunction, point to both senses of the word, it has been argued that in his early (i.e., cynical) poetry Donne appeals to Nature for a "justification of a frankly sexual conception of love" (Bredvold 1923, 474); and that he was a libertine who progressed from "the inconstancy of nature to scepticism to naturalism; then following a profound emotional change . . . from despair at the inconstancy of life to scepticism to religious faith" (Williamson 1934, 290).

According to S. L. Bethell writing in 1948, these opinions were popular in the twenties and the two decades following because "it is—or was—a sceptical age" (78). This generation of critics made Donne a cynical libertine because it wanted him to be one. In fact, however, "Donne was remarkably secure on the subject of marriage and shares with Shake-speare and the Book of Common Prayer the honour of having cleared away a great deal of highfalutin 'Platonic' rubbish and perverted poetry which held in contempt the function of the body in love." Donne was so secure, he continues, that he could write about inconstancy (79). His views of "highfalutin 'Platonic' rubbish" aside, Bethell is partially accurate in his assessment. Believing they had found in Donne a poet troubled by and doubting both his religious heritage and the ability of reason itself to answer his doubts, many critics of the twenties, thirties, and forties molded the poet to fit their own skeptical attitudes toward their changing world. Thus the confusion about Donne's sexual, religious, and philosophical libertinism is increased even more by an association of "libertinism" and "skepticism." The tendency to make Donne a "modern free-thinker" no doubt accounts in part for Louis Bredvold's view of Donne and Donne's contemporaries. In part, however, his view of Donne's skepticism is shaped by a desire to put the pieces of Donne together:

Few subjects of biography are more fascinating than John Donne. . . . The apparent inconsistency in the career of the man who wrote the *Elegies* as well as the *Hymn to God the Father,* only entices one the more to penetrate, if possible, into the innermost secret of his development. However elusive it may be, one feels that there must be some principle of continuity in the intellectual and spiritual history of Donne, some deeper impulse or characteristic which manifested itself in diverse ways. (1923, 471)

The connecting link for Bredvold is Donne's libertinism. In both his skepticism and his "naturalistic conception of the Golden Age, Donne's thought resembled the current 'libertine' ideas of the Renaissance" (493), even though these ideas seem "singularly modern" (501). Donne's idealism and his marriage, however, converted him from this earthly naturalism, making him "a different saint for having passed through his youthful period of hard living and hard thinking" (502).

For a time, this characterization of Donne's thought prevailed. Now his marriage (or alternatively Anne's death) had converted him not simply from a reckless profligate to a loving husband but from a skeptic, a disbeliever, a sensualist to a faithful priest.[7] George Williamson complicates the conversion more than does Bredvold, but his outline of Donne's thought is the same. *Biathanatos,* he says, is "a crucial point in the progress of the soul which converted Jack Donne into Dr. Donne for it marks the end of his naturalistic journey" (1934, 286). After *Biathanatos,* the "world seemed hardly worth scepticism," but Donne found constancy in his love for Anne (289).

Responses to this picture of Donne were not long in coming. Allen Benham (1941, 277–78), R. G. Howarth (in Memorabilist 1945, 257), and Ernest Sprott (1950, 341) stressed the more common meaning of "not dissolute," all agreeing that Baker characterized Donne's personal appearance and all specifically denying sexual promiscuity. In addition, Sprott notes that no one in the seventeenth century used "libertine" to refer to Donne's morality (399–411), as Bredvold and Williamson had implied.[8] Addressing the question of Donne's religious or skeptical thought, Robert Ornstein shows that Donne and Montaigne criticized "natural law," or natural theology, independently of the libertine tradition and of each other (1956, 214).[9]

Nevertheless, Donne the skeptical libertine did not disappear with the skepticism of the twenties and thirties. Instead, discussions of this aspect of his thought and personality became more sophisticated than they had been, while the connection between his supposed sexual freedom and promiscuity and his religious career became more intertwined. Robert Nye, for example, in an essay published in 1972, proposed looking not at Baker's Donne, not at the witty, skeptical, "*fragmented*" Donne of the love poems, whom Eliot and his generation adopted, but at the Christian Donne (345–46). To do this, he says, the division in Donne "between sacred and prophane must be broken down" by following from beginning to end "the seriousness of his commitment to love" (351). Nye's version of Donne departs from that presented by Williamson, Bredvold, Payne, and others—but not radically. The paradox Donne found in his heart, he says, when he looked there to write was the Christian paradox—the Incarnation:

Yet he was sceptical, reluctant, a kind of atheist of love. It is perhaps difficult to *remain* an atheist in love. Truth on a high hill is one thing. Truth in bed with you or active in your life as a sacramental presence is another. Donne may be perceived through two experiences: his experience of love through the person of Anne More, and his experience of love through the Person of Jesus Christ. . . . The former, in its conjunction of opposites, may be supposed to have clarified the latter. (351–52)

A refinement of the earlier Donne Nye's picture certainly is, but it still presents a skeptic—in this case an agnostic—coverted to faith by love for his wife. At the same time, Nye's essay, coming as it did more than seventy years after Gosse had proposed a similar conversion, indicates a "truth" about Donne's thought: that at one time in his life he either questioned the teachings of humanly-ordained institutions or, less probably, doubted the existence of God, a hypothesis supported by the doubts and questioning in *Satyre III*. The distinction between deducing facts about Donne's beliefs regarding women from the *Songs and Sonets* and about his "philosophical" or religious thought from the *Satyres* is hazy, but it is a distinction accepted even by those who eschew biographical readings of the love poems. R. C. Bald, for example, writes:

The tone of the third Satire is, however, less cynical and more mature [than that of such poems as "Womans constancy"]. There is still a sceptical balancing of the adherents of the various sects against one another so that they are all made to seem equally contemptible, along with the man who accepts all the creeds and the man who will have none of any. But the rejection of all the commonly accepted reasons for religious belief does not involve the abandonment of the search for truth. . . . The evidence of the poems, such as it is, suggests that Donne's immersion in controversial divinity resulted in a period of unsettlement during which neither Catholicism nor Protestantism could wholly satisfy him. His natural inclination to scepticism was for a time reinforced by a mood of cynicism in which he flaunted his sense of insecurity. (1970, 71–72)

The question is how profoundly this "period of unsettlement" influenced Donne's later religious faith and how and when he renounced his doubts about a church's authority—and for what. Writing only seven years apart, A. D. Cousins and John Bernard propose very different times for the end of this skepticism. Cousins sees it ending by 1600 (although he does not specifically make the connection, this is of course a year before Donne's marriage) (1979, 98). Bernard, on the other hand, denying the "myth" of Jack and Dr. Donne, believes skepticism consistently informed Donne's thought: "What we are left with when we have done is a mind indefatigably skeptical of its own creative motives. . . . Donne's uncertainties . . . are so profound, his mistrust of the merely fictive so ingrained, that it was inevitable he would come to rest where Authority was greatest," that is, in the church (1972, 388–89). Emphasizing the difficulties of tracing the progress of and changes in Donne's thought, this disagreement also illustrates the problems of deciding Donne's beliefs.

Unlike much scholarship on Donne, that exploring what replaced his skepticism follows basically chronological lines. Unlike the 1960s, those, like Williamson (1934, 286) and Bredvold (1925, 191–232), who believed in an intensely skeptical pre-ordination Donne also posited a fideistic preacher. A mind doubting everything, the theory goes, doubting even knowledge itself, finally can come to rest in a completely nonrational faith. However, this view of Donne has all but disappeared. Even John Carey, who returns to many of the older views on Donne and who emphasizes his skepticism, believes "the simple faith" was "alien to his combative, critical nature" (1981, 34). The failure of reason in matters of faith "frustrated and alarmed him" (253). More positively, Dennis Quinn shows that Donne in his *Sermons* "espouses the rules of faith as well as the rules of good scholarship" (1962, 317).[10] Terry Sherwood also notes that Donne stresses that "rational knowledge is prior, in time, to faith" (1972, 354–55).[11] As a reaction to the Donne created by the preceding generation, assessments such as Sherwood's and Quinn's present a more balanced and now more widely accepted view of the churchman.

Donne's relationship to medieval theology follows a similar chronological pattern. The emphasis, in the twenties, thirties, and forties, on Donne's skepticism rested on a comparison of his to modern thought. That is, one of Donne's attractions for these readers was his doubt, which seemed modern. So Eliot, comparing Donne to Lancelot Andrewes, could say that the latter was more medieval, the former more modern (1926a, 622). Donne, Eliot remarks, "belonged to that class of persons . . . who seek refuge in religion from the tumults of a strong emotional temperament which can find no complete satisfaction elsewhere" (622); he writes sermons as a means to self-expression (622). It did not take Eliot's followers long to cultivate this "modern" aspect of Donne's character, not necessarily denying Donne's reliance on medieval or patristic theology but simply ignoring that possibility. If they mentioned Donne's reliance on medieval thought at all, they concentrated on his innovativeness. Thus, Herbert Read said in 1928 that Donne is "scarcely ever devout because, he is always sceptical" except in his later religious poems (66). He "gave to English poetry the *words* of scholastic philosophy; [but] it is more than this, because Donne's choice of words was an inspired selection" (67). Likewise, Ashley Sampson noted in 1936 that "the resurrection of Donne in our midst to-day owes less to his intrinsic virtues as a poet than to the fact that this generation has endured the pangs which brought Donne to maturity as an individual" (308). Donne witnessed the overthrow of religious civilization, modern poets the overthrow of scientific civilization (312). Fausset in 1931 believed Donne's poetry appealed because his generation was "struggling to free itself from a mental consciousness that has brought spiritual death in its train" (93); whereas for Williamson, writing one year earlier, metaphysical poetry was popular because of its "connections with the strange, unearthly, and terrible nebula of emotion which surrounds our life and bewilders us in the daily papers" (1930, 93).

This emphasis on Donne's modernism would seem to have little to do with his medievalism; in fact, it is a tacit denial of his medieval connections and culminates all the varied effects the New Criticism had on Donne scholarship: Donne, the New Critics believed, was skeptical in the same way they were; thus the actual facts of his life were unimportant; only his thought mattered. He was modern; thus he improved on or rejected all the old poetic forms.

At the same time, however, other scholars were intensely curious about Donne's medieval heritage. Such scholars as Mary Patton Ramsey (1917, 1–3ff.; 1931, 101–20), Evelyn Simpson ([1924] 1948, 118),[12] and Roy Battenhouse (1942, 217–48) wanted to dispute these claims of modernism and show that Donne's world view, while perhaps skeptical, was also profoundly influenced by preceding thinkers. Despite some in the late thirties and forties who disputed Donne's medieval lineage,[13] this is the view of his religion that is current now. Although few scholars of the sixties and seventies have assayed as systematic a study of his relationship to medieval theology as did Ramsey or would accept all her conclusions, Donne's reliance on the patristic tradition is undisputed.[14] Furthermore, studying Donne's theology in the context of Augustinian traditions leads to a new assessment of his principles of scriptural interpretation. Until the fifties, not much attention was paid to Donne's methods of interpretation, to the art involved in his devotional prose. For those writing in Eliot's wake, the *Sermons* and the *Essays in Divinity* were less interesting than the metaphysical poems. By the sixties, however, the complexities of Donne's scriptural method became evident.[15]

Oddly, Eliot saw scholarship on Donne's medieval lineage moving in the opposite direction than that in which it actually moved. In 1931, he wrote: "As long as we thought of Donne as a mediaeval, as a mystic, . . . we did not see his poetry as it is. Donne is not even an absolutely first-rate devotional poet" (13). Later in the same essay he contended that Donne's sermons would disappear as works of art (18–19). Tate agreed, adding that they "have been mildly popular among people who wish to be in the Donne fashion without taking the trouble to read the verse" ([1932] 1959, 328). Surprising as Tate's statement may seem to those who have tried to read the ten volumes of sermons, it, along with Eliot's view, provides the clearest reason for the chronological neatness of theories about Donne's theology. Those wishing to see only the skeptical, modern Donne found in the religious prose a return to orthodoxy, a fellow rebel returning to the fold. Consequently, these works were "ready for oblivion" (Tate [1932] 1959, 328), since they presented a much less interesting person, at least to Eliot and his followers. As reactions against this view of Donne took hold, and as scholarship on the poetry proliferated, later scholars turned to the prose to find it more complex, more interesting, and richer than Eliot's dismissive statements had indicated. As a result, these scholars could allow the several dimensions of Donne's theology to coexist as those earlier often did not.

A corollary to the trend of studies on his medieval thought, the study of Donne's supposed mysticism is, nevertheless, not as neatly chronological because those accepting Eliot's dismissal of medieval elements in Donne's theology did not necessarily accept his dismissal of mysticism. Therefore, while emphasis on Donne's medieval tendencies has grown in the sixties and seventies, emphasis on his supposed mysticism has diminished. In fact, few are interested in even denying his mysticism.[16] Until the mid-fifties, however, there was no definitive pronouncement on his mystical qualities, with some vehemently insisting on them and others just as vehemently denying them.

Since "mysticism" can mean anything from a direct communion with God by way of deep meditation or trance to an intuitive recognition of a reality beyond the things of this world (a definition applicable to any number of poets and people generally), it is not surprising that Donne has often been called a mystic or that individual poems have been labeled mystical. Given the numerous—often loose—meanings given to the term, one wonders what is gained by attempting to "prove" Donne's mysticism. And the answer often is "not much." To maintain, as some critics have, that "The Extasie" is mystical[17] does little to illuminate the poem, since mystical qualities are difficult to define absolutely. Furthermore, although Donne does use mystical language—he speaks of a spiritual marriage in the Holy Sonnet "Batter my heart" and the dark night of the soul in "I am a little world made cunningly," for example—his use of these is unspecific enough to be generally religious without being distinctly mystical. The problems with defining mysticism or with labeling any but a very few poets mystical are accurately summarized by Holman: "*Mysticism* takes many different forms and does not yield itself readily to definition. Objective studies of *mysticism* are impossible, since one not himself a mystic must be content to receive as fact the autobiographical or artistic record of an experience that is, by its very nature, ineffable" (1980, 332–33).

Nevertheless, a number of critics, especially before 1950, were intent on proving or disproving Donne's mysticism. Doing so has led to a great deal of confusion, mainly because the definition of "mysticism" varies from critic to critic. However, the problem with Donne's mysticism also arises because of unanswered questions about the theologian himself. He may have traveled in Spain (Bald 1970, 50–51) and was undoubtedly familiar with Spanish literature, particularly with that of the Spanish mystics, St. John of the Cross and Saint Teresa. To what extent he simply adopted the language of mysticism and to what extent he subscribed to the tenets of mysticism are unclear. But this uncertainty has not prevented critics from defending or refuting Donne's "mystical" qualities.

As sometimes happens when Donne is placed in any tradition, those insisting on his mysticism sometimes fell into the habit of proclaiming him mystical but imperfect. Thus Caroline Spurgeon in 1913 saw Donne's "attitude of mind" as "essentially mystical" but found that Donne "entirely fails to utilise" the mystical and philosophical possibilities of *Metempsychosis* (72–76).[18] That is, she assumes Donne tried to be mystical and failed. More often, however, Donne's mysticism is discussed in relation to his theological beliefs or to his sermons rather than to his secular poetry.[19] Interestingly, belief—or disbelief—in Donne's mysticism follows none of the expected lines. Eliot dismissed Donne's mysticism (1930, 443), but Tate, while agreeing with his mentor's assessment of the *Sermons,* called Donne "a mystical poet" (1927, 45). Williamson, who in his early essays was almost slavishly devoted to Eliot, nevertheless insisted on Donne's mysticism (1930, 17; 1934, 291). Bald, on the other hand, more predictably praised Eliot's influence on Donne studies and denied Donne's mysticism ([1932] 1965, 28). If belief in Donne's medieval theology depended to a large extent on one's relationship to New Criticism, belief in his mysticism apparently did not.

Nor did belief in his medieval tendencies either encourage or preclude belief in his mysticism. Ramsey saw a definite connection between the two (1917, 4), whereas Husain, denying Donne's medieval thought, insisted on his mysticism (1948, 39–46). And Helen White saw Donne as a mystic only in that there are mystical passages in his poetry and prose. At the opposite pole from Ramsey, Moloney denied both Donne's medievalism and his mysticism (1944, 180–95). He put his finger on the problem when he discussed the loose definitions often given to mysticism (165–69). Mahood, on the other hand, insisted that Donne's mysticism could be denied only if the term was given its strictest definition (1950, 121). Similarly, Husain's definition is sufficiently broad to make Donne a mystic. Donne, he says, cannot be theologically related to the medieval scholastics because they could not find Christ's place in the individual soul. Donne, however, "belongs to that line of Christian mystics who, like St. Bernard and St. John of the Cross and St. Teresa and others, have made the adoration of Christ and the contemplation of His Passion the aim of their mystical life" (1948, 103). The question of Donne's mysticism has never been definitively answered because the semantic question is so central. The dearth of scholarly essays about it recently is, I suspect, less a product of resolution than of loss of interest.[20]

A more persistent question than that of Donne's mysticism is that of his religious toleration, which for most critics means his willingness to grant that those attending Puritan services or Catholic mass could still be saved. In 1962, Douglas Bush, after several citations from Donne's *Sermons* to prove his point, said, "It would seem that Dr. Donne's liberal charity is exaggerated" ([1945] 1962, 2d ed., 324–25).[21] In 1948, Herbert Grierson said that when Donne was not speaking in anger, he followed the *via media;* that is, Donne believed all churches preaching a doctrine of salvation to be catholic (309). Before the 1940s, Grierson's position was the more common, subscribed to by Jessopp (1897, 58–72), Krapp (1915, 208–9) Simpson ([1924] 1948, 74–75, 107–11), Leishman (1934, 91–93), Husain (1938, 13), and Battenhouse (1942, 217–18).[22] Unfortunately, Donne often spoke in anger, and unfortunately Bush is not the only scholar to have emphasized Donne's anger more than his moderate writings.

Although Bush's and Grierson's comments address Donne's attitudes toward Puritanism and Catholicism, his attitudes as an Anglican priest toward Catholics are more frequently an issue in criticism and are intricately connected to his own early Catholicism. Since Donne's early education was Catholic and since his mother remained a recusant until her death in 1630/1, most scholars expect Donne to show more evidence of toleration for the Catholic position than did his contemporaries. Thus, when they find evidence, especially in the *Sermons,* of Donne condemning or damning English Catholics, they are often harsher with him than they are with his contemporaries who also preached against Catholicism.

The most striking evidence supporting Donne's religious toleration is the Holy Sonnet, "Show me deare Christ," but an examination of the scholarship reveals that the poem has caused more problems than it has solved. It did not appear in the 1633 edition of Donne's poems, probably indicating that Donne or his son believed it would reflect badly on the poet, and was not published until Gosse did so in 1899. In fact, both because of its sexual imagery and its religious tenets, it continues to cause consternation even in the twentieth century. As many have noted, if this sonnet is to be used to determine Donne's spiritual progress, its date of composition must be fixed more certainly than it has been.[23] If it was written before ordination, then, as Novarr suggests, it reveals one possible reason for Donne's refusing holy orders as long as he did (1980, 118, 133). Many others, however, accept Gardner's post-1620 dating of the sonnet on the basis of its appearance in the Westmoreland MS with "Since she whome I lovd" (dated after 1617 when Anne died) and on the basis of its difference in tone from the twelve *Holy Sonnets* not appearing in the Westmoreland MS (1952, 77–78).

If the post-1620 dating is correct, then apparently, so the argument goes, Donne was still questioning the Anglican church after his ordination in 1615. Gosse and Grierson, for example, see it this way,[24] as does Douglas Bush: "If the philosophic doctrine of the relativity of truth helped to open the doors of the Church, it also left them ajar. 'Show me deare Christ, thy spouse so bright and clear,' Donne could write, two or three years after his ordination, in a sonnet discreetly omitted from his collected *Poems*" ([1945, 1st ed.] 133). Bush's statement appeared in 1945. In 1952, Gardner, disagreeing strongly that the sonnet shows Donne's doubts about the Anglican church, expanded upon Evelyn Simpson's reading of the poem to argue that the sonnet is "a sign of his [Donne's] sympathy with the Anglican refusal to choose one of two mutually exclusive positions" (121, 126). In the revised edition of *English Literature in the Earlier Seventeenth Century* (1962), Bush reversed his position and called Gardner's analysis "convincingly read" (136), although he insisted more on Donne's intolerance in this edition than he did in the 1945 edition.

Others, however, were not so quickly won over to Gardner's views as was Bush. Robert Jackson, in 1970, for example, disagreed strongly with Gardner's interpretation, although he accepted her dating and her conclusions about Donne's "churchmanship" (148). Rather than taking a middle position between Catholicism and Puritanism, Donne "accepted both" (148). Reading the poem in this way will not, Jackson says, "clearly exculpate Donne from the charge of uncertainty about the Anglican church, nor should we" because the "very uncertainties in the poem . . . actually support the assertion of his essential Anglicanism" (151–52). Eventually, Jackson shows the bride in the poem to be "a man, the poet himself, the true bride, the spiritual Israel—yet not a true bride unless actually joined to her counterpart in the opposite gender, the husband-lover, the Lord, who is also the betrayer, the world itself, the external ecclesia, discoverable also as a man and the poet himself in his full complete presence as a body and a soul joined" (172). Thus, in Jackson's view the poem has less to do with Donne's actual attitude toward Rome, Geneva, or Canterbury than with "the discovery of the figure of Christ in his inner life, the completeness with which the inner life now joins the historical church, and the identity of his own integrated person with the marriage between Christ and his bride" (174). As too often happens with discussions of the love poems, this Holy Sonnet becomes a way to characterize the poet rather than to study his theological position.

In a more measured way than Jackson, David Novarr, also disagreeing with Gardner, raises the poem's second problem—its sexual imagery.

Although Donne was probably a liberal Anglican, advocating "Anglican tolerance and comprehensiveness" but rejecting "a self-serving, indiscriminatory latitudinarianism" (1980, 136–37), he was also pragmatic and politically prudent (140). Novarr, quite rightly, illustrates with passages from the *Sermons* that Donne preached both Anglican toleration and the necessity of a state church (137–40). He concludes that if Donne did in fact write "Show me deare Christ" after his ordination, "he had good reason to restrict its circulation" (140): he felt so strongly about the doctrine of One Church that he expressed that belief in his own, very idiosyncratic way— through shocking erotic images (140). Gardner, in her attempt to prove Donne's toleration, euphemizes these images: Donne's "bride" does not simply receive embraces as Gardner glosses the lines; rather, the last line means " 'when she is available to and can be penetrated by the greatest number' " (Novarr, 141). Novarr finds "the physical passion in the language . . . an index of the passionateness of Donne's emotion" (141). Others, however, find this aspect of the poem undercutting whatever universal doctrine Donne may be espousing. De Silva, for example, insists that Donne "makes of Christian faith a more than usually repulsive species of adultery with the Church in the role of profligate wife and Christ as decadent wittol" (1971, 6). William Kerrigan, exploring Donne's use of Christian accommodation (speech that allowed Christians to conceive of God in human terms), finds "Show me deare Christ" a failed sonnet because some men do want wives who are untrue. Thus, "we are left with an awful similarity rather than an awesome discrimination" (1974, 356–60). This sonnet, then, which should conclusively prove Donne's religious toleration, instead leads scholars into discussions of his supposed religious skepticism and sexual decadence.

What disagreements about Donne's toleration (either in this sonnet or, more generally, in his life as a clergyman) ultimately derive from are differing theories about Donne's conversion from Catholicism to Anglicanism. In 1936, at the beginning of her balanced but sympathetic analysis of Donne's religious experience, Helen C. White advised that the most important aspect of Donne's life to remember is that he was born with the possibility of dying for religion and rejected the chance (95). In 1981, near the beginning of the most iconoclastic biographical analysis of Donne in recent years, John Carey said: "The first thing to remember about Donne is that he was a Catholic; the second that he betrayed his faith" (15). Opinions on the effect of Donne's early Catholicism on his work and life are wide-ranging. One can choose from C. S. Lewis's now-famous remark that Donne's Catholicism caused him to suffer from the "sinfulness of sexuality" ([1938] 1962, 90–92) or Marius Bewley's description of the *Songs and Sonets* as "Donne's private guerilla warfare" against his Catholic background (1952, 645) or Louise Guiney's assertion that

"Donne's Catholicism . . . wrought upon him to the end of his life" (1920, 13). One can choose Frederick Rowe's position that Donne the preacher "is firmly Protestant, critical of Rome" (1964, 100) or R. C. Bald's assertion that he hated Jesuits but never Catholics (1970, 66) or Murray Roston's conviction that "there is . . . an unmistakable parallel between the Jesuit concept of prevarication and the witty, quibbling, and shifting wordplay of Donne's verse" (1974, 80). Those emphasizing Donne's "apostasy" and guilt because he forsook the faith of his ancestors generally wrote before 1950.[25] However, that Carey in 1981 could base an entire biography on Donne's continuing Catholic guilt, while perhaps indicating idiosyncracies on Carey's part, underscores the difficulties of shaping a coherent view of Donne's Catholicism.

Thus, even if one disregards such biographical uncertainties as the date of his religious conversion or his feelings after the death of his brother Henry, questions about Donne's theology and religious toleration remain. Middle views, such as Bald's on Donne's hatred of Jesuits but sympathy with Catholics and Novarr's on his tolerant beliefs but political prudence, seem most justified, but the divisions in Donne's mind are often so subtle and so interesting that critics like Carey will probably always emerge to explore only one angle.

Footnotes to Donne's religious beliefs are his alleged melancholy, morbidity, and death-wish. Unfortunately, these as they sometimes appear in the *Holy Sonnets,* some of the *Sermons,* and the St. Paul's statue of Donne in his shroud have throughout this century turned some readers away from Donne, provided additional stimulus for those who want to disparage him, or distressed even sympathetic readers. The prevailing opinion has been that Donne's melancholy and morbidity are different from, more extreme than, these attitudes as they appear in other Jacobean writers, despite Eliot's connection of Webster and Donne in his "Whispers of Immortality":

> Webster was much possessed by death
>
> . . . . . . . . . . . .
> Donne, I suppose, was such another
>
> . . . . . . . . . . . .
> He knew the anguish of the marrow
> The ague of the skeleton;
>
> (1952, 32–33)

Clay Hunt, for example, argued that Donne is different enough from other Renaissance writers on death to seem morbid (1954, 144). His "burrowing into the putrescence of corpses frequently verges on the queer" (143), Hunt maintains, and when he writes about death, he is not as witty as Shakespeare in the "Poor Yorick" speech in *Hamlet* (145). In 1924, Evelyn

Simpson thought it unfortunate that anthologized passages from Donne's prose concentrated on the morbidity rather than the "sanity and beauty of much of his writing" ([1924] 1948, 64). Assuming that mentally healthy people do not dwell on death, she calls the morbid passages:

> almost insane in their emphasis on the horrible. . . . there were certain flaws in a mind which was otherwise sane and healthy. Chief of these was a morbid obsession with the idea of death, especially the physical decay which attends death. One is tempted to think that Donne had seen some horrible sight in his childhood. . . . (65)

For Peter Fiore also, "Donne's use of grotesque is unique. No other poet in the English language could take a traditional Christian concept and intertwine it with such intellectual ingenuity and theological ingeniousness" as Donne could. (1972, 4).[26]

The main importance of Donne's morbidity in commentaries on his thought is that it can be used to "prove" or support a great many theories about that thought. That is, those wishing to illuminate Donne's acceptance of Anglicanism can argue, as Leishman did, that "to triumph over the fear of death, or, rather, over the fear of what may come after death, was for him the supreme test of faith, and it is a battle which he is continually re-fighting, both with himself and with his congregation" (1951, 75).[27] Or, alternatively, his morbidity can be used to illustrate the influence of Catholicism.[28] It can be used as one way to minimize the seeming division between the amorous and divine poems, as Bush used it: "The macabre strain that touched even poems of love has full play in the sinner's preoccupation with death" in the later religious poems (1952, 60).[29] It may provide the *raison d'être* for the love lyrics: "One of the most important sources of Donne's melancholy is a disturbed interest in sex." In his love poetry, he cures the love melancholy through satiric laughter (Stein 1944, 272–73).[30] His wish for and fear of death also caused cynicism toward women[31] and philosophical skepticism.[32] It even contributed to Donne's innovativeness by shaping "the Metaphysical mode of thought . . . the Metaphysical shudder. . . . most precisely concentrated in Donne. In biography it is represented by Donne and his shroud" (Williamson 1930, 90). Given all the theories to which Donne's melancholy and morbidity can be applied, it is no wonder that these have played such a large part in Donne scholarship. They are elements of Donne's thought with which almost every writer on Donne must contend.

However, several scholars have convincingly accounted for or explained these strains in Donne. For some, no further proof of Donne's morbidity is needed than *Deaths Duell,* which Frank Kermode in 1957 called an "appalling sermon" (1957a, 8). However, as our culture changed, death became a more discussable subject than it had been before the sixties;

and, because of this change, Donne's interest in death came to seem more normal. Thus, in 1972, Stanley Fish, while not directly addressing the issue of Donne's morbidity, showed that in *Deaths Duell* "sermon, preacher, and parishioner dissolve together into a self-effacing and saving union" (70). Ten years later Helen Gardner, disagreeing with Fish's reading, nevertheless rejected the notion that *Deaths Duell* is an "example of his terrible morbidity. He was not deliberately shocking his hearers by describing things of which they had no experience" (1982a, 101). In another essay, she also denied Donne's morbidity in posing in his shroud: "I find it strange that the shrouded effigies that are so common in the mid-seventeenth century should be regarded as morbid or macabre" (1979, 36). Her conclusion is long overdue, since Donne's alleged morbidity often seems to point more to the critic's evasion of death than to any obsession Donne might have had.[33] That this was recognized even before the sixties is evident from a moving essay written by Evelyn Simpson in 1951. She accounted for the melancholy of Donne's later sermons (those written between 1625 and 1628) by showing that Donne had good reason for melancholy: Lucy Donne and a number of close friends died during these years (1951, 339–57). Others have related Donne's morbidity to the temper of his age or underplayed it.[34]

If the issue of Donne's attitude toward death and the grave cannot finally be resolved, it has encouraged some of the most idiosyncratic, outrageous, but simultaneously amusing commentary on Donne, especially in the first two or three decades of the century. Edmund Gosse, for example, called Donne's posing in his winding sheet "one of the grimmest freaks that ever entered into a pious mind" ([1981] 1930, 56). In addition, *Deaths Duell* is " 'creepy' " (59). Sir John Collings Squire, after visiting St. Paul's, said that Donne's effigy "is a queer, stark, frozen thing; there is no beauty about it, but a force that makes everything else in the Cathedral seem dead. The sculptor was not a great artist; but he must have been under the spell of Donne when he made it" (1920, 116). Finally, Laurence Housman, constructing a playlet of Donne's final days, has the dean's housekeeper bring his Shrove Tuesday pancakes. After Donne agrees to eat them, adding that it will be the last time, the housekeeper exclaims, " 'Tis always the last time with you, sir. If words could dig a man's grave, you'd have been in it five years ago" (1929, 254). Obviously, these examples have not contributed greatly to a better understanding of Donne, but perhaps they explain the fascination with which readers have approached Donne and with which they attempt to determine his attitudes and thoughts.

One final aspect of Donne's thought that has perplexed twentieth-century scholars is his attitude toward the "New Philosophy." The most judicious approaches bypass the question of whether Donne philosophically accepted or rejected the scientific discoveries of Copernicus, Tycho Brahe, Galileo, and Kepler, emphasizing instead that he used in his poetry images gleaned from new astronomical discoveries and the Ptolemaic universe much as Milton did in *Paradise Lost,* as well as using concepts from numerology and alchemy.[35] From Felix Schelling's statement in 1910 that Donne's adoption of scientific terms was the "natural utterance of a mind accustomed to think in technical terms" (368) to John Carey's seventy-one years later that Donne really did not care if the new theories were true so long as they provided speculation for his works (1981, 249–53), the view of Donne as an impartial reaper of images to illustrate rather than to demonstrate belief has been the most prevalent one.[36] Yet conflicting views about Donne's interest in the New Science and about the influence it had on him persist.[37]

Some of the most illuminating studies have focused on Donne's intense interest in, although not necessarily acceptance of, the New Science. Most outstanding in this area are Evelyn Simpson and Marjorie Hope Nicolson. Simpson says that "Donne stood almost alone among contemporary poets in his perception of the importance of the changes which scientific discovery was bringing about" ([1924] 1948, 118) and shows that he changed some of his imagery after reading Kepler (118–24). Nicolson agrees: "Of all the English poets, there was none who showed a more immediate response to the new discoveries than John Donne, nor is there in English literature a more remarkable example of the immediate effect of *Sidereus Nuncius,*" although she adds that the depth of his interest may be questioned (1935, 449).[38] These conclusions would seem quite modest, given Donne's statements that the "new Philosophy arrests the Sunne" (*"To the Countess of* Bedford," line 37) and the "New starres, and old do vanish from our eyes" (*First Anniversarie,* line 260). Since he was an educated man who described himself as one "diverted by the worst voluptuousness, which is an hydroptic, immoderate desire of human learning and languages—beautiful ornaments to great fortune" (Gosse [1899] 1959, 1 : 191), it seems reasonable to assume that Donne would employ these images with his usual energy and imagination in his poetry and prose.

Some, however, disagree that this is the case. Merritt Hughes, for example, writes: "Setting aside for a moment Donne's intellectual curiosity about the new science, we can make sure that in the depths of his soul he was unmoved by Copernicus" ([1934] 1975, 44). Since Hughes's primary purpose in this essay was objecting to the modern intellectual skeptic that Eliot and the New Critics had made of Donne, his objectivity may be questioned. But he illuminates some of the controversies involved in studying Donne and the New Science. First, he shows that Donne's references to the New Science can produce very different conclusions:

Among laymen, respect for his poetry sometimes proves to be founded upon the illusion that he was a pioneer of the Copernican astronomy in England. Even scholars are not entirely immune to the temptation. Mrs.

Simpson yields to it in some degree. . . . On the other hand, Miss Ramsey counters with the positive statement that Donne was never shaken in his belief in the Ptolemaic system.

In Donne's Sermons there are several passages which may be quoted against Miss Ramsey, but opinions about their real significance will differ. (42)

Hughes's own conclusion is that "from his first literary experiments until he wrote *Death's Duell,* Donne thought of the universe as the Ptolemaic machine pictured by St. Thomas and Dante, and that for him time began and ended with creation" (47). His main reason for reaching this conclusion raises the second complicating feature of studying Donne's alleged Copernican advocacy. "So much," Hughes says, "has been written about Donne's scientific curiosity and his skepticism that we wrap him up in our own modern scientific consciousness" (50). Thus opinions of Donne's scientific sympathies depend in part on the scholar's attitude toward his skepticism—not in this case his doubting of God or of man's churches but rather his epistemological skepticism, his supposed disbelief in man's ability to know.

But once again, opinions vary, with some believing the discoveries of Copernicus, Kepler, and Galileo profoundly influenced him, causing an intellectual skepticism, and others believing he was skeptical of the New Science because of his faith.

Subscribing to the first view, D. H. Roberts wrote in 1976 that Donne was concerned with the "epistemological crisis of the seventeenth century" (1976, 107). Like other "poet-scholars" of his time, he experienced a "growing skepticism about the possibilities of attaining with certainty, metaphysical knowledge" (99). Charles Coffin's position, almost forty years earlier, was similar: to Donne the "appeal to concrete experience" offered by the New Science "met with a sensitive response that argues how deeply the new revelations sank into the marrow of his understanding" (1937a, 81). But the clash between new and old theories of the universe caused Donne to question man's ability to know (103). As Coffin presents the situation, the discoveries by scientists and astronomers in the early seventeenth century caused a break between theology and natural science that had never before existed. Aware of this break, Donne surrendered himself to a wholly nonrational faith. If man could not know how the universe worked, he could not know anything (264). B. I. Evans's outline of Donne's intellectual progress differs in details but not in conclusions. He shows Donne accepting the New Science and the decay of the world wholeheartedly although eventually reasserting "a faith, Catholic in essence. . . . Yet even in this triumph the memory of the anatomizing intellect remains" ([1940] 1964, 47).[39]

In the opposing camp are those who believe that Donne was skeptical of the New Science because of his faith. Mahood's conclusion, for example, differs from Coffin's. Even if Donne in the *Anniversaries* had despaired at finding "a satisfying correspondence" between the physical and spiritual worlds such as Dante and Aquinas had found, by the time of his sermons he had outgrown this despair. They "show him still refusing to accept Bacon's partition of knowledge into the provinces of faith and of reason." Thus he came to view "the findings of the natural philosophies, however discordant with the Book of Genesis, as the symbols of spiritual truths" (1950, 152–53). Bethell agrees: "Donne was not a religious sceptic, but he was sceptical in matters of science . . . his doubts in the field of 'natural philosophy' only served to fortify his religious conviction" (1951, 87). Examples of this line of disagreement could be multiplied, but the point is that Donne's specific attitude toward the new astronomical theories and their specific influence on him remain elusive.

Most scholars of Donne have their own biases regarding his beliefs, but because his belief in the New Science is inextricably linked with so many other strains of Donne's thought, the verdict on the New Philosophy is not yet in. That is, in some studies, evidence about Donne's attitude toward the New Science is used to support a particular theory about his beliefs, but since this evidence is sketchy and often contradictory, it can be used to support almost any other hypothesis, and as such provides a fitting conclusion for the study of twentieth-century interpretations of Donne.

First, a study of his scientific beliefs can lend supporting evidence to contradictory views of Donne's theology. Haydn uses it to prove Donne's fideism; Woodhouse and Hassel to prove his reasoned faith.[40] It can be used (albeit almost exclusively by Empson) to show Donne's doubts about conventional Christianity.[41] It provides reasons for Donne's and his contemporaries' melancholy.[42] It can also explain his attitudes toward women.[43] Besides proving contradictory theories about Donne's thought, a study of his attitudes toward the New Science can be used to show his place in literary traditions, especially the baroque or mannerist styles, or conversely to show his poetic rebelliousness.[44] Those believing Donne is essentially medieval can maintain that he rejected the New Science, while those believing he is akin to the moderns show that he embraced it with open arms.[45] Furthermore, because Donne's supposed belief in the New Science often was used to link him with Eliot, those wishing to disagree with Eliot also used the New Science to dissolve the comparison. After severely criticizing Eliot's phrase "dissociation of sensibility," Stephen Orgel comments: "Donne's famous complaint . . . that 'the new philosophy calls all in doubt' may be an index of his extraordinary awareness; but the feelings generated in him by that awareness are neither inevitable nor justified, logically or dramatically" (1971, 240–41).[46] Finally, Donne's attitude toward the New Science plays a role in biographical speculations, to show his *angst,* his reasons for delaying or finally accepting ordination, or his ambition.[47]

The controversy over Donne's philosophical acceptance of the New Science thus can serve as an epitome of Donne scholarship as a whole. As he does in his letters, Donne provides just enough information to tantalize the reader but not enough to commit himself to a position. As it is possible to see in Donne's letters to his father-in-law, George More, both a contrite, anguished newlywed and a pompous, tactless upstart, so is it possible to see in the *Anniversaries* or *Ignatius his Conclave* a wholehearted supporter of Copernicus and a medievally trained mind distressed by the changing world. Following their practice in other areas of Donne scholarship, the New Critics exploited the poet's seeming doubts about the world to reshape him in their own image, whereas those reacting against the New Critics, while sometimes remaking him to challenge New Critical theories, more often provided a balanced view of the poet. Furthermore, the difficulty of deciding why Donne used scientific imagery is paralleled by the difficulty of determining his literary heritage.

Thus studies of Donne's attitudes toward women, religion, and science clarify and simultaneously confuse critical attitudes toward him. Evidence for both acceptance and rejection of a variety of beliefs, theories, and observations exists, and emphasizing one side over the other, here as in other areas of Donne scholarship, has made that scholarship at once illuminating and problematic.

# Conclusion

Of major English poets, only Shakespeare has had attached to his works more contradictory theories and interpretations than Donne has had attached to his. But whereas Shakespeare has always enjoyed an elevated status, Donne's reputation has suffered during years when he was not accepted as a "competent" poet. Although Donne's reputation has been relatively high since the mid-nineteenth century, the criticism leveled against him by such notable writers as Ben Jonson and Samuel Johnson has had an impact on twentieth-century studies. Furthermore, while biographical studies of Shakespeare's plays and poems have continued, the fact that so much more is known about Donne's life than about Shakespeare's makes biographical studies of Donne's works at once more tantalizing and harder to dismiss. Add to biographical speculation the New Critics' adoption of Donne in order to lend authority and tradition to their own interpretive theories, and it is easy to see why Donne's critical history in the twentieth century has been complex.

The fascinating but seemingly contradictory facts of Donne's life and the sometimes-confessional nature of his poetry have generated their share of idiosyncratic criticism. One author idolizes Donne for his "sincere," passionate feeling; another is angry with Donne for "buying" patronage with extravagant poems or for verifying New Critical theories or for deserting Catholicism; still another is outraged with Donne's death pose or his apparent egocentricity in the religious poems or love lyrics. However, this kind of criticism, while appearing more often than one might like, does not constitute a majority in critical assessments of Donne's life and work. Such scholars as R. C. Bald, Helen Gardner, Louis Martz, John Shawcross, Evelyn Simpson, A. J. Smith, and many others have made outstanding contributions to an understanding of Donne's biography, poetry, and prose. Nevertheless, as the preceding pages have shown, even these scholars sometimes succumb to an emphasis on one feature of Donne's works to the unfortunate exclusion of other equally important features or to a protest against the New Criticism that faults Donne in the process or to an unsubstantiated biographical interpretation of the poetry. John Roberts, who has read more Donne criticism than any other scholar, also recognizes this peculiarity in Donne studies: "I often feel that many

161

books and essays on Donne tell me more about the critics writing them than they do about Donne's poetry" (1982, 60).

That Donne, a major poet and complex personality, has attracted a great deal of critical commentary is to be expected; it would be naive to suppose that scholars can agree on the "meaning" of his poems any more than they can on the "meaning" of *The Wife of Bath's Prologue, Astrophil and Stella,* or "Upon Appleton House," not to mention such works as *Hamlet* and *The Wasteland*. However, to quote Roberts again:

> Although we may be inclined to smile at the utter naiveté of some of our predecessors and may feel even comfortably liberated from their seemingly quaint moral and quixotic literary judgments, perhaps we should resist congratulating ourselves too uncritically and too hastily; for, although often rich and indeed exciting, the enormous body of scholarship and criticism that has been produced on Donne during the past fifty years has not necessarily moved us toward a general consensus about the precise qualities and merits of his poetry. Although we tend to agree that Donne is a major poet, we tend to disagree on exactly what accounts for his greatness or wherein his greatness lies. Therefore, what we have is a mass of criticism that continues to grow but often seems bewildering and even contradictory. (1982, 59)

What then is the future of Donne studies? Some believe all that can be said of Donne's poetry has already been said—a belief reminiscent of Eliot's fifty-seven years ago: "Donne's poetry is a concern for the present and the recent past rather than of the future" (1931, 5). Roberts believes the best course is to return Donne to his readers without, however, abandoning "intellectually demanding and highly sophisticated literary approaches to Donne," if those help elucidate Donne's poetry (66); that is, Roberts wants critics to make "Donne's poetry more, not less accessible to an even wider reading audience than he enjoys at the present time" (67).

One potential obstacle that could stand in the way of Roberts's goal is the theoretical structure proposed by the *avant garde* critics of the seventies and eighties. It is perhaps fortunate for Donne's accessibility that these theorists, who certainly do not write for a wide audience, have largely ignored his poetry. There have been a few reader-response and structuralist evaluations but not many. Since, then, these critics show no particular interest in Donne, there is little danger that they too will kidnap him.

In a more traditional mode of criticism, John Carey's biography of Donne, published in 1981, is certainly one of the most readable books on the poet in recent years and has stimulated controversy on Donne once again, if not among the general reading public then at least among scholars whose primary field of interest is not necessarily seventeenth-century poetry. Unfortunately, however, if Carey's book makes Donne's poetry more accessible to readers, it does so in the context of some odd, often-unacceptable preconceptions about his personality and character. What happens, then, as Patrick Cullen notes, is that Carey returns, obviously with more sophistication and evidence, to the kinds of reactions to Donne that were possible before Eliot and his generation adopted the poet (1982, 171). But even more important, Carey makes Donne into what he wants him to be, and it is this tendency that has plagued Donne criticism for decades.

Fortunately, however, more and more scholars are acknowledging this tendency to create a Donne who fits preconceived notions. Such recognition may encourage scholars to avoid interpreting poetry and letters according to what they want his character to be. For example, Ilona Bell has recently revised the received view of three letters in the Burley manuscript. Arguing that these are not typical Petrarchan compliments to Donne's patronesses, as Evelyn Simpson believed, Bell shows that they may, in fact, be Donne's letters to Anne before their marriage (1986, 25–52). Differing in kind from Milgate and LeComte's disagreement about the marriage date, Bell's view of the letters relies not so much on an interpretation of Donne's character as on a careful reading of the texts with an eye to epistolary conventions.

John Shawcross's "The Argument and Order of Donne's Poems" provides another good example of recent Donne scholarship. Arguing that the order of poems in seventeenth-century manuscripts may contribute to how these poems are read, Shawcross defends this position with a wealth of textual evidence. His theory may eventually cause us to reevaluate our thinking about some of Donne's poems. For example, if three lyrics are grouped together, then, if two are biographical, the third has to be. Equally, if one is judged to be nonbiographical, all three are. Other poems may change their familiar designations as satires, elegies, lyrics (1986, 119–63). These and other studies that depend on biographical, historical, and textual facts rather than on assumptions about Donne's personality will provide a clearer perception of Donne's life, letters, and poetry.

An improved perception, however, may be all that we can achieve, for Donne—who posed for at least five portraits and who adopted countless roles in his poetry—may remain elusive, donning a variety of masks in his personal letters, his poetry, his sermons, and his life.

# Notes

## Introduction

1. See also Stephen Greenblatt, who says, "in the sixteenth century there appears to be an increased self-consciousness about the fashioning of human identity as a manipulable, artful process." Furthermore, "self-fashioning derives its interest precisely from the fact that it functions without regard for a sharp distinction between literature and social life" (1980, 2–3).

## Chapter 1. The Image of Donne from 1633 to 1897

1. See chapter 2 for a fuller discussion of this.

2. All subsequent citations of Donne's poetry will be from this edition, edited by John T. Shawcross, and will be cited parenthetically by line number in the text and will refer to John Donne 1967a.

3. John Shawcross writes that lines 12–16 are probably autobiographical, "although in this poem such background does not alter our reading" (1986, 61).

4. Arthur Nethercot also notes Donne's possible critical comment and his conventional stance (1922a, 469).

5. Most of the pre-twentieth-century commentary on Donne's writings and biography can be found in A. J. Smith's *John Donne: The Critical Heritage* (1975). His book is organized by name and century of the commentator, making entries easy to find. Throughout this book, however, I am citing the originals, unless otherwise noted.

6. Clay Hunt believes Donne's references to his own poems, "even before he came to regret them as early indiscretions, seem guarded and oblique, and apologetic beyond the conventional deprecatory pose of the Renaissance gentleman toward his literary work." He adds that in the letter to Garrard "Donne winces at the criticism of his two Anniversaries" (1954, 180, 251n.).

7. Walter Bate indicates that Johnson marked in his books those passages he wished to use; however, "the illustrative quotations proved far too bulky. Many had to be cut; while still others were added—often from Johnson's own memory" (1955, 26).

8. Samuel Johnson quotes these lines almost word for word; however, in both stanzas he omits the short second line that breaks an otherwise near perfect couplet. In addition, Johnson changes line 10 of "Goe, and catche a falling starre" by adding "see" between "to" and "strange"—an addition which regularizes the meter.

9. Arthur Symons, despite these comments, is not generally favorable toward Donne's poetry.

10. See two major Donne biographies, Edmund Gosse's *Life and Letters* ([1899] 1959, 1:63, and 2:342) and John Carey's *Life, Mind and Art* (1981, 272). A. J. Smith comments: "Johnson's account of Donne and the 'metaphysical' poets . . . was long taken as a definitive dismissal and his analysis of the 'metaphysical' style is still sometimes offered for received truth" (1975, 214).

11. See Frank Warnke (1955, 160–75) and James Mirollo (1963, 244–45), who both dispute the association of Donne and Marino.

12. See A. J. Smith, who says the change in attitudes toward Donne "happened very abruptly" in the last years of the eighteenth century (1975, 18). Kathleen Tillotson, arguing against the idea that Donne was " 'discovered' " in the first decade of the twentieth century,

shows that the period from 1835 to 1875 was as important to Donne's recovery as the late nineteenth century. Unlike Smith, she describes this period as "rather one of a gradual (though not steady) recovery than of a revolutionary discovery" ([1959] 1975, 20). See also Joseph Duncan, who details the increasing numbers of metaphysical poems in nineteenth-century anthologies (1959, 29–30).

13. A. J. Smith points out this connection (1975, 265).

14. See, however, Sidney Gottlieb's (1983) convincing analysis of the "defensiveness" of these elegies.

15. Chapter 5 explores in more detail the controversies about Donne's supposed libertinism.

16. Leigh Hunt describes the elegy "On his Mistress" as containing the "fine ghostly image" of Donne "dissuading his wife from going with him . . . and hopes she will not start in her sleep at night fancying him slain" (1862, 1:148).

17. See Ralph Waldo Emerson (1965, 5:341); Elizabeth Barrett Browning (1842, 522); Thomas deQuincey (1897, 10:101); Dante Gabriel Rossetti (1895, 2, 356); and Sarah Orne Jewett (1911, 60).

## Chapter 2. "I did best when I had least truth": Biographical Criticism

1. See R. C. Bald (1970, 64) and John Carey (1981, 20) for two conflicting views on this.

2. According to Bald (1970), *Satyres 1* and *2* were written while Donne was at Lincoln's Inn (77); *Satyre 3* in 1596 (72); *Satyre 4* in 1597 (86); and *Satyre 5* during his employment by Egerton (100). See *The Complete Poetry* (Donne 1967a, 415) for a different dating of the *Satyres* by John Shawcross.

3. See Louis Bredvold (1924, 160) for an opposing view.

4. According to Bald, Donne may have been one of the attendants who waited outside Essex House when only the councillors were admitted, and he probably assisted the Lord Keeper in examining witnesses and preparing for the trial (1970, 112–13).

5. Egerton said, according to Walton, that "though he was unfeignedly sorry for what he had done, yet it was inconsistent with his place and credit, to discharge and readmit servants at the request of passionate petitioners" ([1670] 1927, 30).

6. For a conflicting view of this traditional story, see Helen Gardner (1979, 29–44).

7. For a fuller discussion of this, see Clement Wyke (1976, 805–19).

8. I am not talking here about Gosse's importance as the publisher of Donne's letters or as the corrector of Walton: his importance in these areas is indisputable. But the effect of his biographical interpretations of the poems on later scholarship has been neglected.

9. See, for examples of the more recent ones, Roger Sharrock (1972, 42–46); S. W. Dawson, Harriet Hawkins, and Roger Elliott (1974, 94–104); Helen Thomas (1976, 183–89); and George Nitchie (1979, 16–21).

10. Not to be confused with Rochester who was also Robert Ker.

11. Donne's statement seems one of the most provocative that a poet has ever made about his work, and it is odd that even more attention has not been devoted to it. Those who do deal with it assume that they rank as best the same poems that Donne did and ignore the double implication of "least"—that is, that some have more truth and that all have some. See, for example, Leah Jonas (1940, 207); J. B. Leishman (1951, 56); Doniphan Louthan (1951, 166); Helen Gardner (1952, xxxvii); "Diverging on Donne" (1972, 1581); and Murray Roston (1974, 7).

12. Raoul Granqvist (1986) argues that Gosse wrote on Donne because he knew Donne was becoming fashionable and that, in fact, Gosse genuinely disliked Donne (see especially pp. 163–64 and 266–67).

13. Gosse means two years: Donne entered the ministry in 1615; Anne died in 1617.

14. Joseph Duncan comments that the "later nineteenth century was fascinated" by the paradoxes in Donne's life (1953a, 661).

15. "The Anagram" can be seen as an exception, although the poet is here telling someone else to "Marry, and love thy *Flavia.*" Several poems may contain puns on Anne More's name, but that is far from certain.

16. For additional comments on Donne's simplicity or lack of it, see also Frederic Carpenter (1909, lvii–lviii); and W. J. Courthope (1903, 3:166).

17. Herbert Grierson identifies these poems as "Sweetest love," "A Valediction: of weeping," "A Valediction: forbidding mourning," "The Canonization," "The Anniversary," and "Elegie: On his Mistris."

18. See also Arthur Quiller-Couch ([1918] 1930, 95–96).

19. Donne himself, of course, began this distinction in a letter to Robert Ker in 1619 that accompanied a copy of *Biathanatos*. He says of the book: "Let any that your discretion admits to the sight of it know the date of it; and that it is a book written by Jack Donne, and not by Dr. Donne" (Gosse [1899] 1959, 2:124).

20. As late as 1926, F. W. Payne, arguing for a biographical reading of the *Songs and Sonets*, says that "there are in the collection poems—unquotable here—which prove that Donne had such experiences" ([1926] 1969, 59).

21. Although Horace Eaton's interest in Donne's sensuality is not unusual, his contention that Donne expresses a "universal mood" is contrary to what most early twentieth-century critics said about Donne's poetry.

22. George Philip Krapp says Donne's delay shows his unwillingness to investigate his feelings toward the profession (1915, 207). See also J. J. Jusserand (1909, 1:421). Felix E. Schelling says his delay reveals Donne's open-mindedness, his ability to see a number of different religious alternatives (1910, 364).

23. See, for example, Frederic Carpenter (1909, lviii).

24. See, for example, Alfred Kazin (1962, 113–18); Nathaniel Weyl (1959, 17); and Peter Viereck (1959, 92–103).

25. It should be noted that Crofts objects specifically to Eliot's praise of Donne.

26. John Sparrow uses this elegy as part of his argument for dating Donne's travels.

27. Twelve years later, Arthur Marotti still maintained that "Donne located the poem's thematic material in an autobiographical context" (1986, 198).

28. Another exception is Alec Brown, who insists that it is only the poet's moaning for the year that is gone rather than for an actual woman (1933, 29).

29. For an exception, see Clay Hunt (1954, viii).

30. See also *The Complete Poetry* (Donne 1967a, 402).

31. Although "Since she whome I lovd" is usually assumed to be about Anne, Donne, unlike Milton in "Me Thought I Saw My Late Espoused Saint," makes no mention of the woman's specific relationship to him.

32. See, for example, Edward LeComte's biography (1965, 55).

33. See, for example, Marius Bewley (1952, 633); Herbert Grierson (1948, 307); and John Carey (1981, 31–32). Grierson, however, is very sympathetic to Donne's position.

34. Some exceptions are Robert Hillyer, who is sympathetic to Donne but points to the influence of his mother in Donne's seeking a position at court (1941, xxi–xxii); L. C. Knights, who sees Donne's "separation" from his mother when she remarried as the cause of his feelings of nothingness (1974, 113); and Leslie Fiedler, who, in exploring the value of biographical interpretation, relates "mummy" in "Loves Alchemie" to Donne's mother and to the "greater Mother, the Roman Church" (1952, 266). The OED, incidentally, does not confirm the maternal meaning of "mummy" in Donne's lifetime.

35. For another set of completely opposite interpretations by these two biographers, see John Carey (1981, 75) and R. C. Bald (1970, 268). Anthony Low comments on the differences between these two biographies, as well as several others; these differences are often the result of an author's own sympathies and mind set (1983, 111–15).

36. See Annabel Patterson (1982) for a discussion of other of Donne's letters.

## Chapter 3. Donne Refashioned: Eliot and the New Critics

1. I use the term in its strict sense in that I mean those who treat literature as an object in itself and use close analyses to interpret it without reference to biography or history. I use it in a loose sense in that I have not, in general, distinguished various theories within this very broad "school," and I have used it to mean both American and English critics, although I realize that technically it refers only to the former. In that sense, it is a term of convenience.

2. The term is A. J. Smith's ([1960] 1962, 174).

3. Edward LeComte gives a complete list of these titles (1965, 237–38).

4. Richard Garnett and Edmund Gosse made the previous charge ([1903] 1904, 2:292).

5. See also, for example, Arthur Nethercot (1922a, 473; 1925a, 132); Affable Hawk (1923, 660); R. L. Megroz (1926, 47); Ashley Sampson (1936, 308); and Theodore Spencer (1939, 3).

6. It is interesting that Sona Raiziss in 1952 still accepts these parallels as valid.

7. See Joseph Duncan (1959, 163–64) for a fuller discussion of this.

8. See F. R. Leavis (1931, 346) and Cleanth Brooks (1939, 74) for two examples.

9. See, especially, chapters 5 and 6.

10. This practice has continued sporadically into the sixties. See, for example, A. Alvarez (1961). In his last chapter, he downgrades Spenser and the Petrarchans for not being Donne.

11. See, especially, "Seventeenth-Century Verse" (1934, 741–42); Louis Untermeyer (1938, 13–18); S. L. Bethell (1948, 83–85); and William Van O'Connor (1948, 92).

12. Actually, the sonnet is not "nominally" about anyone.

13. See, for example, E. M. W. Tillyard's *The Elizabethan World Picture* (1943a) and "A Note on Donne's *Extasie*" (1943b).

14. Three appear in the 1936 edition.

15. See, especially, pp. 140–44 and 327–28.

16. See, for example, F. O. Matthiessen (1947, 150–51) and Cleanth Brooks (1939, 65–67).

17. For an extreme example, see Sacheverell Sitwell (1930).

18. See also Robert Gorham Davis et al. (1949, 514).

19. In "The Metaphysical Man: John Donne" (1959) Louis Untermeyer professes an appreciation of Donne's poetry, but his scholarship is so shoddy that his praise seems mere lip service to a fad. See, especially, pp. 124–25.

20. See, for example, F. W. Bateson (1951; 1952); Harold Wendell Smith (1951); Eric Thompson (1952); A. E. Malloch (1953); Robert Martin Adams (1954); Arnold Stein (1960); F. M. Kuna (1963); and Haskell M. Block (1967).

21. For a similar example, see J. B. Leishman (1951, 99–100).

22. See, for example, Leslie Fiedler (1952, 253–56); Roger Sharrock (1972, 35); and Patrick Cullen (1982, 171).

23. The phrase is Helen Gardner's, in the introduction to *John Donne: A Collection of Critical Essays* (1962, 9).

24. Marius Bewley's thesis is more closely and carefully argued eighteen years later in a revised version of this essay (1970).

25. Helen Gardner disagrees with Cleanth Brooks's argument that because of ambiguity and paradox the babe represents both innocence and vengeance. Instead, "it is the judgement of the human heart that Macbeth fears here, and the punishment which the speech foreshadows is not that he will be cut down by Macduff but that having murdered his own humanity he will enter into a world of appalling loneliness of meaningless activity, unloved himself, and unable to love" (1959b, 61).

26. The title further reflects A. J. Smith's disagreement with the New Critics, parodying as it does the title of Eliot's 1931 essay.

27. Donne, of course, nowhere claims that his poetry is new.

28. See, for example, Henry Wells ([1924] 1961); Robert Sharp (1935); Milton Rugoff (1939); and Alice Brandenburg (1942).

# Chapter 4. Donne and Literary Tradition

1. For two such exceptions, see J. S. Harrison (1903, 141–66) and Ernest Rhys ([1913] 1973, 196–99). Rhys maintains that Donne took some ideas from Sidney, Spenser, Quarles, and the Fletchers.

2. See also George Williamson (1931, 155–76).

3. This is the date of Merritt Hughes's essay "Kidnapping Donne." See text below.

4. See, for example, Herbert Read (1923, 256); Beatrice Johnson (1928, 1098–1109); Elizabeth Holmes (1929, 1–2); and Douglas Bush ([1932] 1963, 118). Read believes Donne's "philosophical spirit" derives from Dante and the early Italian poets; Johnson discusses Donne's classical allusions; Holmes finds a direct connection between the Elizabethan poets

and Donne; and Bush notes a similarity between Spenser's *Mutability Cantos* and Donne's *Anniversaries.*

5. See, for an example of this kind of treatment of Donne, Sacheverell Sitwell (1930).

6. Obviously, Donne's early education was Catholic, as that of many of his contemporaries was not. However, Donne, like many of his contemporaries, had a university education.

7. Lu Emily Pearson, in 1933—several years ahead of her time—also explores this connection ([1933] 1966).

8. Donald Guss's approach ignores the tradition of flea poems, which, Helen Gardner notes, were popular "all over Europe in the sixteenth century" (1965, 174). More recently, Anne Lake Prescott has shown Donne's affinities with Ronsard (1978, 115–16).

9. Dennis McKevlin notes the same objection to Andreasen's misreading of "The Extasie," which is due to her attempt to associate Donne exclusively with the Christian Platonism of Ficino" (1984, 80).

10. See, for example, N. J. C. Andreasen (1967, 130–90) and Patricia Garland Pinka (1982, 27–33).

11. The refrain is italicized in this edition by John Shawcross.

12. J. S. Harrison uses "Platonism" to mean that "body of thought" that "latter-day criticism has named Neo-platonism" (1903, viii).

13. See, for example, Clay Hunt, who shows that Donne attacks Neoplatonic thought (1965, 33–40); Eleanor McCann, who believes Donne's purpose in "The Extasie" is "to subvert the tradition of Platonic love" (1954, 127); and A. J. Smith, who demonstrates that Donne's poetry differs fundamentally from Neoplatonism (1972a, 89–131).

14. Gardner adds that if the poem is justifying physical love, then the arguments do not logically lead to the poem's concluding lines (1959a, 244).

15. Gardner defines "sex" in lines 31–32, "Wee see by this, it was not sexe, / Wee see, we saw not what did move," as "gender" (1959a, 252–53); that is, it was not their maleness and femaleness that caused their love. Not only does this reading contradict a majority of this poem's readers, but it also is at variance with the OED editor, who uses these lines to illustrate the first time "sex" was used to denote intercourse rather than gender.

16. See Stanley Archer for one example of disagreement with Helen Gardner's and Louis Martz's theories about the *Holy Sonnets*. He argues that these poems are instead modelled on the strophe, antistrophe, and epode of the Greek chorus (1961, 147).

17. See, for example, Rosalie Colie (1964, 165); Raymond Anselment (1971, 199); and Patrick Mahoney (1972, 235).

18. W. M. Lebans puts them into the tradition of classical funeral elegy and notes that this does not rule out the meditative tradition (1972, 552).

19. See also Mario Praz (1964, 175, 179); Austin Warren, who, however, is not interested in discussing Donne as a baroque poet (1939, 98–101); Wylie Sypher, who contends that Donne's baroque is different from Milton's and that Milton is in the mainstream of the baroque (1944, 3–7); and Frank Warnke, who sees Donne's metaphysical style as different from "High Baroque" style (1961, 3–6), but in a later essay points to similarities between the two (1967, 38–48).

20. Murray Roston states that mannerism finds "its fulfillment in self-criticism and in a refined, sensitive spirituality," and the baroque reaffirms "through its wealth and splendour the exclusive and unquestionable authority of Rome" (1974, 29).

21. See, for example, William Rooney ([1962] 1971, 386); George Levine (1971, 384–87); and Elaine Hoover (1978, 28ff.).

22. For the sake of brevity, I am limiting this discussion to Donne's poetry with only occasional references to his prose. However, much that I argue about the poetry is also applicable to his prose works.

23. Although a few writers classified by C. S. Lewis as "Golden" poets are "plain stylists" to Yvor Winters (Greville is probably the best example), in general the two categories overlap considerably. Furthermore, Lewis's definition of "Drab" writers (1954, 222) and Winters's of "plain stylists" ([1939] 1967, 95–96) are very similar.

24. See Heather Dubrow (1979, 77–83); John Peter (1956, 133, 299); and Emory Elliott (1976, 110).

25. Douglas Bush is an early example of one who believes he was not essentially Ovidian ([1932] 1963, 102, 232–33). For later examples, see Roma Gill (1973, 167–78); she argues that the best *Elegies* are not Ovidian. See also A. J. Peacock (1975, 20–29); he shows Donne's reliance on Ovid and others but concentrates on Donne's originality.

26. "The Message," "The Baite," "Communitie," "Confined Love," "The Expiration," "The Apparition," "Breake of day," "Song: Sweetest love, I do not goe," "Goe, and catche a falling starre."

27. See Rosalie Colie (1964, 154); Barbara Lewalski (1971, 46–47); and W. M. Lebans (1972, 545–46).

28. See Elizabeth Wiggins (1945, 41–42); Concetta Greenfield (1976, 427–28); and Thomas Sloan (1963, 31–44).

29. See Ronald McFarland (1977, 392); and Walter Beale (1976, 380–81).

30. See Elizabeth Wiggins (1945, 43); and John Mulder (1969, 42–47).

## Chapter 5. Donne's Views on Women, Religion, and Science

1. Although love poets are by nature egocentric in their love poems, the amount of criticism concentrating on Donne's egocentricity in the *Songs and Sonets* indicates that rightly or wrongly he seems to many more self-involved than Petrarch, Sidney, and others.

2. See William Empson (1981, 42–43); Christopher Ricks (1981, 7); and Gerald Guinness and Andrew Hurley (1986, 137–55).

3. J. B. Leishman (1934, 28–29); see also O. P. Titus (1942, 177); Helen Gardner (1965, xxvii–xxix); and Molly Mahood (1950, 105). Mahood argues that Donne's marriage changed him from a humanist to an antihumanist.

4. See also Richard Hughes (1968, 44–45).

5. See, for example, Theodore Redpath, who says that even in the most passionate of the *Songs and Sonets,* there are hints or overtones of cynicism: "This strengthens the poems: for just as when a hard man weeps it is impressive, so it is when a sceptical or cynical man loves" (1956, xxx); Lynne Molella, who argues that "the tension in 'A Lecture' is largely caused by Donne's ambivalent attitude toward the possibility of maintaining any ideal state in the world of change" (1962, 76); Barbara Everett, who says that in both the cynical and mutual love poems, Donne adopts "that amiable rancour, that wary civility, that distinguishes the tone of English social convention" (1972, 18); and Dwight Cathcart, who argues that the speaker in the *Songs and Sonets* is cynical because he skeptically disregards the "identity of the 'you'" (1975, 45).

6. Other possibilities for linking these two areas of Donne's life are presented by Alan Porter, who argues that Donne was always more interested in the struggle than in the victory. Thus, in his *Sermons* Donne tries to talk himself into surrendering the world, but "he preached to himself as he wrote to himself. Even his love poems are self-involved. They were never written to win the favor of a lady" (1931, 539); and by J. B. Broadbent, who argues that in Donne's public poems Donne made a religion of women: "You can say they satisfied the latent Mariolatry of a lapsed Catholic" (1964, 230).

7. See, for example, F. W. Payne ([1926] 1969, 88); and Fletcher Henderson (1937, 280).

8. See Ernest Sprott (1950, 339–41); Louis Bredvold (1923, 499–502); and George Williamson (1934, 279).

9. John Klause maintains that Donne's *Metempsychosis* was directly inspired by Donne's reading Montaigne's *Essais* (1986, 431–33). These encouraged Donne to question and doubt (442). Although he kept reading them late into his life, he no longer relied on them (443).

10. See also Dennis Quinn ([1960] 1971, 358).

11. Terry Sherwood (1972) quotes Donne: "*Knowledge* cannot save us, but we cannot be saved without Knowledge; Faith is not on this side of Knowledge, but beyond it; we must necessarily come to *Knowledge* first" ("Preached at Saint Pauls upon Christmasse day, 1621," in Donne 1962, 3:359). See also Irving Lowe (1961, 389–92).

12. Evelyn Simpson says that Donne is neither completely medieval nor completely modern.

13. See, for example, Michael Moloney (1944, 15, 73, 105); and John Moore (1936, 290).

14. See, for example, Dennis Quinn (1969, 626–32); Patrick Grant (1971, 544–49); and Achsah Guibbory (1980, 261–65).

15. See Dennis Quinn (1962, 313–29); Gerard Cox III (1973, 331–51); and Joan Webber (1963, 123–42).

16. For three who do not take up this question and deny Donne's mysticism, see Robert Collmer (1961, 33–33); René Graziani (1968, 124); and Bruce Henrickson (1972, 5).

17. Eleanor McCann relates Donne's "Extasie" directly to Teresa's *Vida* (1954, 125–32).

18. See also Arthur Quiller-Couch ([1918] 1930, 130).

19. For exceptions, see Elbert Thompson (1921, 192–94); Robert George (1925, 28–83); and R. L. Mégroz (1926, 47–51).

20. Oddly, most who have recently believed in Donne's mysticism are Japanese scholars. Elizabeth McLaughlin, who sees a parallel between Donne and mystics (1970, 77–78), and Robert Jackson, who does not use the term, but advocates a Donne who "hopes to contact God directly" (1970, 34) are two exceptions.

21. This sentence does not appear in Douglas Bush's first edition, published in 1945.

22. Those who deny Donne's religious toleration include E. G. Lewis (1938, 255–58); Marius Bewley (1952, 621–22); and Clay Hunt (1954, 171–72).

23. See, for example, David Novarr (1980, 119); and Robert Jackson (1970, 146–48).

24. Edmund Gosse ([1899] 1959, 2:109–10); and Herbert Grierson (1912, 2:235–36). Grierson says that the sonnet reveals Donne, "already three years in orders, as still conscious of all the difficulties involved in a choice between the three divisions of Christianity" (235).

25. Marius Bewley and Clay Hunt are two exceptions.

26. See also John Carey (1981, 191–201).

27. See also Rose Macauley (1931, 84–91).

28. See Donald Roberts (1947, 973–74); and John Carey (1981, 191–226).

29. See also Robert Hillyer (1941, xx–xxi).

30. See also Arnold Stein (1946, 118); and Donald Roberts (1947, 975).

31. See D. W. Harding (1951, 433–38); and Robert Hillyer (1941, xxix).

32. See Theodore Spencer (1931, 180–95); and Arnold Stein (1944, 278–80).

33. See Terry Sherwood for a similar interpretation of Donne's death pose (1984, 193–95).

34. See Joan Bennett (1934, 36–38); and Helen White (1951a, 365; 1931, 254).

35. Edgar Hill Duncan (1942, 257–85); Joseph Mazzeo (1957, 103–23); and John Freccero (1963, 335–76).

36. See, for example, Evelyn Simpson ([1924] 1948, 130); Francis Johnson ([1937] 1968, 243); F. P. Wilson (1945, 10); Michael Roberts (1937, 88–90); and Douglas Bush (1950, 33–35).

37. I use the term "New Science" to mean the astronomical discoveries about the position and motions of the earth and sun. Although Copernicus's theories were not new in Donne's time, they were becoming visually real—and often disturbing—because of the discovery and increasing use of the telescope.

38. See also Marjorie Nicolson (1950, 170–74). In both studies, Nicolson demonstrates Donne's progress from indifference and even rejection of the New Science in *Ignatius his Conclave* to interest in his later works. Others who demonstrate Donne's interest in the New Science include F. R. Johnson ([1937] 1968, 243); and Robert Ellrodt (1964, 187–90). Others disagree that Donne was as interested in the New Science as Nicolson and Simpson suggest, but they agree that he used the imagery. See Herschel Baker (1952, 59); and Ralph Crum ([1931] 1966, 42–47).

39. See also Hiram Haydn ([1950] 1966, 652).

40. Hiram Haydn ([1950] 1966, 23, 113–15); A. S. P. Woodhouse (1965, 48); and R. Chris Hassel, Jr. (1971, 329–37).

41. William Empson (1930b, 73–84, 133–83; 1957, 337–99).

42. George Williamson (1935, 121–50); and Arnold Stein (1944, 269–80).

43. Charles Coffin, broadening his definition of the New Science to include a new philosophy bent on overthrowing Medieval rationalism and attempting "to revise the conception of the nature of knowledge and to discover the ultimate grounds of truth" (1937a, 214), shows that Donne's inclination "to look realistically at a subject ridden by convention and falsified by romantic illusion" fits exactly his acceptance of the "new philosophy" (221–22).

44. Molly Mahood (1950, 145–53); Murray Roston (1974, 18–19, 212); and Patrick Cruttwell (1954, 50–55).

45. Those on the medieval side include George Shuster (1940, 83–84); Frank Kermode (1957a, 13–15); Michael Macklem (1958, 93); and John Thomas (1976, 91). Those on the modern side include Maurice Evans (1955, 174–75); Mario Praz (1931, 61); Robert Adams (1954, 286–89); and Josephine Miles (1971, 218–19).

46. See also J. E. V. Crofts ([1937] 1962, 86–89); E. M. W. Tillyard (1943a, 108); and Douglas Bush (1950, 33–36).

47. O. P. Titus (1942, 176–77); Judah Stampfer (1970, 33n.); and John Carey (1981, 248–53).

# Works Cited

Adams, Robert Martin. 1954. "Donne and Eliot: Metaphysicals." *Kenyon Review* 16:278–91.

Affable Hawk [Desmond MacCarthy, pseud.]. 1923. "Books in General." *The New Statesman* 20:660.

Aiken, Conrad. 1919. "The Ivory Tower: Louis Untermeyer As Critic." In *Scepticisms: Notes on Contemporary Poetry*, 258–71. New York: Alfred A Knopf.

Aikin, John. 1810. *Vocal Poetry: Or A Select Collection of English Songs*. London: J. Johnson.

Alden, Raymond MacDonald. 1917. "The Lyrical Conceit of the Elizabethans." *Studies in Philology* 14:129–52.

———. 1920. "The Lyrical Conceits of the 'Metaphysical Poets.'" *Studies in Philology* 17:183–98.

Alford, Henry, ed. 1839. *The Works of John Donne, D. D., Dean of St. Paul's, 1621–1631, with a Memoir of his Life*. London: John W. Parker, West Strand.

Allen, Don Cameron. 1941. "Donne's Suicides." *Modern Language Notes* 56:129–33.

Alvarez, A. 1961. *The School of Donne*. London: Chatto and Windus.

Andreasen, N. J. C. 1967. *John Donne: Conservative Revolutionary*. Princeton: Princeton University Press.

Anselment, Raymond A. 1971. "'Ascensio Mendax, Descensio Crudelis': The Image of Babel in the *Anniversaries*." *ELH* 38:188–205.

Archer, Stanley. 1961. "Meditation and the Structure of Donne's 'Holy Sonnets.'" *ELH* 28:137–47.

Bailey, John. 1920. "The Sermons of a Poet." *Quarterly Review* 233:317–28.

Baker, Herschel. 1952. *The Wars of Truth: Studies in the Decay of Christian Humanism in the Earlier Seventeenth Century*. Cambridge: Harvard University Press.

Baker, Richard. 1643. *A Chronicle of the Kings of England from the Time of the Romans Government unto the Raigne of our Soveraigne Lord King Charles*. London.

Bald, R. C. [1932] 1965. *Donne's Influence in English Literature*. Morpeth: St. John's College Press, 1932. Reprint. Gloucester, Mass.: Peter Smith, 1965.

———. 1959. *Donne and the Drurys*. Cambridge: Cambridge University Press.

———. 1970. *John Donne: A Life*. Edited by Wesley Milgate. London: Oxford University Press.

Bate, Walter Jackson. 1955. *The Achievement of Samuel Johnson*. New York: Oxford University Press.

Bateson, F. W. 1951. "Contributions to a Dictionary of Critical Terms. II. Dissociation of Sensibility." *Essays in Criticism* 1:302–12.

———. 1952. "The Critical Forum: 'Dissociation of Sensibility.'" *Essays in Criticism* 2:213–14.

Battenhouse, Roy W. 1942. "The Grounds of Religious Toleration in the Thought of John Donne." *Church History* 11:217–48.

Beale, Walter H. 1976. "On Rhetoric and Poetry: John Donne's 'The Prohibition' Revisited." *Quarterly Journal of Speech* 62:376–86.

Bell, Ilona. 1983. "The Role of the Lady in Donne's *Songs and Sonets.*" *Studies in English Literature* 23:113–29.

———. 1986. " 'Under Y$^e$ Rage of a Hott Sonn & Y$^r$ Eyes': John Donne's Love Letters to Ann More." In *The Eagle and the Dove,* 25–52. See Claude J. Summers and Ted-Larry Pebworth 1986.

Bell, Robert. *Lives of the Most Eminent Literary and Scientific Men of Great Britain.* Vol. 1. London: Longman, Orme, Brown, Green, and Longmans.

Bellew, John Chippendall Montesquieu. 1868. *Poet's Corner. A Manual for Students in English Poetry.* London: George Routledge and Sons.

Benham, Allen R. 1941. "The Myth of John Donne the Rake." In *Renaissance Studies in Honor of Hardin Craig,* edited by Baldwin Maxwell et al., 273–81. Stanford: Stanford University Press.

Bennett, Joan. 1934. *Four Metaphysical Poets: Donne, Herbert, Vaughan, Crashaw.* Cambridge: Cambridge University Press.

———. [1938] 1962. "The Love Poetry of John Donne. A Reply to Mr. C. S. Lewis." In *Seventeenth Century Studies Presented to Sir Herbert Grierson.* Oxford: Clarendon Press, 1938. Reprint in *Seventeenth-Century English Poetry,* 1st ed., 111–31. See William Keast [1962] 1971.

Benson, Donald R. 1971. "Platonism and Neoclassic Metaphor: Dryden's *Eleonora* and Donne's *Anniversaries.*" *Studies in Philology* 68:340–56.

Bernard, John. 1972. "Orthodoxia Epidemica: Donne's Poetics and 'A Valediction: Of My Name in the Window.' " *South Atlanta Quarterly* 71:377–89.

Bethell, S. L. 1948. "Two Streams from Helicon." In *Essays on Literary Criticism and the English Tradition,* 53–87. London: Dennis Dobson.

———. *The Cultural Revolution of the Seventeenth Century.* London: Dennis Dobson.

Bewley, Marius. 1952. "Religious Cynicism in Donne's Poetry." *Kenyon Review* 14:619–46.

———. 1970. "The Mask of John Donne." In *Masks and Mirrors: Essays in Criticism,* 3–49. New York: Atheneum. [Revised version of 1952 essay.]

Block, Haskell M. 1967. "The Alleged Parallel of Metaphysical and Symbolist Poetry." *Comparative Literature Studies* 4:145–59.

*Book of the Poets, Chaucer to Beattie.* 1842. London: Scott, Webster and Geary.

Borgerhoff, E. B. O. 1953. " 'Mannerism' and 'Baroque': A Simple Plea." *Comparative Literature* 5:323–31.

Brandenburg, Alice Stayert. 1942. "The Dynamic Image in Metaphysical Poetry." *PMLA* 57:1039–45.

Bredvold, Louis I. 1923. "The Naturalism of Donne in Relation to Some Renaissance Traditions." *Journal of English and Germanic Philology* 22:471–502.

———. 1924. "Sir T. Egerton and Donne." *TLS,* 13 March, 160.

———. 1925. "The Religious Thought of Donne in Relation to Medieval and Later Traditions." In *Studies in Shakespeare, Milton and Donne,* University of Michigan Publications, Language and Literature, no. 1, 191–232. New York and London: Macmillan.

Broadbent, J. B. 1964. *Poetic Love.* London: Chatto and Windus.

Brooke, Rupert. [1913] 1973. "John Donne." *Poetry and Drama* 1 (1913): 185–88. Reprint in *Donne, Songs and Sonets,* 100–104. See Julian Lovelock 1973.

Brooks, Cleanth. 1939. *Modern Poetry and the Tradition.* Chapel Hill: University of North Carolina Press.

———. [1942] 1947. "The Language of Paradox." In *The Language of Poetry,* edited by Allen Tate, 37–61. Princeton: Princeton University Press, 1942. Reprint in *The Well Wrought Urn: Studies in the Structure of Poetry,* 3–21. New York and London: Harcourt Brace Jovanovich, 1947.

———. "Milton and the New Criticism." *Sewanee Review* 59:1–22.

————, and Robert Penn Warren. 1938. *Understanding Poetry: An Anthology for College Students.* New York: Henry Holt.

————, John Thibaut Purser, and Robert Penn Warren. [1936] 1952. *An Approach to Literature: A Collection of Prose and Verse with Analyses and Discussions.* 3d ed. 1936. Reprint. Baton Rouge: Louisiana State University Press, 1952.

Brown, Alec. 1933. "Some Notes on Scientific Criticism in Connection with the Clarendon Edition of Donne." *Dublin Magazine* 8(2): 20–31.

Browning, Elizabeth Barrett. 1842. Anonymous review of *Book of the Poets. Athenaeum* no. 763, 11 June, 522.

Bullough, Geoffrey. 1962. "The Poetry of the Soul's Instruments During the Renaissance." In *Mirror of Minds: Changing Psychological Beliefs in English Poetry,* 1–47. Toronto: University of Toronto Press; London: Athlone Press.

Bush, Douglas. [1932] 1963. *Mythology and the Renaissance Tradition in English Poetry.* Minneapolis: University of Minnesota Press; London: Humphrey Milford, Oxford University Press, 1932. Reprint. New York: W. W. Norton, 1963.

————. [1945] 1962. *English Literature in the Earlier Seventeenth Century, 1600–1660.* 1945. 2d. ed., rev., Oxford: Oxford University Press, 1962.

————. 1950. "The New Science and the Seventeenth-Century Poets." In *Science and English Poetry: A Historical Sketch, 1590–1950,* 27–50. New York: Oxford University Press.

————. 1952. *English Poetry: The Main Currents from Chaucer to the Present.* New York: Oxford University Press.

————. 1958. "Tradition and Experience." In *Literature and Belief,* English Institute Essays, 1957, edited by M. H. Abrams, 31–52. New York: Columbia University Press.

Campbell, Thomas. 1875. *Cyclopaedia of English Poetry. Specimens of the British Poets: Biographical and Critical Notices, and An Essay on English Poetry.* 2d ed. Philadelphia: J. B. Lippincott.

Carey, John. 1963. "John Donne." *Time and Tide* 44(14): 24, 36.

————. 1981. *John Donne: Life, Mind and Art.* London and Boston: Faber and Faber.

Carpenter, Frederic Ives. 1909. Introduction to *English Lyric Poetry, 1500–1700,* edited by C. H. Herford, lvi–lx. London: Blackie and Son.

Cathcart, Dwight. 1975. *Doubting Conscience: Donne and the Poetry of Moral Argument.* Ann Arbor: University of Michigan Press.

Cattermole, Richard. 1844. *The Literature of the Church of England.* Vol. 1. London: John W. Parker.

Chalmers, Alexander, ed. 1810. *The Works of the English Poets from Chaucer to Cowper in 21 Volumes.* Vol. 5. London: J. Johnson; J. Nichols and Son; R. Baldwin et al.

Chambers, Robert. [1843] 1902. *Chambers Cyclopaedia of English Literature.* Vol. 1. 1843. Reprint. Edited by David Patrick. Philadelphia: J. B. Lippincott, 1902.

Clive, Mary. 1966. *Jack and the Doctor.* London: Macmillan; New York: St. Martin's Press.

Coffin, Charles M. 1937a. *John Donne and the New Philosophy.* Morningside Heights, N.Y.: Columbia University Press.

————. 1937b. "Donne's Astronomy." *TLS,* 18 September, 675.

————, ed. 1952. *The Complete Poetry and Selected Prose of John Donne.* New York: Modern Library.

Coleridge, Samuel Taylor. [1836] 1967. *The Literary Remains of Samuel Taylor Coleridge.* Vol. 1. Edited by Henry Nelson Coleridge. 1836. Reprint. New York: AMS Press, 1967.

————. 1853. *Notes, Theological, Political, and Miscellaneous.* London: Edward Moxon.

————. 1955. *Coleridge on the Seventeenth Century.* Edited by R. F. Brinkley. Durham, N.C.: Duke University Press.

————. 1969. *The Collected Works of Samuel Taylor Coleridge, The Friend.* Vol. 1. Edited by Barbara E. Rooke. London: Routledge and Kegan Paul.

Colie, Rosalie L. 1964. "The Rhetoric of Transcendence." *Philological Quarterly* 43:145–70.

———. 1966. *Paradoxia Epidemica: The Renaissance Tradition of Paradox.* Princeton: Princeton University Press.

Collmer, Robert G. 1961. "The Meditation on Death and Its Appearance in Metaphysical Poetry." *Neophilologus* 45:323–33.

Corrigan, Robert A. 1969. "Ezra Pound and the Bollingen Prize Controversy." In *The Forties: Fiction, Poetry, Drama,* edited by Warren French, 287–95. Deland, Fla.: Everett/Edwards.

Courthope, W. J. 1903. *History of English Poetry.* Vol. 3. London: Macmillan.

Cousins, A. D. 1979. "The Coming of Mannerism: The Later Ralegh and the Early Donne." *English Literary Renaissance* 9:86–107.

Cox, Gerard H., III. 1973. "Donne's *Devotions:* A Meditative Sequence on Repentance." *Harvard Theological Review* 66:331–51.

Crofts, J. E. V. [1937] 1962. "John Donne." *Essays and Studies* of 1936, 22 (1937): 128–43. Reprint as "John Donne: A Reconsideration." In *A Collection of Critical Essays,* 77–89. See Helen Gardner 1962.

Crum, Ralph B. [1931] 1966. "Poetry and the New Science." In *Scientific Thought in Poetry.* New York: Columbia University Press, 1931. Reprint. New York: AMS Press, 1966, 40–60.

Cruttwell, Patrick. 1954. *The Shakespearean Moment and Its Place in the Poetry of the 17th Century.* London: Chatto and Windus.

———. 1970. "The Love Poetry of John Donne: Pedantique Weedes or Fresh Invention?" In *Metaphysical Poetry,* edited by Malcolm Bradbury and David Palmer, 11–39. Bloomington and London: Indiana University Press.

Cullen, Patrick. 1982. "Recent Studies in the Renaissance." *Studies in English Literature* 22:157–85.

Cunningham, Francis, ed. 1875. *The Works of Ben Jonson.* 9 vols. Vol. 9. London: Bickers and Son.

Dark, Sidney. 1928. *Five Deans: John Colet, John Donne, Jonathan Swift, Penrhyn Stanley, William Ralph Inge,* 54–108. New York: Harcourt, Brace and Co.

Datta, Kitty. 1977. "Love and Asceticism in Donne's Poetry: The Divine Analogy." *Critical Quarterly* 19(2): 5–25.

Davis, Robert Gorham, et al. 1949. "The Question of the Pound Award." *Partisan Review* 16:344–47, 512–22.

Dawson, S. W., Harriet Hawkins, and Roger Elliott. 1974. "As We Read the Living?" *Essays in Criticism* 24:94–104.

Dean, John. 1972. "The Two Arguments of Donne's 'Air and Angels.'" *Massachusetts Studies of English* 3:84–90.

deQuincey, Thomas. 1897. *The Collected Writings of Thomas deQuincey.* Vol. 10. Edited by David Masson. London: A & C Black.

De Silva, D. M. 1971. "John Donne—An Un-metaphysical Perspective." *Ceylon Journal in Humanities* 2:3–14.

"Diverging on Donne." 1972. *TLS,* 29 December, 1581–82.

Divine, May D. 1973. "Compass and Circle in Donne's 'A Valediction: Forbidding Mourning.'" *Papers on Language and Literature* 9:78–80.

Doebler, Bettie Anne. 1972. "Donne's Incarnate Venus." In *Essays in the Renaissance in Honor of Allan H. Gilbert,* edited by Philip J. Traci and Marilyn L. Williamson. *South Atlanta Quarterly* 71(4): 502–12.

Doggett, Frank A. 1934. "Donne's Platonism." *Sewanee Review* 42:274–92.

Donne, John. [1633] 1970. *Poems with Elegies on the Author's Death.* 1633. Reprint. The English Experience, no. 240. New York: Da Capo Press, 1970.

———. 1962. *The Sermons of John Donne.* 10 vols. Edited by Evelyn M. Simpson and George R. Potter. Berkeley and Los Angeles: University of California Press.

———. 1967a. *The Complete Poetry of John Donne.* Edited by John T. Shawcross. Garden City, N.Y.: Doubleday.

———. 1967b. *John Donne: Selected Prose.* Chosen by Evelyn Simpson. Edited by Helen Gardner and Timothy Healy. Oxford: Clarendon Press.

"Donne's Poetry." 1956. *TLS,* 27 April, 253.

Douds, John Boal. 1937. "Donne's Technique of Dissonance." *PMLA* 52:1051–61.

Drake, Nathan. [1838] 1969. *Shakespeare and His Times.* 1838. Reprint. New York: Burt Franklin, 1969.

Dryden, John. [1693] 1958. *A Discourse Concerning the Original and Progress of Satire.* 1693. In *The Poems of John Dryden.* Vol. 2. Edited by James Kinsley. Oxford: Oxford University Press.

Dubrow, Heather. 1979. " 'No man is an island': Donne's Satires and Satiric Traditions." *Studies in English Literature* 19:71–83.

Duncan, Edgar Hill. 1942. "Donne's Alchemical Figures." *ELH* 9:257–85.

Duncan, Joseph E. 1953. "The Revival of Meatphysical Poetry, 1872–1912." *PMLA* 68:658–71.

———. 1959. *The Revival of Metaphysical Poetry: The History of a Style, 1800 to the Present.* Minneapolis: University of Minnesota Press.

Eaton, Horace Ainsworth. 1914. "*The Songs and Sonnets* of John Donne." *Sewanee Review* 22:50–72.

Eliot, T. S. 1921. "The Metaphysical Poets." *TLS,* 20 October, 669–70.

———. 1926a. "Lancelot Andrewes." *TLS,* 23 September, 621–22.

———. 1926b. "Note sur Mallarmé et Poe." Translated by Ramon Fernandez. *Nouvelle Revue Francaise* 27:524–26.

———. 1930. "Thinking in Verse: A Survey of Early Seventeenth-Century Poetry." *The Listener* 3:441–43.

———. 1931. "Donne in Our Time." In *A Garland for John Donne,* 3–19. See Theodore Spencer 1931.

———. 1952. *The Complete Poems and Plays, 1909–1950.* New York: Harcourt, Brace, and World.

———. 1957. *On Poetry and Poets.* New York: Farrar, Straus, and Cudahy.

Elliott, Emory. 1976. "The Narrative and Allusive Unity of Donne's *Satyres.*" *Journal of English and Germanic Philology* 75:105–16.

Ellrodt, Robert. 1964. "Scientific Curiosity and Metaphysical Poetry in the Seventeenth Century." *Modern Philology* 61:180–97.

Emerson, Ralph Waldo, ed. 1875. *Parnassus.* Boston: James R. Osgood.

———. 1965. *The Journals and Miscellaneous Notebooks of Ralph Waldo Emerson.* Vol. 5. Edited by Merton M. Sealts, Jr. Cambridge, Mass.: Belknap Press.

Empson, William. [1930]a 1962. *Seven Types of Ambiguity.* London: Chatto and Windus, 1930. Reprint in *A Collection of Critical Essays,* 52–60. See Helen Gardner 1962.

———. 1930b. *Some Versions of Pastoral.* London: Chatto and Windus.

———. 1957. "Donne the Space Man." *Kenyon Review* 19:337–99.

———. 1966. "Donne in the New Edition." *Critical Quarterly* 8:255–80.

———. 1967. "Donne." *Critical Quarterly* 9:89.

———. 1981. " 'There Is No Penance Due to Innocence.' " *New York Review of Books* 28, no. 19 (3 December) 42–50.

Evans, B. Ifor. [1940] 1964. "Donne to Milton." In *Tradition and Romanticism Studies in English Poetry from Chaucer to W. B. Yeats.* London: Methuen; New York: Longmans, Green and Co., 1940. Reprint. London and Hamden, Conn.: Archon Books, 1964, 44–60.

Evans, Maurice. 1955. "Donne and the Elizabethans." In *English Poetry in the Sixteenth Century,* 161–75. London: Hutchinson's University Library.

Everett, Barbara. 1972. *Donne: A London Poet.* From the Proceedings of the British Academy, Vol. 58. London: Oxford University Press.

Fausset, Hugh I'Anson. 1931. "The Poet and His Vision." *The Bookman* (London) 79:341–42.

Ferriar, John. 1813. *An Essay Towards a Theory of Apparitions,* London: J. and J. Haddock.

Ferry. Anne [D.] 1975. *All in War with Time: Love Poetry of Shakespeare, Donne, Jonson, Marvell.* Cambridge: Harvard University Press.

Fiedler, Leslie. 1952. "Archetype and Signature: A Study of the Relationship Between Biography and Poetry." *Sewanee Review* 60:253–73.

Fiore, Peter Amadeus. 1972. "John Donne Today." In *Just So much Honor: Essays Commemorating the Four-Hundredth Anniversary of the Birth of John Donne,* 1–8. Edited by Peter A. Fiore. University Park and London: Pennsylvania State University Press.

Fish, Stanley E. 1972. *Self-Consuming Artifacts: The Experience of Seventeenth-Century Literature.* Berkeley, Los Angeles, London: University of California Press.

Flynn, Dennis. 1986. "Donne the Survivor." In *The Eagle and the Dove,* 15–24. See Claude J. Summers and Ted-Larry Pebworth 1986.

Forsythe, R. S. 1925. "The Passionate Shepherd; and English Poetry." *PMLA* 40:692–742.

Fox, Ruth A. 1971. "Donne's *Anniversaries* and the Art of Living." *ELH* 38:528–41.

Freccero, John. 1963. "Donne's 'Valediction: Forbidding Mourning.' " *ELH* 30:335–76.

Friederich, Reinhard H. 1978. "Expanding and Contracting Space in Donne's *Devotions.*" *ELH* 45:18–32.

Gardner, Helen, ed. 1952. *The Divine Poems.* Oxford: Clarendon Press.

———. 1956. "Donne and the Church." *TLS,* 25 May, 320.

1957. "Another Note on Donne: 'Since she whome I lov'd.' " *Modern Language Review* 52:564–65.

———. [1959a] 1975. "The Argument about 'The Ecstasy.' " In *Elizabethan and Jacobean Studies,* 279–306. Oxford: Clarendon Press, 1959. Reprint in *Essential Articles,* 239–58. See John Roberts 1975.

———. 1959b. "Interpretation." In *The Business of Criticism,* 52–75. Oxford: Clarendon Press.

———, ed. 1962. *John Donne: A Collection of Critical Essays.* Englewood Cliffs, N.J.: Prentice-Hall.

———. ed. 1965. *John Donne: The Elegies and The Songs and Sonnets.* Oxford: Clarendon Press.

———. 1979. "Dean Donne's Monument in St. Paul's." In *Evidence in Literary Scholarship: Essays in Memory of James Marshall Osborn,* edited by René Wellek and Alvaro Ribeiro, 29–44. Oxford: Clarendon Press.

———. 1982a. *In Defence of the Imagination.* Cambridge: Harvard University Press.

———. 1982b. " 'A Nocturnal upon St. Lucy's Day, being the shortest day.' " In *Poetic Traditions of the English Renaissance,* edited by Maynard Mack and George deForest Lord, 181–201. New Haven and London: Yale University Press.

———, and J. B. Leishman. 1956. "Poetic Tradition in Donne." *TLS,* 11 May, 283.

Garnett, Richard, and Edmund Gosse. [1903] 1904. *English Literature, An Illustrated Record in Four Volumes.* Vol. 2. London: Heinemann, 1903. Reprint. New York: Grosset and Dunlap, 1904.

*Gems of Sacred Poetry.* 1841. Vol. 1. London: Standidge and Co.

George, Robert Esmonde Gordon. 1925. *Outflying Philosophy: A Literary Study of the Religious Element in the Poems and Letters of John Donne and in the Works of Sir Thomas Browne and of Henry Vaughan the Silurist.* London: Simpkin, Marshall and Co.

Gill, Roma. 1973. "As We Read the Living? An Argument." *Essays in Criticism* 23:167–78.

Goldberg, M. A. 1956. "Donne's 'A Lecture Upon the Shadow.' " *Explicator* 14, Item 50.

Gosse, Edmund. [1891] 1930. *Gossip in a Library.* 1891. Reprint. New York: Lovell, Coryell, and Co., 1930.

———. [1899] 1959. *The Life and Letters of John Donne, Dean of St. Paul's.* Dodd, Mead, and Co., 1899. Reprint. Gloucester, Mass.: Peter Smith, 1959.

———. 1921. "The Sepulchral Dean." In *Books on the Table,* 185–89. London: William Heinemann.

———. 1923. "Metaphysical Poetry." In *More Books on the Table,* 307–13. New York: Charles Scribner's Sons.

Gottlieb, Sidney. 1983. "*Elegies upon the Author:* Defining, Defending, and Surviving Donne." *John Donne Journal* 2:23–38.

Granger, James. [1769] 1775. *A Biographical History of England, from Egbert the Great to the Revolution.* Vol. 1. 2d ed. 1769. Reprint. London, 1775.

Granqvist, Raoul. 1986. "Edmund Gosse: The Reluctant Critic of John Donne." *Neuphilologische Mitteilungen* 87:262–71.

Gransden, K. W. 1954. *John Donne.* London and New York: Longmans, Green, and Co.

Grant, Patrick. 1971. "Augustinian Spirituality and the *Holy Sonnets* of John Donne." *ELH* 38:542–61.

Graziani, René. 1968. "John Donne's 'The Extasie' and Ecstasy." *Review of English Studies* 19:121–36.

Greenblatt, Stephen. 1980. *Renaissance Self-Fashioning: From More to Shakespeare.* Chicago and London: University of Chicago Press.

Greenfield, Concetta C. 1976. "Principles of Coherence in Spenser and Donne." *Lingua e Stile* 11:427–38.

Grierson, Sir Herbert J. C. 1909. *Cambridge History of English Literature, IV,* 196–223. Cambridge: Cambridge University Press.

———, ed. 1912. *The Poems of John Donne.* Oxford: Oxford University Press.

———, ed. 1921. *Metaphysical Lyrics & Poems of the Seventeenth Century: Donne to Butler.* Oxford: Clarendon Press.

———. 1929. "Love Poetry." In *Cross Currents in English Literature of the XVIIth Century.* London: Chatto and Windus.

———. 1943. "A Spirit in Conflict." *Spectator* 170:293.

———. 1948. "John Donne and the 'Via Media.' " *Modern Language Review* 43:305–14.

Groom, Bernard. 1955. "The Spenserian Tradition and Its Rivals up to 1660." In *The Diction of Poetry from Spenser to Bridges,* 48–73. Toronto: University of Toronto Press; London: Geoffrey Cumberlege, Oxford University Press.

Grosart, Alexander B., ed. 1872. *The Complete Poems of John Donne, D.D.* London: Robson and Sons.

*The Guardian.* 1713. 30 March, no. xvi.

Guibbory, Achsah. 1980. "John Donne and Memory as 'the Art of *Salvation.*' " *Huntington Library Quarterly* 43:261–74.

Guiney, Louise I. 1920. "Donne as a Lost Catholic Poet." *The Month* 136:13–19.

Guinness, Gerald. 1986. "Playing for Life in Donne's Elegies, Songs and Sonnets." In *Auctor Ludens: Essays on Play in Literature,* edited by Gerald Guinness and Andrew Hurley, 137–55. Philadelphia: Benjamins.

Guss, Donald L. 1966. *John Donne, Petrarchist: Italianate Conceits and Love Theory in The Songs and Sonets.* Detroit: Wayne State University Press.

Harding, D. W. 1951. "Coherence of Theme in Donne's Poetry." *Kenyon Review* 13:427–44.

Hardison, O. B. 1962. "The Idea of Elizabeth Drury." In *The Enduring Monument: A Study* in the *Idea of Praise in Renaissance Literary Theory and Practice*, 163–86. Chapel Hill: University of North Carolina Press.

Hardy, Barbara. 1977. "Thinking and Feeling in the Songs and Sonnets of John Donne." In *The Advantage of Lyric: Essays on Feeling in Poetry*, 18–32. Bloomington: Indiana University Press; London: Athlone Press.

Hardy, Evelyn. 1942. *Donne: A Spirit in Conflict*. London: Constable and Co.

Harris, Victor. 1949. *All Coherence Gone*. Chicago: University of Chicago Press.

Harrison, J. S. 1903. *Platonism in English Poetry of the 16th and 17th Centuries*. New York: Columbia University Press.

Hassel, R. Chris, Jr. 1971. "Donne's *Ignatius His Conclave* and the New Astronomy." *Modern Philology* 68:329–37.

Haydn, Hiram. [1950] 1966. *The Counter Renaissance*. New York: Charles Scribner's Sons, 1950. Reprint. Gloucester, Mass.: Peter Smith, 1966.

Hazlitt, William. [1818, 1819] 1930. *Lectures on the English Poets* [1818] and *Lectures on the Comic Writers* [1819]. Reprint in *The Complete Works of William Hazlitt*, vols. 5 and 6, edited by P. P. Howe. London: J. M. Dent and Sons, 1930.

Henderson, Fletcher Orpin. 1937. "Traditions of *Précieux* and *Libertin* in Suckling's Poetry." *ELH* 4:274–98.

Henrickson, Bruce. 1972. "Donne's Orthodoxy." *Texas Studies in Literature and Language* 14:5–16.

Herz, Judith Scherer. 1986. " 'An Excellent Exercise of Wit That Speaks So Well of Ill': Donne and the Poetics of Concealment." In *The Eagle and the Dove*, 3–14. See Claude J. Summers and Ted-Larry Pebworth 1986.

Hester, M. Thomas. 1978. " 'All our Soules Devotion': Satire as Religion in Donne's *Satyre III*." *Studies in English Literature* 18:35–55.

———. 1982. *Kinde Pitty and Brave Scorn: John Donne's Satyres*. Durham, N.C.: Duke University Press.

Hillyer, Robert Silliman. 1941. Introduction to *The Complete Poetry and Selected Prose of John Donne and The Complete Poetry of William Blake*. New York: Modern Library.

———. 1949. "Treason's Strange Fruit." *Saturday Review of Literature* 32 (11 June): 9–11, 28.

Holman, C. Hugh. 1980. *A Handbook to Literature*. 4th ed. Indianapolis: Bobbs-Merrill Educational Publishing.

Holmes, Elizabeth. 1929. *Aspects of Elizabethan Imagery*. Oxford: Blackwell.

Hoover, L. Elaine. 1978. *John Donne and Francisco de Quevedo: Poets of Love and Death*. Chapel Hill: University of North Carolina Press.

Housman. A. E. 1933. *Name and Nature of Poetry*. New York: Macmillan; Cambridge, England: University Press.

Housman, Laurence. 1929. *Cornered Poets. A book of Dramatic Dialogues*, 237–56. London: Jonathan Cape.

Hughes, Merritt Y. 1932. "The Lineage of 'The Extasie.' " *Modern Language Review* 27:1–5.

———. [1934] 1975. "Kidnapping Donne." *University of California Publications in English* 4 (1934): 61–89. Reprint in *Essential Articles*, 37–57. See John Roberts 1975.

———. 1958. "The Seventeenth Century." In *Contemporary Literary Scholarship: A Critical Review*, edited by Lewis Leary, 67–82. New York: Appleton-Century-Crofts.

———. [1960] 1975. "Some of Donne's 'Ecstasies.' " *PMLA* 75 (1960): 509–18. Reprint in *Essential Articles*, 259–70. See John Roberts 1975.

Hughes, Richard E. 1965. "John Donne's 'Nocturnall Upon S. Lucies Day': A Suggested Resolution." *Cithara* 4(2): 60–68.

———. 1968. *The Progress of the Soul: The Interior Career of John Donne*. New York: William Morrow.

Hume, David. [1778] 1983. *The History of England from the Invasion of Julius Caesar to the Revolution in 1688.* 6 vols. Vol. 5. 1778. Reprint. N.p.: Liberty Classics, 1983.

Hunt, Clay. 1954. *Donne's Poetry: Essays in Literary Analysis.* New Haven: Yale University Press.

Hunt, Leigh. 1862. *The Correspondence of Leigh Hunt.* Vol. 1. Edited by Thorton Hunt. London: Smith, Elder and Co.

Hunter, Jim. 1965. *The Metaphysical Poets.* Literature in Perspective. London: Evans Brothers.

Huntington, John. 1977. "Philosophical Seduction in Chapman, Davies, and Donne." *ELH* 44:40–59.

Hurd, Richard. 1753. *Q. Horatii Flacci Epistola ad Augustum. With an English Commentary and Notes To which is added a Discourse Concerning Poetical Imitation.* Vol. 2. London: n.p.

Husain, Itrat. 1938. *The Dogmatic and Mystical Theology of John Donne.* London: Society for Promoting Christian Knowledge; New York: Macmillan.

———. 1948. *The Mystical Element in the Metaphysical Poets of the Seventeenth Century.* Edinburgh: Oliver and Boyd.

Ince, Richard. 1939. *Angel from a Cloud Wherein Is Presented the Romantic Career of John Donne.* London: Massie.

Jackson, Robert S. 1968. " 'Doubt Wisely': John Donne's Christian Skepticism." *Cithara* 8(1): 39–46.

———. 1970. *John Donne's Christian Vocation.* Evanston, Ill.: Northwestern University Press.

Jameson, Anna Murphy. [1829] 1857. *Memoirs of the Loves of the Poets.* 1829. Reprint. Boston: Ticknor and Fields, 1857.

Jenkins, Raymond. 1923. "Drayton's Relation to the School of Donne, as Revealed in the *Shepheards Sirena.*" *PMLA* 38:557–87.

Jessopp, Augustus. 1897. *John Donne: Sometime Dean of St. Paul's.* London: Methuen.

Jewett, Sarah Orne. 1911. *Letters of Sarah Orne Jewett.* Edited by Annie Fields. Boston: Houghton Mifflin.

"John Donne and His Contemporaries." 1900. *Quarterly Review* 192:217–40.

Johnson, Beatrice. 1928. "Classical Allusions in the Poetry of Donne." *PMLA* 43:1098–1109.

Johnson, Francis R. [1937] 1968. "The Quest for Physical Confirmation of the Earth's Motion." In *Astronomical Thought in Renaissance England: A Study of the English Scientific Writings from 1500 to 1645.* Baltimore: Johns Hopkins Press; London: Humphrey Milford, Oxford University Press, 1937. Reprint. New York: Octagon Books, 211–47, 1968.

Johnson, Samuel. [1755] 1967. *A Dictionary of the English Language in Two Volumes.* Vol. 2. London: W. Straham, 1755. Reprint. New York: AMS Press, 1967.

———. 1825. *The Works of Samuel Johnson, LL.D.* Vol. 7. Oxford: Talboys and Wheeler.

Jonas, Leah. 1940. "John Donne." In *The Divine Science: The Aesthetic of Some Representative Seventeenth-Century English Poets.* Columbia University Studies in English and Comparative Literature, 151, pp. 201–10. New York: Columbia University Press.

Jonson, Ben. 1966. *Notes of Conversations with Ben Jonson made by William Drummond of Hawthornden, January 1619.* In *Discoveries, Conversations with William Drummond of Hawthornden,* edited by G. B. Harrison. Elizabethan and Jacobean Quartos. New York: Barnes and Noble.

Jusserand, J. J. 1909. *A Literary History of the English People.* Vol. 1, 420–32. London: G. P. Putnam's Sons.

Kazin, Alfred. 1962. "The Youngest Man who Ever Was." In *Contemporaries,* 113–18. Boston and Toronto: Little, Brown.

Keast, William R. 1950. "Johnson's Criticism of the Metaphysical Poets." *ELH* 17:59–70.

———, ed. [1962] 1971. *Seventeenth-Century English Poetry: Modern Essays in Criticism.* 1962. 2d ed., rev. New York: Oxford University Press, 1971.

Kermode, Frank. 1957a. *John Donne.* Writers and Their Works, No. 86. London: Longmans, Green, and Co.

———. 1957b. "Dissociation of Sensibility." *Kenyon Review* 19:169–94.

———. 1971. *Shakespeare, Spenser, Donne: Renaissance Essays.* London: Routledge and Kegan Paul; New York: Viking.

Kerrigan, William W. 1974. "The Fearful Accommodations of John Donne." *English Literary Renaissance* 4:337–63.

———. 1987. "What Was Donne Doing?" *South Central Review* 4(2): 2–15.

Kippus, Andrew. [1973] 1974. *Biographia Britannica.* Vol. 5. 1793. Reprint. New York: Georg Olms Verlag Hildesheim, 1974.

Klause, John. 1986. "The Montaigneity of Donne's *Metempsychosis.*" In *Renaissance Genres: Essays on Theory, History, and Interpretation,* edited by Barbara Kiefer Lewalski, 418–43. Cambridge: Harvard University Press.

Knights, L. C. 1974. "All or Nothing: A Theme in John Donne." In *William Empson: The Man and His Work,* edited by Roma Gill, 109–16. London: Routledge and Kegan Paul.

Krapp, George Philip. 1915. *The Rise of English Literary Prose.* New York: Oxford University Press.

Kuna, F. M. 1963. "T. S. Eliot's Dissociation of Sensibility and the Critics of Metaphysical Poetry." *Essays in Criticism* 13:241–52.

Lander, Clara. 1971. "A Dangerous Sickness Which Turned to a Spotted Fever." *Studies in English Literature* 11:89–108.

Lang, Andrew. 1912. *History of English Literature from 'Beowulf' to Swinburne.* London: Longmans, Green, and Co.

Leavis, F. R. 1931. "The Influence of Donne on Modern Poetry." *The Bookman* (London) 79:346–47.

———. [1935] 1936. "English Poetry in the Seventeenth Century." *Scrutiny* 4 (1935): 236–56. Reprint in *Revaluation: Tradition and Development in English Poetry,* 10–41. London: Chatto and Windus, 1936.

———. 1936. "Milton's Verse." In *Revaluation: Tradition and Development in English Poetry,* 42–67. London: Chatto and Windus.

———. 1952. "Reality and Sincerity." *Scrutiny* 19:90–98.

———. 1969. " 'English'—Unrest and Continuity." *TLS,* 29 May, 509(3): 569–72.

Lebans, W. M. 1972. "Donne's *Anniversaries* and the Tradition of Funeral Elegy." *ELH* 39:545–59.

LeComte, Edward S. 1965. *Grace to a Witty Sinner: A Life of Donne.* New York: Walker.

———. 1968. "The Date of Donne's Marriage." *Etudes Anglaises* 21:168–69.

———. 1972. "Jack Donne: From Rake to Husband." In *Just So much Honor,* 9–32. See Peter Fiore 1972.

Legouis, Pierre. 1928. *Donne the Craftsman: An Essay upon the Structure of the Songs and Sonnets.* Paris: Henri Didier; London: Humphrey Milford and Oxford University Press.

Leishman, J. B. 1934. *The Metaphysical Poets: Donne, Herbert, Vaughan, Traherne.* Oxford: Clarendon Press.

———. 1950. "Was John Donne a Metaphysician?" *The Listener* 43:747–48.

———. 1951. *The Monarch of Wit: An Analytical and Comparative Study of the Poetry of John Donne.* London: Hutchinson University Library.

———. 1961. *Themes and Variations in Shakespeare's Sonnets.* London: Hutchinson and Co.

Levine, George R. 1971. "Satiric Intent and Baroque Design in Donne's 'Go and Catch a Falling Star.'" *Die neueren sprachen* 20:384–87.

Lewalski, Barbara K. 1971. "Donne's Poetry of Compliment: The Speaker's Stance and the Topoi of Praise." In *Seventeenth-Century Imagery: Essays on Uses of Figurative Language from Donne to Farquhar,* edited by Earl Miner, 45–67. Berkeley and Los Angeles: University of California Press.

———. 1973a. *Donne's 'Anniversaries' and the Poetry of Praise: The Creation of a Symbolic Mode.* Princeton: Princeton University Press.

———. 1973b. "A Donnean Perspective on 'The Extasie.'" *English Language Notes* 10:258–62.

Lewis, C. S. [1938] 1962. "Donne and Love Poetry in the Seventeenth Century." In *Seventeenth Century Studies Presented to Sir Herbert Grierson.* Oxford: Clarendon Press, 1938. Reprint in *A Collection of Critical Essays,* 90–99. See Helen Gardner 1962.

———. 1954. *English Literature in the Sixteenth Century.* Oxford: Oxford University Press.

Lewis, E. G. 1938. "The Question of Toleration in the Works of John Donne." *Modern Language Review* 33:255–58.

Louthan, Doniphan. 1951. *The Poetry of John Donne: A Study in Explication.* New York: Bookman Associates.

Love, Harold. 1966. "The Argument of Donne's *First Anniversary.*" *Modern Philology* 64:125–31.

Lovelock, Julian, ed. 1973. *Donne, Songs and Sonets: A Casebook.* London: Macmillan.

Low, Anthony. 1983. "John Carey and John Donne." *John Donne Journal* 2(1): 111–17.

Lowe, Irving. 1961. "John Donne: The Middle Way. The Reason-Faith Equation in Donne's Sermons." *Journal of the History of Ideas* 22:389–97.

Lynd, Robert. 1920. "John Donne." *London Mercury* 1:29–48.

McAdams, James R. 1972. "A Mixed Success." *JGE: Journal of General Education* 24:206–13.

McCann, Eleanor M. 1954. "Donne and St. Teresa on the Ecstasy." *Huntington Library Quarterly* 17:125–32.

Macaulay, Rose. 1931. "Anglican and Puritan." In *Some Religious Elements in English Literature,* 84–126. London: Hogarth Press.

McFarland, Ronald E. 1977. "Figures of Repetition in John Donne's Poetry." *Style* 11:391–406.

McGrath, Lynette. 1980. "John Donne's Apology for Poetry." *Studies in English Literature* 20:73–89.

McKevlin, Dennis S. 1984. *A Lecture in Love's Philosophy: Donne's Vision of the World of Human Love in 'Songs and Sonets.'* Lanham, Md.: University Press of America.

Macklem, Michael. 1958. *The Anatomy of the World: Relations Between Natural and Moral Law from Donne to Pope.* Minneapolis: University of Minnesota Press.

McLaughlin, Elizabeth. 1970. " 'The Extasie'—Deceptive or Authentic?" *Bucknell Review* 18(3): 55–78.

Mahoney, Patrick. 1969. "*The Anniversaries:* Donne's Rhetorical Approach to Evil." *Journal of English and Germanic Philology* 68:407–13.

———. 1972. "The Structure of Donne's *Anniversaries* as Companion Poems." *Genre* 5:235–56.

Mahood, Molly M. 1950. *Poetry and Humanism.* New York: W. W. Norton.

Malloch, A. E. 1953. "The Unified Sensibility and Metaphysical Poetry." *College English* 15:95–101.

Manley, Frank, ed. 1963. *John Donne: The Anniversaries.* Baltimore: The Johns Hopkins University Press.

Marilla, E. L. 1962. "Some Vagaries in Modern Literary Criticism: Some Instances Touching the Renaissance." In *Studies in English Renaissance Literature,* edited by Waldo F. McNeir, 168–80. Louisiana State University Studies. Humanities Series, no. 12. Baton Rouge: Louisiana State University Press.

Marotti, Arthur F. 1974. "Donne and 'The Extasie.' " In *The Rhetoric of Renaissance Poetry from Wyatt to Milton,* edited by Thomas O. Sloan and Raymond B. Waddington, 149–73. Berkeley: University of California Press.

———. 1986. *John Donne, Coterie Poet.* Madison: University of Wisconsin Press.

Martz, Louis L. 1947. "John Donne in Meditation: The *Anniversaries.*" *ELH* 14:247–73.

———. 1954. *The Poetry of Meditation: A Study in English Religious Literature of the Seventeenth Century.* Yale Studies in English, 125. New Haven: Yale University Press; London: Oxford University Press.

———. 1959. "Donne and the Meditative Tradition." *Thought* 34: 269–78.

———. 1960. "John Donne: The Meditative Voice." *Massachusetts Review* 1:326–42.

———. 1969. *The Wit of Love: Donne, Carew, Crashaw, Marvell.* Ward Phillips Lectures in English Language and Literature, 3. Notre Dame, Ind.: University of Notre Dame Press.

Matthiessen, F. O. 1947. *The Achievement of T. S. Eliot: An Essay on the Nature of Poetry.* New York and London: Oxford University Press.

Mauch, Katharine. 1977. "Angel Imagery and Neoplatonic Love in Donne's 'Air and Angels.' " *Seventeenth-Century News* 35:106–11.

Mazzeo, Joseph Anthony. 1957. "Notes on John Donne's Alchemical Imagery." *Isis* 48: 103–23.

Mégroz, R. L. 1926. "The Wit and Fantasy of Donne." *Dublin Magazine,* n.s. 1(2): 47–51.

Memorabilist. 1945. "Sir Richard Baker on John Donne." *Notes and Queries* 188:257.

Miles, Josephine. 1971. "Twentiety-Century Donne." In *Twentieth-Century Literature in Retrospect,* edited by Reuben Brower, 205–24. Harvard English Studies, no. 2. Cambridge: Harvard University Press.

Milgate, Wesley, ed. 1967. *John Donne: The Satires, Epigrams and Verse Letters.* Oxford: Clarendon Press.

———. 1969. "The Date of Donne's Marriage: A Reply." *Etudes Anglaises* 22:66–67.

———. 1972. " 'Aire and Angels' and the Discrimination of Experience." In *Just So much Honor,* 149–76. See Peter Fiore 1972.

Milman, Henry Hart, D.D. 1868. *Annals of S. Paul's Cathedral.* London: John Murray.

Mirollo, James V. 1963. *The Poet of the Marvelous: Giambattista Marino.* New York: Columbia University Press.

———. 1972. "The Mannered and the Mannerist in Late Renaissance Literature." In *The Meaning of Mannerism,* edited by F. W. Robinson and S. G. Nichols, 7–24. Hanover, N.H.: University Press of New England.

Molella, Lynne. 1962. "Donne's 'A Lecture upon the Shadow.' " *Thoth* 3:69–77.

Moloney, Michael F. 1944. *John Donne: His Flight from Mediaevalism.* Illinois Studies in Language and Literature, 29, no. 2–3. Urbana: University of Illinois Press.

Montgomery, James. 1828. *The Christian Poet.* 3d ed. Glasgow: W. Collins and Co.

*Monthly Review.* 1756. January–June, xiv, no. 91, 535.

Moore, John F. 1936. "Scholasticism, Donne and the Metaphysical Conceit." *Revue Anglo-Américaine* 13:289–96.

Morley, Christopher. 1926. "Every Tuesday." In *The Romany Stain,* 205–10. Garden City, N.Y.: Doubleday, Page and Co.

Mourgues, Odette de. 1953. *Metaphysical Baroque and Précieux Poetry.* Oxford: Clarendon Press.

Mueller, Janel M. 1968. "The Exegesis of Experience: Dean Donne's *Devotions upon Emergent Occasions.*" *Journal of English and Germanic Philology* 67:1–19.

———. 1972. "Exhuming Donne's Enigma." *Modern Philology* 69:231–49.

Mueller, William R. 1961. "Donne's Adulterous Female Town." *Modern Language Notes* 76:312–14.

———. 1962. *John Donne: Preacher.* Princeton: Princeton University Press.

Mulder, John R. 1969. *The Temple of the Mind: Education and Literary Taste in Seventeenth-Century England.* New York: Pegasus.

Nelson, Lowry J. 1961. "Poems of Donne." In *Baroque Lyric Poetry,* 121–37. New Haven and London: Yale University Press.

Nethercot, Arthur H. 1922a. "The Reputation of John Donne as Metrist." *Sewanee Review* 30:463–74.

———. 1922b. "The Term 'Metaphysical Poets' before Johnson." *Modern Language Notes* 37:11–17.

———. 1924. "The Reputation of the 'Metaphysical Poets' during the Seventeenth Century." *Journal of English and Germanic Philology* 23:173–98.

———. 1925a. "The Reputation of the 'Metaphysical Poets' during the Age of Johnson and the 'Romantic Revival.'" *Studies in Philology* 22:81–132.

———. 125b. "The Reputation of the 'Metaphysical Poets' during the Age of Pope." *Philological Quarterly* 4:161–79.

Nicolson, Marjorie Hope. 1935. "The 'New Astronomy' and English Literary Imagination." *Studies in Philology* 32:428–62.

———. 1950. *The Breaking of the Circle: Studies in the Effect of the "New Science" upon Seventeenth Century Poetry.* Evanston: Northwestern University Press.

Nitchie, George W. 1979. "Donne in Love: Some Reflections on 'Loves Alchemie.'" *Southern Review* 15:16–21.

Novarr, David. 1980. *The Disinterred Muse: Donne's Texts and Contexts.* Ithaca and London: Cornell University Press.

Nye, Robert. 1972. "The body is his book: the Poetry of John Donne." *Critical Quarterly* 14:345–60.

Orgel Stephen. 1971. "Affecting the Metaphysics." In *Twentieth Century Literature in Retrospect,* edited by Reuben Brower, 225–45. Harvard English Studies, no. 2. Cambridge: Harvard University Press.

Ornstein, Robert. 1956. "Donne, Montaigne, and Natural Law." *Journal of English and Germanic Philology* 55:213–29.

Ousby, Heather Dubrow. 1976. "Donne's 'Epithalamion made at Lincolnes Inne': An Alternative Interpretation." *Studies in English Literature* 16:131–43.

Palgrave, Francis Turner, ed. 1890. *The Treasury of Sacred Song.* Oxford: Clarendon Press.

———, ed. 1964. *The Golden Treasury of the Best Songs and Lyrical Poems in the English Language.* 5th ed. London: Oxford University Press.

Parish, John E. 1957. "Donne as a Petrarchan." *Notes and Queries,* n.s. 4:377–78.

Patterson, Annabel. 1982. "Misinterpretable Donne: The Testimony of the Letters." *John Donne Journal* 1:39–53.

Payne, F. W. [1926] 1969. *John Donne and his Poetry.* London: George G. Harrap, 1926. Reprint. Folcroft Press, 1969.

Peacock, A. J. 1975. "Donne's Elegies and Roman Love Elegy." *Hermathena* 119:20–29.

Pearson, Lu Emily. [1933] 1966. "John Donne's Love Lyrics." In *Elizabethan Love Conventions.* Berkeley: University of California Press; London: Cambridge University Press, 1933. Reprint. New York: Barnes and Noble, 1966, 223–30.

*The Penny Cyclopaedia of the Society for the Diffusion of Useful Knowledge.* 1837. Vol. 9. London: Charles Knight.

Peter, John. 1956. *Complaint and Satire in Early English Literature.* Oxford: Clarendon Press.

Peterson, Douglas L. 1959. "John Donne's *Holy Sonnets* and the Anglican Doctrine of Contrition." *Studies in Philology* 56:504–18.

——. 1967. *The English Lyric from Wyatt to Donne: A History of the Plain and Eloquent Styles.* Princeton: Princeton University Press.

Pinka, Patricia Garland. 1982. *This Dialogue of One: The "Songs and Sonnets" of John Donne.* Alabama: University of Alabama Press.

"Poetic Tradition in Donne." 1956. *TLS,* 16 March, 164.

"Poetic Tradition in Donne." 1956. *TLS,* 11 May, 283.

Porter, Alan. 1931. "Dean Donne." *Spectator* 146:539–40.

Potter, George Reuben. 1934. "John Donne's Discovery of Himself." *University of California Publications in English* 4:3–23.

——. 1936. "Donne's *Extasie,* Contra Legouis." *Philological Quarterly* 15:247–53.

——. 1941. "A Protest Against the Term *Conceit.*" In *Renaissance Studies in Honor of Hardin Craig,* edited by Baldwin Maxwell, et al, 282–91. Stanford: Stanford University Press.

Praz, Mario. 1931. "Donne's Relation to the Poetry of His Time." In *A Garland for John Donne,* 53–72. See Theodore Spencer 1931.

——. 1961. "Literary Resurrections." *English Studies* 42:357–62.

——. 1964. "Baroque in England." *Modern Philology* 61:169–79. Translated from "Il Barocco in Inghilterra." In *Mannerismo, Barocco, Rococo: Concetti e Termini.* Problemi Attuali di Scienza e di Cultura, No. 52, 129–46. Roma: Accademia Nazionale dei Lincei, 1962.

Prescott, Anne Lake. 1978. *French Poets and the English Renaissance: Studies in Fame and Transformation.* New Haven and London: Yale University Press.

Price, Daniel. 1613. *Tears Shed Over Abner, The Sermon Preached on the Sunday Before the Prince his funerall in St. James Chappell before the body.* Oxford: Joseph Barnes.

Quiller-Couch, Arthur. [1918] 1930. *Studies in Literature.* 1st series. 1918. Reprint. Cambridge University Press, 1930.

——. 1929. "The English Elegy (II)." In *Studies in Literature: Third Series,* 23–50. Cambridge: Cambridge University Press; New York: G. P. Putnam's Sons.

Quinn, Dennis. [1960] 1971. "Donne's Christian Eloquence." *ELH* 27 (1960): 279–97. Reprint in *Seventeenth-Century Prose: Modern Essays in Criticism,* edited by Stanley E. Fish, 353–74. New York: Oxford University Press, 1971.

——. 1962. "John Donne's Principles of Biblical Exegesis." *Journal of English and Germanic Philology* 41:313–29.

——. 1969. "Donne and the Wane of Wonder." *ELH* 36:626–47.

Raine, Kathleen. 1945. "John Donne and the Baroque Doubt." *Horizon* 11:371–95.

Raiziss, Sona. 1952. *The Metaphysical Passion: Seven Modern American Poets and the Seventeenth-Century Tradition.* Philadelphia: University of Pennsylvania Press.

Ramsey, Mary Paton. 1917. *Les Doctrines Médiévales Chez Donne, Le Poète Métaphysicien de l'Angleterre (1573–1631).* London: Oxford University Press.

——. 1931. "Donne's Relation to Philosophy." In *A Garland for John Donne,* 101–20. See Theodore Spencer 1931.

Ransom, John Crowe. [1938] 1938. "Shakespeare at Sonnets." *Southern Review* 3 (1938): 531–55. Reprint in *The World's Body,* 27–303. New York: Charles Scribner's Sons, 1938.

——. [1941] 1941. "Eliot and the Metaphysicals." *Accent* 1 (1941): 148–56. Reprint in *The New Criticism,* 175–92. Norfolk, Conn.: New Directions, 1941.

Read, Herbert. 1923. "The Nature of Metaphysical Poetry." *The Criterion* (London) 1:246–66.

——. 1928. *Phases of English Poetry.* London: Hogarth Press.

Rebhorn, Wayne A. 1978. *Courtly Performances: Masking and Festivity in Castiglione's "Book of the Courtier."* Detroit: Wayne State University Press.

Redpath, Theodore, ed. 1956. *The Songs and Sonets of John Donne.* An *Editio minor.* London: Methuen.

Reed, Edward Bliss. 1912. *English Lyrical Poetry From Its Origins to the Present Time*. New Haven: Yale University Press.

Rhys, Ernest. [1913] 1973. *Lyric Poetry*. London and Toronto: J. M. Dent and Sons, 1913. Reprint. New York: AMS Press, 1973.

Richmond, H. M. 1964. *The School of Love: The Evolution of the Stuart Love Lyric*. Princeton: Princeton University Press.

———. 1973. "Donne's Master: The Young Shakespeare." *Criticism* 15:126–44.

Ricks, Christopher. 1981. "Donne's Will to Power." *London Review of Books* 3(11): 7–8 (18 June).

Robbins, Rossell Hope. 1951. *The T. S. Eliot Myth*. New York: Henry Schuman.

Roberts, D. H. 1976. " 'Just Such Disparitie': The Real and the Representation in Donne's Poetry." *South Atlantic Bulletin* 41(4): 99–108.

Roberts, Donald R. 1947. "The Death Wish of John Donne." *PMLA* 62: 958–76.

Roberts, John R., ed. 1975. *Essential Articles for the Study of John Donne's Poetry*. Hamden, Conn.: Shoe String, Archon.

———. 1982. "John Donne's Poetry: An Assessment of Modern Criticism." *John Donne Journal* 1:55–67.

Roberts, Michael. 1937. "The Seventeenth Century: Metaphysical Poets and the Cambridge Platonists." In *The Modern Mind*, 88–117. New York: Macmillan; London: Faber and Faber.

Rooney, William J. 1956. " 'The Canonization'—The Language of Paradox Reconsidered." *ELH* 23:36–47.

———. [1962] 1971. "John Donne's 'Second Prebend Sermon'—A Stylistic Analysis." *Texas Studies in Literature and Language* 4 (1962): 24–34. Reprint in *Seventeenth-Century Prose: Modern Essays in Criticism*, edited by Stanley E. Fish, 375–87. New York: Oxford University Press, 1971.

Rossetti, Dante Gabriel. [1985] 1970. *Dante Gabriel Rossetti: His Family-Letters with A Memoir by William Michael Rossetti*. Vol. 2. 1895. Reprint. New York: AMS Press, 1970.

Roston, Murray. 1974. *The Soul of Wit: A Study of John Donne*. Oxford: Clarendon Press.

Rowe, Frederick A. 1964. *I Launch at Paradise: A Consideration of John Donne, Poet and Preacher*. London: Epworth Press.

Ruffo-Fiore, Silvia. 1976. *Donne's Petrarchism: A Comparative View*. Florence: Grafica Toscana.

Rugoff, Milton Allan. 1939. *Donne's Imagery: A Study in Creative Sources*. New York: Corporate.

Russell, John D. 1958. "Donne's 'A Lecture Upon the Shadow.' " *Explicator* 17, Item 9.

Saintsbury, George. [1980] 1907. *A History of Elizabethan Literature*. 2d ed. 1890. Reprint. London: Macmillan, 1907.

———. [1896] 1962. "John Donne." Preface to *The Poems of John Donne*. 2 vols. Edited by E. K. Chambers. London: n.p., 1896. Reprint in *A Collection of Critical Essays*, 13–21. See Helen Gardner 1962.

———. 1908. *A Short History of English Literature*. London: Macmillan.

———. 1921a. "The Metaphysical Poets." *TLS*, 27 October, 698.

———. 1921b. "The Metaphysical Poets." *TLS*, 10 November, 734.

Sampson, Ashley. 1936. "The Resurrection of Donne." *London Mercury* 33:307–14.

Sanders, Wilbur. 1971. *John Donne's Poetry*. London: Cambridge University Press.

Schelling, Felix E. 1910. *English Literature during the Lifetime of Shakespeare*. New York: Henry Holt.

———. 1913. *The English Lyric*. Boston: Houghton Mifflin.

Seccombe, T., and J. W. Alden. 1903. *The Age of Shakespeare*. Vol. I. Poetry and Prose. London: George Bell and Sons.

Selden, Raman. 1975. "John Donne's 'Incarnational Conviction.'" *Critical Quarterly* 17:55–73.

"Seventeenth-Century Verse." 1934. *TLS*, 1 November, 741–42.

Shapiro, Karl. 1952. *In Defense of Ignorance*. New York: Random House.

Sharp, Robert Lathrop. 1934. "Some Light on Metaphysical Obscurity and Roughness." *Studies in Philology* 31:497–518.

———. 1935. "Observations on Metaphysical Imagery." *Sewanee Review* 43:464–78.

Sharrock, Roger. 1972. "Wit, Passion and Ideal Love: Reflections on the Cycle of Donne's Reputation." In *Just So much Honor*, 33–56. See Peter Fiore 1972.

Shawcross, John T. 1965. "Donne's 'A Nocturnall Upon S. Lucies Day.'" *Explicator* 23, Item 56.

———. 1986a. "The Arrangement and Order of John Donne's Poems." In *Poems in Their Place: The Intertextuality and Order of Poetic Collections*, edited by Neil Freistat, 119–63. Chapel Hill: University of North Carolina Press.

———. 1986b. "Poetry, Personal and Impersonal: The Case of Donne." In *The Eagle and the Dove*, 53–66. See Claude J. Summers and Ted-Larry Pebworth 1986.

Sherwood, Terry G. 1972. "Reason in Donne's Sermons." *ELH* 39:353–74.

———. 1984. *Fulfilling the Circle: A Study of John Donne's Thought*. Toronto: University of Toronto Press.

Shuster, George N. 1940. "Milton and the Metaphysical Poets." In *The English Ode from Milton to Keats*. Columbia University Studies in English and Comparative Literature, 150, pp. 64–92. New York: Columbia University Press.

Simpson, Evelyn M. [1924] 1948. *A Study of the Prose Work of John Donne*. 1924. Reprint. Oxford: Clarendon Press, 1948.

———. 1931. "Donne's 'Paradoxes and Problems.'" In *A Garland for John Donne*, 23–49. See Theodore Spencer 1931.

———. 1951. "The Biographical Value of Donne's Sermons." *Review of English Studies*, n.s. 2: 339–57.

———, ed. 1952. *Essays in Divinity*. Oxford: Clarendon Press.

———. 1956. "Donne and the Church." *TLS*, 25 May, 320.

———, ed. 1963. *John Donne's Sermons on the Psalms and Gospels; With a Selection of Prayers and Meditations*. Berkeley: University of California Press; London: Cambridge University Press.

Sitwell, Sacheverell. 1930. *Doctor Donne and Gargantua: The First Six Cantos*. London: Gerald Duckworth and Co.; New York: Houghton Mifflin.

Sloan[e], Thomas O. 1963. "The Rhetoric in the Poetry of John Donne." *Studies in English Literature* 3:31–44.

———. 1985. *Donne, Milton, and the End of Humanist Rhetoric*. Berkeley: University of California Press.

Smith, A. J. 1956. "Two Notes on Donne." *Modern Language Review* 51:405–7.

———. 1957a. "Donne in His Time: A Reading of 'The Extasie.'" *Rivista di Letterature Moderne e Comparate* (Firenze) 10:260–75.

———. 1957b. "Sources of Difficulty and of Value in the Poetry of John Donne." *Letterature Moderne* 7:182–90.

———. 1958. "The Metaphysic of Love." *Review of English Studies*, n.s. 9:362–75.

———. [1960] 1962. "New Bearings in Donne: *Aire and Angels*." *English* 13 (1960): 49–53. Reprint in *A Collection of Critical Essays*, 171–79. See Helen Gardner 1962.

———. 1972a. "The Dismissal of Love or, Was Donne a Neoplatonic Lover?" In *John Donne: Essays in Celebration*, edited by A. J. Smith, 89–131. London: Methuen.

———. 1972b. "Donne's Reputation." In *John Donne: Essays in Celebration*, edited by A. J. Smith, 1–27. London: Methuen.

————. 1975. *John Donne: The Critical Heritage*. London and Boston: Routledge and Kegan Paul.

Smith, G. Gregory, ed. 1904. *Elizabethan Critical Essays*. Vol. 1. Oxford: Clarendon Press.

Smith, Hallett. 1952. *Elizabethan Poetry: A Study in Conventions, Meaning, and Expression*. Cambridge: Harvard University Press.

Smith, Harold Wendall. 1951. " 'The Dissociation of Sensibility.' " *Scrutiny* 18:175–88.

Smith, James. 1933. "On Metaphysical Poetry." *Scrutiny* 2:222–39.

Smith, Logan Pearsall. 1937. *Reperusals and Re-collections*. New York: Harcourt, Brace and Co.

————. 1941. *Milton and His Modern Critics*. Boston: Little, Brown.

Southey, Robert. 1807. *Specimens of the Later English Poets*. Vol. 1. London: S. Hollingsworth.

Sparrow, John. 1931. "The Date of Donne's Travels." In *A Garland for John Donne*, 123–51. See Theodore Spencer 1931.

————. 1934. *Sense and Poetry: Essays on the Place of Meaning in Contemporary Verse*. New Haven: Yale University Press.

Spencer, Theodore. 1931. "Donne and His Age." In *A Garland for John Donne, 1631–1931*, edited by Theodore Spencer, 179–202. Cambridge: Harvard University Press; London: Humphrey Milford, Oxford University Press.

————. 1939. "Recent Scholarship in Metaphysical Poetry." In *Studies in Metaphysical Poetry: Two Essays and a Bibliography*, edited by Theodore Spencer and Mark Van Doren. New York: Columbia University Press.

Sprott, J. Ernest. 1950. "The Legend of Jack Donne the Libertine." *University of Toronto Quarterly* 19:335–53.

Spurgeon, Caroline F. E. 1913. *Mysticism in English Literature*. Cambridge: Cambridge University Press.

[Squire, Sir John Collings]. 1920. "Dr. Donne's Tomb." In *Books in General by Solomon Eagle*. 2d ed., 115–18. New York: Alfred Knopf.

Stampfer, Judah. 1970. *John Donne and the Metaphysical Gesture*. New York: Funk and Wagnalls.

Stein, Arnold. 1944. "Donne and the Satiric Spirit." *ELH* 11:266–82.

————. 1946. "Donne's Obscurity and the Elizabethan Tradition." *ELH* 13:98–118.

————. 1960. "Donne and the 1920's: A Problem in Historical Consciousness." *ELH* 27:16–29.

————. 1962. *John Donne's Lyrics: The Eloquence of Action*. Minneapolis: University of Minnesota Press.

Stephens, James. [1946] 1964. "John Donne." In *James, Seumas and Jacques: Unpublished Writings of James Stephens*, edited by Lloyd Frankenburg. 1946. Reprint. New York: Macmillan, 1964, 202–6.

————. 1974. *Letters of James Stephens*. Edited by Richard J. Finnernan. New York: Macmillan.

Summers, Claude J., and Ted-Larry Pebworth, eds. 1986. *The Eagle and the Dove: Reassessing John Donne*. Columbia: University of Missouri Press.

Symons, Arthur. [1899] 1916. *Figures of Several Centuries*. 1899. Reprint. London: Constable; New York: E. P. Dutton, 1916.

Sypher, Wylie. 1944. "The Metaphysicals and the Baroque." *Partisan Review* 11:3–17.

————. 1955. *Four Stages of Renaissance Style: Transformations in Art and Literature 1400–1700*. Anchor A44. Garden City, N.Y.: Doubleday.

Taine, H. A. [1863–64] 1873. *Histoire de la littérature anglaise*. Vol. 2. 1863–64. Reprint. Edinburgh: Edmonston and Douglas, 1873.

Tate, Allen. 1927. "Poetry and the Absolute." *Sewanee Review* 35:41–52.

———. [1932] 1959. "A Note on Donne." *The New Republic* 70 (1932): 212–13. Reprint in *Collected Essays*, 325–32. Denver: Alan Swallow, 1959.

———. 1933. "A Note on Elizabethan Satire." *The New Republic* 74:128–30.

———. [1938] 1959. "Tension in Poetry." *Southern Review* 4 (1938): 101–15. Reprint in *Collected Essays*, 75–90. Denver: Alan Swallow, 1959.

———. [1949] 1953. "Johnson on the Metaphysicals." *Kenyon Review* 11 (1949): 379–94. Reprint in *The Forlorn Demon: Didactic and Critical Essays*, 112–30. Chicago: Henry Regnery, 1953.

———. [1953] 1953. "The Point of Dying: Donne's 'Virtuous Men.'" *Sewanee Review* 61 (1953): 76–81. Reprint in *The Forlorn Demon: Didactic and Critical Essays*, 171–76. Chicago: Henry Regnery, 1953.

Taylor, Rev. Harry. 1949. Letter. *Saturday Review of Literature* 32 (16 April): 31.

Theobald, Lewis. [1733] 1949. Preface to *The Works of Shakespeare*. 1733. Reprint. The Augustan Reprint Society, no. 20. Los Angeles: University of California Press, 1949.

Thomas, Helen S. 1976. "The Concept of the *Persona* in John Donne's Religious Poetry." *The Southern Quarterly* 14(3): 183–89.

Thomas, John A. 1976. "The Circle: Donne's Underlying Unity." In *"The Need Beyond Reason" and Other Essays*, 89–103. College of Humanities Centennial Lectures 1975–76. Provo: Brigham Young University Press.

Thompson, Elbert N. S. 1921. "Mysticism in Seventeenth-Century English Literature." *Studies in Philology* 18:170–231.

Thompson, Eric. 1952. "The Critical Forum: 'Dissociation of Sensibility.'" *Essays in Criticism* 2:207–13.

Tillotson, Kathleen. [1959] 1975. "Donne's Poetry in the Nineteenth Century (1800–1872)." *Elizabethan and Jacobean Studies* 21 (1959): 307–26. Reprint in *Essential Articles*, 20–33. See John Roberts 1975.

Tillyard, E. M. W. 1943a. *The Elizabethan World Picture*. London: Chatto and Windus.

———. 1943b. "A Note on Donne's *Extasie*." *Review of English Studies* 19:67–70.

———. 1956. *The Metaphysicals and Milton*. London: Chatto and Windus.

Titus, O. P. 1942. "Science and John Donne." *The Scientific Monthly* 54:176–78.

Trench, Richard Chenevix. 1870. *A Household Book of English Poetry*. 2d ed. London: Macmillan.

Tuve, Rosemond. 1947. *Elizabethan and Metaphysical Imagery: Renaissance Poetic and Twentieth-Century Critics*. Chicago and London: University of Chicago Press.

Unger, Leonard. 1950. *Donne's Poetry and Modern Criticism*. Chicago: Henry Regnery.

———. 1956. *The Man in the Name: Essays on the Experience of Poetry*. Minneapolis: University of Minnesota Press.

*The Universal Spectator and Weekly Journal*. 1733. Edited by Henry Stonecastle. No. 260, 29 September.

Untermeyer, Louis. 1938. "Wit and Sensibility: Metaphor into Metaphysics." In *Play in Poetry*, 3–24. New York: Harcourt, Brace and Co.

———. 1959. "The Metaphysical Man: John Donne." In *Lives of the Poets: The Story of One Thousand Years of English and American Poetry*, 122–36. New York: Simon and Shuster.

Ure, Peter. 1948. "The 'Deformed Mistress' Theme and the Platonic Convention." *Notes and Queries* 193:269–70.

Van O'Connor, William. 1948. *Sense and Sensibility in Modern Poetry*. Chicago: University of Chicago Press.

Vickers, Brian. 1972. "The 'Songs and Sonnets' and the Rhetoric of Hyperbole." In *Essays in Celebration*, 132–74. See A. J. Smith 1972.

Viereck, Peter. 1959. "Pure Poetry, Impure Politics, and Ezra Pound: The Bollingen Prize Controversy Revisited." In *A Casebook on Ezra Pound*, edited by William Van O'Connor and Edward Stone, 92–103. New York: Thomas Y. Crowell.

Vining, Elizabeth Gray. 1964. *Take Heed of Loving Me*. Philadelphia and New York: J. B. Linnincott.

Walton, Izaak. [1670] 1927. *The Lives of John Donne, Sir Henry Wotton, Richard Hooker, George Herbert, and Robert Sanderson*. 1670. Reprint. London: Oxford University Press, 1927.

———. 1876. *The Complete Angler: or The Contemplative Man's Recreation*. London: Elliot Stock.

Warnke, Frank J. 1955. "Marino and the English Metaphysicals." *Studies in the Renaissance* 2:160–75.

———. 1961. *European Metaphysical Poetry*. The Elizabeth Club Series, 2. New Haven and London: Yale University Press.

———. 1967. "Baroque Poetry and the Experience of Contradiction." *Colloquia Germanica* 1:38–48.

Warren, Austin. 1939. *Richard Crashaw: A Study in Baroque Sensibility*. Ann Arbor: University of Michigan Press.

———. 1958. "Donne's 'Extasie.'" *Studies in Philology* 55:472–80.

Warton, Joseph. 1762, 1782. *An Essay on the Genius and Writings of Pope*. 2d ed. Vol. 1, 1762. Vol. 2, 1782. London.

Watkins, W. B. C. 1936. "Spenser to the Restoration (1579–1660)." In *Johnson and English Poetry Before 1660*, 58–84. Princeton: Princeton University Press.

Webber, Joan. 1963. *Contrary Music: The Prose Style of John Donne*. Madison: University of Wisconsin Press.

Webster, Grant. 1979. *The Republic of Letters: A History of Post-war American Literary Opinion*. Baltimore and London: The Johns Hopkins University Press.

Wellek, René. 1956. "The Criticism of T. S. Eliot." *Sewanee Review* 64:398–443.

———, and Austin Warren. 1956. *Theory of Literature*. 3d ed. New York: Harcourt, Brace and World.

Wells, Henry W. [1924] 1961. *Poetic Imagery: Illustrated from Elizabethan Literature*. New York: Columbia University Press, 1924. Reprint. New York: Russell and Russell, 1961.

Wendell, Barrett. 1904. *The Temper of the Seventeenth-Century in English Literature*. New York: Charles Scribner's Sons.

Weyl, Nathaniel. 1959. "The Strange Case of Ezra Pound." In *A Casebook on Ezra Pound*, edited by William Van O'Connor and Edward Stone, 5–18. New York: Thomas Y. Crowell.

Whipple, Edwin Percy. [1869] 1899. *The Literature of the Age of Elizabeth*. 1869. Reprint. Boston: Houghton Mifflin, 1899.

White, Helen C. 1931. *English Devotional Literature [Prose] 1600–1640*. University of Wisconsin Studies in Language and Literature, no. 29. Madison: University of Wisconsin Press.

———. 1936. *The Metaphysical Poets: A Study in Religious Experience*. New York: Macmillan.

———. 1951a. "John Donne and the Psychology of Spiritual Effort." In *The Seventeenth-Century: Studies in the History of English Thought and Literature from Bacon to Pope*, by Richard Foster Jones and Others Writing in His Honor, 355–68. Stanford: Stanford University Press; London: Oxford University Press.

———. 1951b. "John Donne in the Twentieth Century." *Seventeenth-Century News* 9:2.

Wiggins, Elizabeth Lewis. 1945. "Logic in the Poetry of John Donne." *Studies in Philology* 42:41–60.

Williamson, George. 1927. "The Talent of T. S. Eliot." *Sewanee Review* 35:284–95.

———. 1928. "The Nature of the Donne Tradition." *Studies in Philology* 25:416–38.

———. 1930. *The Donne Tradition: A Study in English Poetry from Donne to the Death of Cowley*. Cambridge: Harvard University Press; Oxford: Oxford University Press.

———. 1931. "Donne and the Poetry of Today." In *A Garland for John Donne,* 155–76. See Theodore Spencer 1931.

———. 1934. "The Libertine Donne." *Philological Quarterly* 13:276–91.

———. 1935. "Mutability, Decay, and Seventeenth-Century Melancholy." *ELH* 2:121–50.

———. 1936. "Strong Lines." *English Studies* 18:152–59.

———. 1960. "The Convention of *The Extasie.*" In *Seventeenth-Century Contexts,* 63–77. London: Faber and Faber; Chicago: University of Chicago Press.

———. 1963. "The Design of Donne's *Anniversaries.*" *Modern Philology* 60:183–91.

Wilson, F. P. 1945. *Elizabethan and Jacobean.* Oxford: Clarendon Press.

Winters, Yvor. [1939] 1967. "The Sixteenth Century Lyric in England: A Critical and Historical Reinterpretation." *Poetry* 53 (1939): 258–72. Reprint in *Elizabethan Poetry: Modern Essays in Criticism,* edited by Paul J. Alpers, 92–125. New York: Oxford University Press, 1967.

Woodhouse, A. S. P. 1965. "The Seventeenth Century: Donne and His Successors." In *The Poet and His Faith: Religion and Poetry in England from Spenser to Eliot and Auden,* 42–89. Chicago and London: University of Chicago Press.

Woods, Susanne. 1982. "Reassessing Donne's Versification." Paper presented at conference, The Eagle and the Dove: Reassessing John Donne, University of Michigan-Dearborn, 16 October.

Wyatt, Sir Thomas. 1975. *Collected Poems.* Edited by Joost Daalder. London, Oxford, New York: Oxford University Press.

Wyke, Clement H. 1976. "Edmund Gosse as Biographer and Critic of Donne: His Fallible Role in the Poet's Rediscovery." *Texas Studies in Literature and Language* 17:805–19.

# Works Consulted

Adams, Robert Martin. 1958. *Strains of Discord: Studies in Literary Openness.* Ithaca: Cornell University Press.

Allen, Don Cameron. 1943. "Dean Donne Sets His Text." *ELH* 10:208–29.

———. 1943. "John Donne's Knowledge of Renaissance Medicine." *Journal of English and Germanic Philology* 42:322–42.

———. 1952. "The Double Journey of John Donne." In *A Tribute to George Coffin Taylor,* edited by Arnold Williams, 83–99. Chapel Hill: University of North Carolina Press.

———. 1959. *Four Poets on Poetry.* Baltimore: The Johns Hopkins University Press.

Altizer, Alma B. 1973. *Self and Symbolism in the Poetry of Michaelangelo, John Donne, and Agrippa d'Aubigné.* International Archives of the History of Ideas, ser. minor 10, 69–100. The Hague: Nijhoff.

Anonymous. 1899. Untitled. *Athenaeum* 11 November and 16 December, 645–46, 836.

Ashley-Montagu, M. F. 1937. "Donne the Astronomer." *TLS,* 7 August, 576.

Atkins, J. W. H. 1951. *English Literary Criticism: 17th and 18th Centuries.* London: Methuen.

Ayres, Philip J. 1976. "Donne's 'The Dampe,' Engraved Hearts, and the 'Passion' of St. Clare of Montefalco." *English Language Notes* 13:173–75.

Babb, Lawrence. 1941. "Melancholy and the Elizabethan Man of Letters." *Huntington Library Quarterly* 4:247–61.

Bateson, F. W. 1934. "Elizabethans, Metaphysicals, Augustans." In *English Poetry and the English Language: An Experiment in Literary History,* 26–64. Oxford: Clarendon Press.

Bellette, Anthony F. 1975. "Art and Imitation in Donne's Anniversaries." *Studies in English Literature* 15:83–96.

———. 1975. " 'Little Worlds Made Cunningly': Significant Form in Donne's *Holy Sonnets* and 'Goodfriday, 1613.' " *Studies in Philology* 72:322–47.

Blanchard, Margaret M. 1964. "The Leap into Darkness: Donne, Herbert, and God." *Renascence* 17:38–50.

Bolton, Joseph S. G., ed. 1928. *Melanthe: A Latin Pastoral Play of the Early Seventeenth Century.* By Samuel Brooke. Yale Studies in English, no. 79. New Haven: Yale University Press; London: Humphrey Milford and Oxford University Press.

Borges, Jorge Luis. [1952] 1964. "El 'Biathanatos.' " In *Otras Inquisiciones (1937–1952).* Buenos Aires: Sur, 1952. Reprint translated by Ruth L. C. Simms. In *Other Inquisitions (1937–1952),* 89–92. Austin: University of Texas Press, 1964.

Bozanich, Robert. 1975. "Donne and Ecclesiastes." *PMLA* 90:270–76.

Bradbury, Malcolm, and David Palmer, eds. 1970. *Metaphysical Poetry.* Bloomington and London: Indiana University Press.

Bradford, Gamaliel. [1888] 1926. *A Naturalist of Souls: Studies in Psychography.* Houghton Mifflin, 1888. Reprint. New York and Boston: Houghton Mifflin, 1926.

Brower, Reuben Arthur. 1951. *The Fields of Light: An Experiment in Critical Reading.* New York: Oxford University Press.

Bullough, Geoffrey. 1972. "Donne the Man of Law." In *Just So much Honor,* 57–94. See Peter Fiore 1972.

Carey, John. 1981. "John Donne's Newsless Letters." In *Essays and Studies, 1981*, collected by Anne Barton, 45–65. Atlantic Highlands, N.J.: Humanities Press.

Carlson, Norman E. 1973. "Donne's 'Holy Sonnets, XIX.'" *Explicator* 32, Item 19.

Carrithers, Gale H., Jr. 1972. *Donne at Sermons: A Christian Existential World*. Albany: State University of New York Press.

Chambers, E. K. 1910. "John Donne, Diplomatist and Soldier." *Modern Language Review* 5:492–93.

———. 1933. "The Disenchantment of the Elizabethans." In *Sir Thomas Wyatt and Some Collected Studies*, 181–204. London: Sidgwick and Jackson.

Cirillo, A[lbert] R. 1969. "The Fair Hermaphrodite: Love Union in the Poetry of Donne and Spenser." *Studies in English Literature* 9:81–95.

Clair, John A. 1965. "Donne's 'The Canonization.'" *PMLA* 80:300–302.

Colvin, Sir Sidney. 1915. "On Concentration and Suggestion in Poetry. *English Association Pamphlet*, no. 32: 17–19.

Cooper, Harold. 1942. "John Donne and Virginia in 1610." *Modern Language Notes* 57:661–63.

Cox, R. G. 1956. "The Poems of John Donne." In *From Donne to Marvell*, edited by Boris Ford, 98–115. The Pelican Guide to English Literature, no. 3. Baltimore: Penguin Books.

———. 1956. "A Survey of Literature from Donne to Marvell." In *From Donne to Marvell*, edited by Boris Ford, 43–85. The Pelican Guide to English Literature, no. 3. Baltimore: Penguin Books.

Cruttwell, Patrick. 1951. "Physiology and Psychology in Shakespeare's Age." *Journal of the History of Ideas* 12:75–89.

Daiches, David. 1972. "A Reading of the 'Good-morrow.'" In *Just So much Honor*, 177–88. See Peter Fiore 1972.

Daniells, Roy. 1945. "Baroque Form in English Literature." *University of Toronto Quarterly* 14:393–408.

Danby, John F. [1950] 1952. "Jacobean Absolutists: The Placing of Beaumont and Fletcher." *Cambridge Journal* 3(1950): 515–40. Reprint as "Beaumont and Fletcher: Jacobean Absolutists." In *Poets on Fortune's Hill: Studies in Sidney, Shakespeare, Beaumont, and Fletcher*, 152–83. London: Faber and Faber, 1952.

Davies, Hugh Sykes. 1965. "Text or Context?" *Review of English Literature* 6(1): 93–107.

"Devotional Poetry: Donne to Wesley: The Search for an Unknown Eden." 1938. *TLS*, 24 December, 814, 816.

Draper, John W. 1929. *The Funeral Elegy and the Rise of English Romanticism*. New York: New York University Press.

Drew, Elizabeth. 1933. *Discovering Poetry*. New York: W. W. Norton.

Duncan, Joseph E. 1953. "The Intellectual Kinship of John Donne and Robert Browning." *Studies in Philology* 50:81–100.

Dunn, Esther Cloudman. 1936. "A Note on John Donne." In *The Literature of Shakespeare's England*, 158–63. New York: Charles Scribner's Sons.

Durand, Laura G. 1969. "Sponde and Donne: Lens and Prism." *Comparative Literature* 21:319–36.

Dyson, A. E., and Julian Lovelock. 1973. "Contracted Thus: 'The Sunne Rising.'" In *Donne, Songs and Sonets: A Casebook*, 185–92. See Julian Lovelock 1973.

Eliot, T. S. 1920. "Imperfect Critics." In *The Sacred Wood: Essays on Poetry and Criticism*, 17–46. London: Methuen.

———. 1921. "The Metaphysical Poets." *TLS*, 3 November, 716.

———. 1923. "John Donne." *Nation and Athenaeum* 33:331–32.

———. 1929. "The Prose of the Preacher: The Sermons of Donne." *The Listener* 2 (3 July): 22–23.

———. 1930. "The Devotional Poets of the Seventeenth Century: Donne, Herbert, Crashaw." *The Listener* 3:552–53.

———. 1930. "Rhyme and Reason: The Poetry of John Donne." *The Listener* 3:502–3.

Ellrodt, Robert. 1960. "Chronologie des poèmes de Donne." *Etudes Anglaises* 13:452–63.

———. 1960. *L'Inspiration personelle et l'esprit du temps chez les poètes métaphysique anglais.* Paris: Jose Corti.

———. 1961. "La vogue de l'image scientifique dans la poésie anglaise du dix-septième siècle." *Etudes Anglaises* 14:346–47.

Elton, Oliver. 1933. "Poetry, 1600–1660." In *The English Muse: A Sketch,* 202–31. London: G. Bell and Sons.

Empson, William. 1972. "Rescuing Donne." In *Just So much Honor,* 95–148. See Peter Fiore 1972.

Evans, Gillian R. 1982. "John Donne and the Augustinian Paradox of Sin." *Review of English Studies,* n.s. 33: 1–22.

Fausset, Hugh I'Anson. [1924] 1967. *John Donne: A Study in Discord.* New York: Russell and Russell, 1924. Reprint. New York: Russell and Russell, 1967.

———. 1947. "Donne's *Holy Sonnets.*" In *Poets and Pundits: Essays and Addresses,* 130–34. London: Jonathan Cape.

Flynn, Dennis. 1979. "Donne's First Portrait: Some Biographical Clues?" *Bulletin of Research in the Humanities* 82:7–17.

Foster, Thomas. 1931. "The Tragedy of John Donne." *The Month* (London) 157:404–9.

Frere, W. H. 1904. *A History of the English Church In the Reigns of Elizabeth and James I, 1558–1625.* London: Macmillan.

Friedman, Donald M. 1973. "Memory and the Art of Salvation in Donne's Good Friday Poem." *English Literary Renaissance* 3:418–42.

Fuson, Benjamin Willis. 1948. *Browning and His English Predecessors in the Dramatic Monolog.* State University of Iowa Humanistic Studies, vol. 8, edited by Frank H. Potter. Iowa City: State University of Iowa.

Gardner, Helen. 1972. "The 'Metempsychosis' of John Donne." *TLS,* 29 December, 1587–88.

Garrod, H. W. 1929. "Cowley, Johnson, and the 'Metaphysicals.'" In *The Profession of Poetry and Other Lectures,* 110–30. Oxford: Clarendon Press.

———. 1945. "Donne and Mrs. Herbert." *Review of English Studies* 29:161–73.

Gegenheimer, Albert Frank. 1947. "They Might Have Been Americans." *South Atlanta Quarterly* 46:511–23.

Goldberg, Jonathan S. 1971. "Donne's Journey East: Aspects of a Seventeenth-Century Trope." *Studies in Philology* 68:470–83.

———. 1971. "The Understanding of Sickness in Donne's *Devotions.*" *Renaissance Quarterly* 24:507–17.

Grant, Patrick. 1974. *The Transformation of Sin: Studies in Donne, Herbert, Vaughan, and Traherne.* Montreal and London: McGill-Queen's University Press; Amherst: University of Massachusetts Press.

Grundy, Joan. 1956. "Donne's Poetry." *TLS,* 27 April, 253.

Hamilton, G. Rostrevor. 1926. "Wit and Beauty: A Study of Metaphysical Poetry." *London Mercury* 14:606–20.

———. 1949. "The Tell-Tale Article." In *The Tell-Tale Article: A Critical Approach to Modern Poetry,* 3–59. London: William Heinemann.

Harris, Victor. 1962. "John Donne and the Theatre." *Philological Quarterly* 41:257–69.

Hathaway, C. M. 1904. "The Compass Figure Again." *Modern Language Notes* 19:192.

Häublein, Ernst. 1979. "King Imagery in the Poetry of John Donne." *Anglia* 97:94–115.

Hayward, John. 1931. "A Note on Donne the Preacher." In *A Garland for John Donne*, 75–97. See Theodore Spencer 1931.

Hebel, William J. 1924. "Drayton's 'Sirena.'" *PMLA* 39:814–36.

Henrickson, Bruce. 1975. "The Unity of Reason and Faith in Donne's Sermons." *Papers on Language and Literature* 11:18–30.

Henry, Nat. 1962. "Donne's 'Lecture Upon the Shadow.'" *Explicator* 20, Item 60.

Hester, M. Thomas. 1977. "Henry Donne, John Donne and the Date of *Satyre II*." *Notes and Queries* 24:524–27.

―――. 1979. "Donne's *Apologia*." *Papers on Language and Literature* 15:137–58.

Heywood, Terrence. 1940. "Some Notes on English Baroque." *Horizon* 2:267–70.

Hodgson, Geraldine E. 1922. "Anglo-Catholic Mystics and Others." In *English Mystics*, 208–72. London: A. R. Mowbray.

Holland, Norman. 1964. "Clinical, Yes. Healthy, No." *Literature and Psychology* 14:121–25.

Hollander, John. 1972. "Donne and the Limits of Lyric." In *Essays in Celebration*, 259–72. See A. J. Smith 1972.

Huxley, Aldous. 1919. "Ben Jonson." *London Mercury* 1:184–91.

"Ill Donne: Well Donne." 1967. *TLS*, 6 April, 277–80.

"John Donne." 1931. *TLS*, 26 March, 241–42.

Johnson, Stanley. 1948. "Sir Henry Goodere and Donne's Letters." *Modern Language Notes* 63:38–43.

Kemper, Susan C. 1976. "Donne's 'The Extasie,' 6." *Explicator* 35(2): 2–3.

Kermode, Frank. 1961. "Interesting but Tough." *Spectator* 206:298–99.

Knights, L. C. 1945. "On the Social Background of Metaphysical Poetry." *Scrutiny* 13:37–52.

Korkowski, Eugene. 1975. "Donne's *Ignatius* and Menippean Satire." *Studies in Philology* 72:419–38.

Krieger, Murray. 1956. *The New Apologists for Poetry*. Minneapolis: University of Minnesota Press.

Labriola, Albert C. 1973. "Donne's 'The Canonization': Its Theological Context and Its Religious Imagery." *Huntington Library Quarterly* 36:327–39.

Lauritsen, John R. 1976. "Donne's *Satyres*: The Drama of Self-Discovery." *Studies in English Literature* 16:117–30.

Lawniczak, Donald A. 1969. "Donne's Sainted Lovers—Again." *Serif* 6(1): 12–19.

Lea, Kathleen M. 1925. "Conceits." *Modern Language Review* 20:389–406.

Lederer, Josef. 1946. "John Donne and the Emblematic Practice." *Review of English Studies* 22:182–200.

Legouis, Pierre. 1952. "L'État présent des controverse sur la poésie de Donne." *Etudes Anglaises* 5:97–106.

―――. 1957. "Donne, l'amour et les critiques." *Etudes Anglaises* 10:115–22.

Lerner, Laurence. 1960. "The Truest Poetry is the Most Feigning." In *The Truest Poetry; An Essay on the Question: What is Literature?*, 204–18. London: Hamish Hamilton.

Lewalski, Barbara K. 1976. "Donne's Epideictic *Personae*." *The Southern Quarterly* 14(3): 195–202.

Lowes, John Livingston. 1919. *Convention and Revolt in Poetry*. Boston and New York: Houghton Mifflin.

MacColl, Alan, and Mark Roberts. 1967. "The New Edition of Donne's Love Poems." *Essays in Criticism* 17:258–78.

McColley, Grant. 1932. "The Theory of a Plurality of Worlds." *Modern Language Notes* 47:319–25.

Marotti, Arthur F. 1968. "Donne's 'Loves Progress,' 11. 37–38, and Renaissance Bawdry." *English Language Notes* 6:24–25.

Mary Caroline, Sister. 1968. "The Existentialist Attitude of John Donne." *Xavier University Studies* 7(1): 37–50.

Matthiessen, F. O. 1941. *American Renaissance: Art and Expression in the Age of Emerson and Whitman.* London, Toronto, New York: Oxford University Press.

Mazzeo, Joseph Anthony. [1952] 1971. "A Critique of Some Modern Theories of Metaphysical Poetry." *Modern Philology* 50 (1952): 89–96. Reprint in *Seventeenth-Century English Poetry*, 77–88. See William Keast [1962] 1971.

Melton, W. F. 1906. *The Rhetoric of John Donne's Verse.* Baltimore: J. H. Furst.

Memorabilist. 1943. "Some Notes on Donne." *Notes and Queries* 184:77, 165–66.

Merrill, Thomas F. 1968. "John Donne and the Word of God." *Neuphilologische Mitteilungen* 69:597–616.

Miles, Josephine. 1946. "Major Adjectives in English Poetry from Wyatt to Auden." In *Vocabulary of Poetry, Three Studies.* University of California Publications in English, 12 (1942–1946), 305–426. Berkeley and Los Angeles: University of California Press.

———. 1951. "The Language of the Donne Tradition." *Kenyon Review* 13:37–49.

Milgate, Wesley. 1942. "Donne the Lawyer." *TLS,* 1 August, 379.

Mitchell, Charles. 1968. "Donne's 'The Extasie': Love's Sublime Knot." *Studies in English Literature* 8:91–101.

Moloney, Michael F. 1947. "John Donne and the Jesuits." *Modern Language Quarterly* 8:426–29.

———. 1950. "Donne's Metrical Practice." *PMLA* 65:232–39.

More, Paul Elmer, and Frank Leslie Cross. 1935. *Anglicanism: The Thought and Practice of the Church of England, Illustrated from the Religious Literature of the Seventeenth Century.* Milwaukee: Morehouse Publishing; London: Society for Promoting Christian Knowledge.

Morgan, Evan. 1928 and 1935. *Some Aspects of Mysticism in Verse [and] John Donne—Lover and Priest: Two Lectures.* Delivered before the Royal Society of Literature on 28 November 1928 and 29 October 1935. [Printed in Great Britain].

Morley, Christopher. 1937. "Courting John Donne." *Saturday Review of Literature,* 1 May, 10, 16.

Murray, W. A. [1959] 1975. "What Was the Soul of the Apple?" *Review of English Studies,* n.s. 10 (1959): 141–55. Reprint in *Essential Articles,* 462–74. See John Roberts 1975.

Nathanson, Leonard. 1957. "The Context of Dryden's Criticism of Donne's and Cowley's Love Poetry." *Notes and Queries,* n.s. 4:56–59.

Novak, Lynn Taylor. 1976. "Response to G. T. Wright's 'The Personae of Donne's Love Poems.'" *The Southern Quarterly* 14(3): 179–81.

Novarr, David. 1952. "Donne's Letters." *TLS,* 24 October, 700.

———. 1964. "The Two Hands of John Donne." *Modern Philology* 62:142–54.

Parker, Barbara L., and J. Max Patrick. 1975. "Two Hollow Men: The Pretentious Wooer and the Wayward Bridegroom of Donne's 'Satyre I.'" *Seventeenth Century News* 33, 10–14.

Parker, Derek. 1975. *John Donne and His World.* London: Thames and Hudson.

Patrick, Stanley R. 1977. "Understanding Understanding Poetry." *Computers and the Humanities* 11:217–21.

Perrine, Laurence. 1963. "Donne's 'A Lecture upon the Shadow.'" *Explicator* 21, Item 40.

Phelps, Gilbert. 1956. "The Prose of Donne and Browne." In *From Donne to Marvell,* edited by Boris Ford, 116–30. The Pelican Guide to English Literature, no. 3. Baltimore: Penguin Books.

"Poets and Editors." 1950. *TLS,* 22 September, 597.

Power, Helen W. 1972. "The Speaker as Creator: The Voice in Donne's Poems." *Xavier University Studies* 11(1): 21–28.

Praz, Mario. 1951. "The Critical Importance of the Revived Interest in Seventeenth-Century Metaphysical Poetry." In *English Studies Today,* edited by C. L. Wren and G. Bullough, 158–66. London: Oxford University Press.

Press, John. 1958. *The Chequer'd Shade: Reflections on Obscurity in Poetry.* New York, London, Toronto: Oxford University Press.

Pritchard, R. E. 1985. "Dying in Donne's 'The Good Morrow.' " *Essays in Criticism* 35: 213–22.

Quinn, Dennis. 1960. "Donne and 'Tyr.' " *Modern Language Notes* 75: 643–44.

Richards, I. A. 1929. *Practical Criticism: A Study of Literary Judgment.* New York: Harcourt, Brace and Co.

Richmond, H. M. 1959. "The Intangible Mistress." *Modern Philology* 56: 217–23.

Roberts, John R. 1973. *John Donne: An Annotated Bibliography of Modern Criticism, 1912–1967.* Columbia: University of Missouri Press.

———. 1982. *John Donne: An Annotated Bibliography of Modern Criticism, 1968–1978.* Columbia and London: University of Missouri Press.

Roberts, Mark. 1966. "If It Were Donne When 'Tis Done. . . ." *Essays in Criticism* 16: 309–29.

Rogers, Robert. 1964. "Literary Value and the Clinical Fallacy." *Literature and Psychology* 14: 116–21.

Roscelli, William John. 1967. "The Metaphysical Milton (1625–1631)." *Texas Studies in Literature and Language* 8: 463–84.

Ross, Malcolm M. 1953. "A Note on the Metaphysicals." *Hudson Review* 6: 106–13.

Routh, H. V. 1947. "The Nineteenth Century and After, II." *The Year's Work in English Studies* 28: 249–68.

Saltmarshe, Christopher. 1931. "John Donne: The Man and His Life." *The Bookman* (London) 79: 343–44.

Saunders, J. W. 1953. "Donne and Daniel." *Essays in Criticism* 3: 109–14.

Schleiner, Winfried. 1970. *The Imagery of John Donne's Sermons.* Providence, R.I.: Brown University Press.

Scott, Walter Sidney. 1945. *The Fantasticks: Donne, Herbert, Crashaw, Vaughan.* London: John Westhouse.

Scrymgeour, Daniel, ed. 1852. *The Poetry and Poets of Britain from Chaucer to Tennyson.* 4th ed. Edinburgh: Adam and Charles Black, North Bridge.

Sellin, Paul R. 1976. "John Donne: The Poet as Diplomat and Divine." *Huntington Library Quarterly* 39: 267–75.

Serrano Poncela, Segundo. 1966. "John Donne o la sensualidad." *Insula* 21: 1, 12.

Shami, Jeanne M. 1980. "Donne on Discretion." *ELH* 47: 48–66.

Sharp, Robert Lathrop. 1934. "The Pejorative Use of *Metaphysical.*" *Modern Language Notes* 49: 503–5.

———. 1940. *From Donne to Dryden: The Revolt Against Metaphysical Poetry.* Chapel Hill: University of North Carolina Press.

Sicherman, Carol M. 1969. "The Mocking Voices of Donne and Marvell." *Bucknell Review* 17(2): 32–46.

Siegel, Paul N. 1949. "Donne's Paradoxes and Problems." *Philological Quarterly* 28: 507–11.

Sloan, Thomas O. [1965] 1975. "The Persona as Rhetor: An Interpretation of Donne's *Satyre III.*" *The Quarterly Journal of Speech* 51 (1965): 14–27. Reprint in *Essential Articles,* 424–38. See John Roberts 1975.

Sloane, Mary C. 1974. "Emblem and Meditation: Some Parallels in John Donne's Imagery." *South Atlantic Bulletin* 39(2): 74–79.

Smalling, Michael. 1976. "The Personae in Donne's Epideictic Verse: A Second Opinion." *The Southern Quarterly* 14(3): 203–6.

Snyder, Susan. 1973. "Donne and Du Bartas: *The Progresse of the Soule* as Parody." *Studies in Philology* 70:392–407.

Sparrow, John, ed. 1923. *Devotions Upon Emergent Occasions by John Donne*. Cambridge: Cambridge University Press.

Spenko, James L. 1975. "Circular Form in Two Donne Lyrics." *English Language Notes* 13:103–7.

Spingarn, J. E., ed. [1908] 1957. *Critical Essays of the Seventeenth Century*. Vol. 1, 1605–1650. Oxford: Clarendon Press, 1908. Reprint. Bloomington: Indiana University Press, 1957.

Spitzer, Leo. 1962. "Three Poems on Ecstasy: John Donne, St. John of the Cross, Richard Wagner." In *Essays on English and American Literature,* edited by Anna Hatcher. 139–79. Princeton: Princeton University Press.

Stauffer, Donald A. 1946. *The Nature of Poetry*. New York: W. W. Norton.

Stein, Arnold. 1942. "Donne and the Couplet." *PMLA* 57:676–96.

———. 1944. "Donne's Prosody." *PMLA* 59:373–97.

Stephens, James. 1947. "The 'Prince of Wits': An Appreciation of John Donne." *The Listener* 37:149–50.

Stringer, Gary. 1976. "Donne's Religious *Personae:* A Response." *The Southern Quarterly* 14(3): 191–94.

Summers, Joseph H. 1970. "The Heritage of Donne and Jonson." *University of Toronto Quarterly* 39:107–26.

Sunne, Richard. 1931. "Books in General." *The New Statesman and Nation,* n.s. 1:222.

Tepper, Michael. 1976. "John Donne's Fragment Epic: 'The Progresse of the Soule.'" *English Language Notes* 13:262–66.

Thomas, [Philip] Edward. 1912. *The Tenth Muse*. London: Martin Secker.

Thomason, Katherine T. 1982. "Plotinian Metaphysics and Donne's 'Extasie.'" *Studies in English Literature* 22: 91–105.

Thompson, Elbert N. S. 1924. "Familiar Letters." In *Literary Bypaths of the Renaissance,* 91–126. New Haven: Yale University Press; London: Oxford University Press.

Thompson, Patricia. 1952. "The Literature of Patronage, 1580–1630." *Essays in Criticism* 2:267–84.

Tillyard, E. M. W. [1934] 1959. *Poetry Direct and Oblique*. 1934. Reprint. New York: Barnes and Noble, 1959.

Tjarks, Larry D. 1976. "Donne's 'Loves Usury' and a Self-Deceived Persona." *The Southern Quarterly* 14(3): 207–13.

Tomkinson, Cyril. 1931. "A Note on the Personal Religion of Dr. Donne." *The Bookman* (London) 79:345–46.

Turnell, Martin. 1950. "John Donne and the Quest for Unity." *Nineteenth Century and After* 147:262–74.

———. 1961. "The Changing Pattern: Contrasts in Modern and Medieval Poetry." In *Modern Literature and Christian Faith,* 1–21. London: Darton, Longman and Todd; Westminster, Md.: Newman Press.

Umbach, Herbert H. 1937. "The Rhetoric of Donne's Sermons." *PMLA* 52:354–58.

Untermeyer, Louis, ed. 1948. *The Love Poems of Robert Herrick and John Donne*. New Brunswick, N.J.: Rutgers University Press.

Van O'Connor, William. 1948. "The Influence of the Metaphysicals on Modern Poetry." *College English* 9:180–87.

Waller, G. F. 1974. "John Donne's Changing Attitudes to Time." *Studies in English Literature* 14:79–89.

Wallerstein, Ruth C. [1949] 1965. "Rhetoric in the English Renaissance: Two Elegies." In *English Institute Essays* of 1948, edited by D. A. Robertson, Jr. New York: Columbia University Press, 1949. Reprint. New York: AMS Press, 1965, 153–78.

———. 1950. *Studies in Seventeenth-Century Poetic.* Madison: University of Wisconsin Press.

Wanamaker, Melissa C. 1975. *Discordia Concors: The Wit of Metaphysical Poetry.* Port Washington, N.Y.: Kennikat.

Ward, Thomas Humphry, ed. 1891. *The English Poets, Vol. I, Early Poetry: Chaucer to Donne.* London and New York: Macmillan.

Warren, Austin. 1954. "The Very Reverend Dr. Donne." *Kenyon Review* 16:268–77.

Webber, Joan. 1968. *The Eloquent 'I': Style and Self in Seventeenth-Century Prose.* Madison: University of Wisconsin Press.

Wells, Henry W. 1940. *New Poets from Old: A Study of Literary Genetics.* New York: Columbia University Press.

White, Harold Ogden. 1935. "The Theory of Imitation from Jonson Onward." In *Plagiarism and Imitation During the English Renaissance: A Study in Critical Distinctions,* 120–202. Cambridge: Harvard University Press.

Whitlock, Baird W. 1954. "The Dean and the Yeoman." *Notes and Queries,* n.s. 1:374–75.

———. 1955. "Yᵉ Curioust Scholer in Cristendom." *Review of English Studies,* n.s. 6:365–71.

———. 1959. "The Heredity and Childhood of John Donne." *Notes and Queries,* n.s. 6:257–62, 348–53.

———. 1967. "From the Counter-Renaissance to the Baroque." *Bucknell Review* 15:46–60.

Whittier, John Greenleaf, ed. 1879. *Songs of Three Centuries.* Boston: Houghton, Osgood and Co.

Wiley, Margaret L. [1950] 1952. "John Donne and the Poetry of Scepticism." *Hibbert Journal* 48 (1950): 163–72. Reprint in *The Subtle Knot: Creative Scepticism in Seventeenth-Century England,* 120–36. London: George Allan and Unwin, 1952.

Williamson, George. 1936. "Senecan Style in the Seventeenth Century." *Philological Quarterly* 15:321–51.

———. 1951. *The Senecan Amble: A Study in Prose Form from Bacon to Collier.* Chicago: University of Chicago Press.

———. 1961. *The Proper Wit of Poetry.* Chicago: University of Chicago Press; London: Faber and Faber; Toronto: University of Toronto Press.

Willmott, Richard, ed. 1985. *Four Metaphysical Poets: An Anthology of Poetry by Donne, Herbert, Marvell, and Vaughan.* Cambridge: Cambridge University Press.

Wilson, G. R., Jr. 1969. "The Interplay of Perception and Reflection: Mirror Imagery in Donne's Poetry." *Studies in English Literature* 9:107–21.

Wilson, Scott W. 1980. "Process and Product: Reconstructing Donne's Personae." *Studies in English Literature* 20:91–103.

Woods, Susanne. 1984. *Natural Emphasis: English Versification from Chaucer to Dryden.* San Marino: The Huntington Library.

Woolf, Virginia. 1932. "Donne after Three Centuries." In *The Second Common Reader,* 20–37. London: Leonard and Virginia Woolf at the Hogarth Press; New York: Harcourt, Brace and Co.

Wright, George T. 1976. "The Personae of Donne's Love Poems." *The Southern Quarterly* 14(3): 173–77.

Wyld, Henry Cecil. 1923. *Studies in English Rhymes from Surrey to Pope: A Chapter in the History of English.* London: John Murray.

Zuberi, Itrat-Husain. 1965. "John Donne's Concept of Toleration in Church and State." *University of Windsor Review* 1:147–58.

# Index